THE END OF AMERICAN LYNCHING

D1558659

THE END OF AMERICAN LYNCHING

ASHRAF H. A. RUSHDY

RUTGERS UNIVERSITY PRESS
NEW BRUNSWICK, NEW JERSEY, AND LONDON

Library of Congress Cataloging-in-Publication Data

Rushdy, Ashraf H. A., 1961–
    The end of American lynching / Ashraf H. A. Rushdy.
        p. cm.
    Includes bibliographical references and index.
    ISBN 978–0–8135–5291–0 (hbk. : alk. paper) — ISBN 978–0–8135–5292–7
(pbk. : alk. paper) — ISBN 978–0–8135–5293–4 (e-book)
    1. Lynching—United States—History.   2. Hate crimes—United States—History.
I. Title.
    HV6457.R87   2012
    364.1'34—dc23

                                                            2011035600

A British Cataloging-in-Publication record for this book is available from the British
Library.

Frontispiece photos, top, ca. 1920s, published in *Minnesota History* 59, no. 1 (Spring
2004), courtesy of Minnesota Historical Society; bottom, lynching in Marion, Indiana,
August 7–8, 1930, photo by Lawrence Beitler, courtesy of the Indiana Historical Society.

Visit our website: http://rutgerspress.rutgers.edu

Manufactured in the United States of America

To my beloved wife, Kidan, and our beloved sons,
Zidane and Aziz

CONTENTS

PREFACE

When Clarence Thomas accused the Senate Judiciary Committee of conducting what he called a "high-tech lynching" during the hearings for his Supreme Court nomination on October 11, 1991, his comments resonated powerfully with one part of the American population.[1] Indeed, pundits and pollsters immediately noted the subsequent spike in support for Thomas among African Americans (while they ignored the insistent protest against his nomination by African American women). At the same time, his comments fell on deaf or unhearing ears in the larger part of the American population. Thomas's comment—and the pollsters' response of tracing the ways it influenced black popular opinion—explicitly made clear that "lynching" referred preeminently to the practice of terrorism against African Americans. At the time of the hearings, it was not clear that a majority of white Americans made that association with the word "lynching." In the introduction of a superb and prizewinning book on lynching that was likely in press at the time of the hearings, Fitzhugh Brundage speculated that "for many modern-day white Americans, lynch mobs conjure up images of cowboys, cattle rustlers, and a generally wholesome tradition of frontier justice."[2] For these many white Americans, presumably, the word did not conjure up another unwholesome tradition of frenzied white Americans ritually dismembering and murdering African Americans at the rate of one person every five days for five decades (1880–1930).

It is certainly true that the historiography of lynching lagged far behind the study of other periods and institutions in American and African American life. In 1991, there were innumerably more books on slavery, Reconstruction, the Harlem Renaissance, and the civil rights and Black Power movements than there were on lynching. Lynching seemed simply to be an ignored or forgotten part of the American past. Indeed, Brundage concluded his book by noting that "nothing about the history of mob violence in the United States is more surprising than how quickly an understanding of the full horror of lynchings has receded from the nation's collective historical memory."[3]

Although that national collective historical memory is divided, of course, and lynching had not receded from the memory of African American writers, like John Hope Franklin or Walter White, or leftist white writers, like Herbert Aptheker and Ralph Ginzburg, who were working and publishing in independent venues, it had seemingly become a lacuna in the mainstream and institutionalized historical profession. Nobody made a more earnest effort to understand how he personally had failed to comprehend the significance of lynching as a form of racial terrorism in American history than the distinguished historian Joel Williamson, who had, in fact, published one of the most highly regarded studies of the intellectual background and social relations in the period between the end of Reconstruction and the beginning of World War I, an era that can rightly be called the "age of lynching."[4]

In his personal essay, Williamson traces his own exposure to the history of lynching, which he first encountered in the 1940 novel and 1943 film *The Ox-Bow Incident*. Having "associated lynching primarily with the frontier," then, Williamson did not learn about how "white people massively lynch[ed] black people" until he was a scholar in the mid-1960s studying the origins of segregation. The discovery of the horrors of lynching—ritual dismemberment, a savage and cruel death, the white mob's morbid search for relics—was almost more than Williamson could bear. "Nothing in my living experience as a southerner and an American," he writes, "nothing in my training and practice as a historian and professor, had prepared me for this."

He then examines all the foundational works of American history that formed his generation's understanding of the national past and finds there the absence of record that at least partly explained why he was so ill-prepared to discover what he came to call this American "holocaust." Williamson acknowledges that there did eventually emerge a body of historical writing on lynching but maintains nonetheless that the subject remains the one "most tenuously held" among those who studied African American and American history. "I know of no one who has devoted a scholarly life to the study of lynching, and only two or three have worked at it for a decade," he notes, which certainly cannot be said of slavery, say, or Reconstruction or the civil rights movement, historical periods that several historians have devoted careers to elucidating in serially published books. "The writing of the history of lynching," he concludes, "has been strangely disjointed and discontinuous."[5]

The End of American Lynching is an attempt to explain at least one source of that collective American amnesia about the history and practice of lynching. In the introduction, I spell out in detail the terms of my argument. Here, I would like to explain why this book focuses almost exclusively on the lynching of African Americans. One of the most signal achievements of the last decade in scholarship on lynching has been the attention paid to explicating the meaningful ways that lynching both resulted from and formed an American culture of violence against people who were thought of in some way as a "minority," because of their ethnic, racial, or class position in the society. Much of the most promising recent work has been specifically on the ways that lynching was used against Mexicans, Mexican Americans, Chinese Americans, and Native Americans.[6]

While I learned a great deal from the works that expand our focus to the lynching of other ethnic and racial groups, I have retained the focus on whites' lynching of black Americans because I believe it best serves the point of this specific study, that it best reveals just what dynamic informs American thinking about what and when a lynching is. There are a couple of reasons for my choice. First, for the last century and a half, since the end of the Civil War to the present, the most frequent dynamic in American lynchings has been that of whites killing black people. We can most insightfully understand the phenomenon of lynching, I think, by examining more closely the most common practice, which can then help us appreciate the dynamic that informs the lynchings of other ethnic and racial minorities, a practice less common but no less heinous and criminal. Second, the lynching of African Americans occupies a unique intellectual space in the American imagination because lynchers and their apologists created a mythic apparatus to justify it (chivalry) while hiding its more easily discernible motives (white supremacy and social control over a formerly enslaved labor pool). And those myths that white Americans generate about black Americans are as informative for the student as they are delusive for those who generate and believe them, since they reveal just what factors are most salient and most repressed in American thinking about race and sex and power.

There is no doubt in my mind that a thorough history of American violence has to take up how that violence is directed in different ways toward diverse groups in particular circumstances. This study, I hope, helps us get closer to that encompassing historical vision by identifying some of the key patterns of American thinking about the lynching of African Americans in the long twentieth century.

ACKNOWLEDGMENTS

I feel particularly fortunate and honored to be publishing this book with Rutgers University Press. For many, many years, I have been reading the acknowledgments of Rutgers authors who have praised the thoughtfulness, generosity, and editorial acumen of Leslie Mitchner, one of those legendary names in academic publishing. I have happily discovered that those authors were all correct. It has been a rare and wonderful privilege to work under her guiding hand, and to be the beneficiary of her professionalism and remarkably sharp mind. I thank her for making this a better book. I would also like to thank Marilyn Campbell, Lisa Boyajian, and Katie Keeran at RUP for all their assistance in the preparation of the manuscript. Finally, I would like to thank India Cooper, who copyedited this manuscript with wonderful good humor and remarkable care and respect and attention.

I started writing this book at the National Humanities Center during a yearlong fellowship that gave me time to think and read and talk with colleagues, some of whom have since become deeply important friends. There are many people who make the National Humanities Center one of the premier academic centers in the world, and I have thanked them elsewhere. I would like to take this opportunity especially to thank Kent Mullikin, its vice president and deputy director, who has been at the center since its conception and is retiring this year. I feel honored to have been a fellow when he was there, and I thank him for his wonderful stories, gregarious spirit, and unfailing good humor.

Many librarians at many institutions made this book possible, and I am sorry that I cannot thank them all by name. They know who they are, and they know how much I appreciate them. I am especially grateful for the work performed by the interlibrary loan office at Wesleyan University, the librarians at Yale University's Sterling Library, and the peerless group of librarians at the National Humanities Center.

This book was written largely at Wesleyan University, where I am blessed with gifted students and generous colleagues. I would like to thank Jan Willis, Rob Rosenthal, and Krishna Winston for their support, friendship, and inspiration. I would like to thank Khachig Tölölyan for more things than I can name. I would also like to thank the administrative assistants who make all things possible—Joan Chiari in the Center for African American Studies and Elizabeth Tinker in the English Department.

I would like to thank Suzanne Hahn of the Indiana Historical Society and Jennifer McElroy of the Minnesota Historical Society for helping me procure images for this book.

I am profoundly grateful for a set of friends, some of whom are former students and former colleagues, who have inspired me by their own work and their undeviating support of mine. In particular I thank Shani Mott, Nathan Connolly, Erness and Nat Brody, Cynthia Horan, and Nancy Lewis.

I would like to thank in particular Leigh Raiford, who read the manuscript with exquisite attention and intelligence. I am indebted to her for her superb work on lynching photographs, and equally indebted to her for her generous and thoughtful commentary on this book. She challenged me to sharpen my arguments and expand my scope, and she has thereby made this a stronger book.

Rochelle Gurstein generously read the entire manuscript of multiple drafts, and her questions, observations, and comments immeasurably helped me catch and correct flaws and develop and enhance my arguments. Rochelle is an outstanding reader and a consummate intellect. I was fortunate in having her as one of the first readers of this book, and considerably more fortunate in having her as one of my most loved friends.

I would like to thank three far-flung families who have been a source of joy and support and love for many, many years. The friendship of Robert Greenhill and Estelle Metayer in Switzerland has enriched my life for so long that I cannot imagine a time when I did not have it. I thank them for everything they have done. Ted Abel and Noreen O'Connor-Abel and Annie Abel in Philadelphia have been steadfast believers in my work since graduate school, and unflagging supporters of this project in particular. Jeff Kerr-Ritchie and Elizabeth Lundquist of Durham, North Carolina, have likewise been generous and thoughtful and wonderful friends for decades. Each of these families has brightened my life with their children: Arthur and Josephine, Seamus, and Nelson and Alexander. I am honored that two of those children are my godsons: Arthur and Alexander.

My own family has been there from the beginning and has been infinitely patient, ceaselessly thoughtful and supportive, and compassionate in a way that no reasonable person could expect. I thank my mother and father, Hassan and Amal, for teaching and showing me the value of intellectual pursuits. Khalo Mohsen and Felicity, my uncle and aunt, have encouraged me in every way in the writing of this book, and been role models for what a life looks like when it is devoted to ideas and social justice advocacy. My brother and sister, Amgad and Janice, and my niece and nephew, Anna and Alex, have been a necessary antidote to the tribulations of writing this book. I am fortunate in having them as an escape and relief, and an infinite source of love and care. I would also like to thank my Tante Nabila and my aunts and uncles and cousins all over the world.

Finally, I would like to thank my wife, Kidan, who did everything she could to create a perfect work environment, and everything possible to give me time to devote to writing. I would also like to thank our two sons, Zidane and Aziz, the two most precious, wonderful, and radiant presences in our life, who did everything they could to render their mother's work futile. Fortunately, the boys' grandfather and grandmother, Kassahun Checole and Nevolia Ogletree, and their aunt and my sister, Senait, have been there every step of the way to provide exemplary support. And even more than support with the children, they have provided me with care and love and good food and good cheer through the whole process. I am indeed fortunate, incredibly fortunate, in having such a family.

I wrote parts of this book while each of our sons played under and around my writing desk, uncomfortably shielding their toddler eyes from the photographs I was studying on my computer screen, and sometimes even the words I was writing and reading. I hope and expect they will grow up in a world that has more justice and peace in it than the ones about which I write, and do everything in my power to make that possible. I dedicate this book to them, and to my most profoundly beloved wife, Kidan, who is a blessing in my life and a steadfast partner in all we do. She made this book possible, and that has been the least of her accomplishments of our life together.

THE END OF AMERICAN LYNCHING

INTRODUCTION

WHEN IS AN AMERICAN LYNCHING?

The End of American Lynching is a study of two relatively hidden discourses of lynching in the long twentieth century. The first discourse is hidden because it was overshadowed by a considerably more dominant discourse of lynching, the second because it has not been subject to much debate or critique and has quietly assumed the place of "common sense" so that a majority of people would not contest its presuppositions and tenets. It is the argument of this book that these two discourses expose opposing ways of thinking about the dynamics of lynching, about what lynchings mean to the society where they occur, about what lynchings are, and *when* they are, that is, when it is that particular events *become* lynchings.

By "discourse," as I am using it here, I mean structured ways of organizing thinking and talking about a subject. The historian Daniel Jonah Goldhagen provides a succinct definition of "discourse" as "a discussion structured by a stable framework with widely accepted reference points, images, and explicit elaborations."[1] The two points I wish to emphasize about the operation of discourses involve their emergence and their dynamic. In the case of lynching, discourses emerge from heated debates about the meaning of the practice, and these debates change over the long history of lynching in America. Second, the dynamic of discourses is that they enable discussions of a given subject, but they also circumscribe and delimit ways of thinking and talking about the subject as much as they inform it. Discourses, then, evolve out of historical debates and come to operate as a set of accepted premises that can generate some arguments and render others unpersuasive or, worse, unimportant. It is also worth noting that discourses are not discrete or autonomous things but frequently overlap in time and content.

The two discourses I examine in this study are organized around the concepts of complicity and denial. Briefly, the first is the discourse of complicity— what I will call the *complicity models* (for there are several of them)—which

1

arose at the same time as the more dominant discourse of the 1880s and 1890s, the lynching-for-rape discourse. The complicity models raise a different set of questions than the dominant discourse. Where the lynching-for-rape discourse was mobilized through questions of chivalry, community, and race, the complicity models took on issues of responsibility, how to define it, how to measure it, and how to understand it in a phenomenon of collective action.

The second is what I am calling the *end-of-lynching discourse*, which arose in the 1930s and 1940s and continues to determine how we think and talk about lynchings in the first decades of the twenty-first century. This discourse emerged as the kinds of lynchings common from Reconstruction to the Depression declined in frequency and changed in form. In the face of this decline, the numerous groups committed to recording, studying, and agitating against lynching engaged in a debate about the meaning of this social change and whether or not lynching had been or soon would be eradicated. I will discuss this discourse more fully in chapters 2, 3, and 4, but we can note briefly here that this discourse established the terms of debate that would determine how lynchings after 1940 were discussed and disputed. The major tenets of the end-of-lynching discourse were that lynching had to be defined narrowly rather than capaciously, that each alleged lynching needed to be investigated in order to show how it was indeed some other kind of activity (not a lynching), and that lynching was in fact a dying if not dead practice. Those who opposed the tenet that lynchings had ended made the argument that lynchings had evolved, "gone underground," and assumed a different form and shape, while serving the same purpose as "traditional" lynchings had done. Even though it is not nearly as readily recognized as the lynching-for-rape discourse that it uneasily coexists with, this discourse has largely governed the ways we have thought about lynching for the past seventy years or so.

I here discuss the tenets and mobilization of these two discourses through the twentieth century—one based on the concept of complicity that raises questions about the wider range of responsibility in an action, and one based on denying transformation or formal change in order to insist on a narrower range of action that can be called lynching. I will return to these two discourses and the concepts that give them life, but first we need to see how discourses of lynching developed out of the persistent debates about the meaning of lynching that have attended the practice since it first developed on American soil during the Revolutionary War. Over the course of two and a half centuries, those debates have been involved and complex, raising issues about the society in which these events occur—issues over the political stability of the society, its racial and gender dynamics, and its sense of the relationship of individual to collective responsibility. These debates over lynching reveal a great deal about the society's larger social relations, beginning with the American Revolution itself, as the nation was considering what formal relations would exist among citizen, state, and nation, and continuing as the nation expanded over the next century, each frontier providing another moment of negotiation between the forces advocating popular and those advocating state sovereignty. At each of those moments in American history, these debates have reflected and helped form ways of thinking and talking about the place of extralegal collective action in a governed society. In other words, what began as debates became discourses—that is, an evolving set of myths, narratives, and imagery that serve as a background to intellectual discussion of the subject of lynching.

———

To get a sense of the evolving and overlapping nature of discourses of lynching, we can briefly examine three key moments in the history of American lynching.

The first moment occurred during the Revolutionary War, in 1780, when the militia of Bedford County, Virginia, hanged an "insurgent" Tory and whipped two others, all without the benefit of trial. A member of the militia, Colonel William Campbell, justified the hanging of the "insurgent" by declaring that it was done "I believe with the joint consent of near three hundred men."[2] The leader of that militia was Colonel Charles Lynch. Although Governor Thomas Jefferson commended the militia's actions in a letter to Charles Lynch, he nonetheless suggested that in the future Lynch resort less to his own law and more to that of the Commonwealth. "The method of seizing them at once which you have adopted is much the best," he noted. "You have only to take care that they be regularly tried after," he continued, suggesting that Lynch consult the attorney for the Commonwealth in Bedford County about how to proceed in those trials.[3] The "joint consent" of the people, apparently, was not a force to replace the structured legal system of the Commonwealth.

Charles Lynch was not overly careful in heeding Jefferson's cautionary note. He continued to resort to extrajudicial forms of examination and punishment in what he called "trying torys &c &c," and two years later he started using the term "Lynchs Law" to describe the violent suppression of Welsh lead miners and advocating the same rough justice for other enemies of the state, including those who traded illegally in slaves.[4] Historians of lynching have rightly called Charles Lynch "the first lyncher" and noted that the term "Lynch law" entered local parlance in the James River region of Virginia shortly after he coined it, spreading as far west as Indiana by the 1820s, but neither replacing other terms for popular or vigilante justice nor appearing too frequently in print prior to the 1830s.[5]

We can find in the Revolutionary-era origin of lynching the germ of a variety of the themes and tensions that would manifest themselves in its later development. First, we can note that the first American lynchers borrowed the language of democratic revolution in order to claim sanction for their extralegal actions. Colonel Campbell's claim that the militia acted with the "joint consent" of the people suggests that their actions were not only those of military officers but of representatives of the people whose "consent" they enjoyed. The governor who urged them to employ trials in the future had four years earlier penned a Declaration stating the "Right of the People" to be governed by their "consent." It was the language of the anti-monarchists in England in the 1640s, of the Puritans in colonial Massachusetts (John Winthrop's "consent of a certaine companie of people"), and of the very governor whose counsel to keep within established legal order they defied.[6] In an age of the emergent idea of popular sovereignty, in a war against monarchists defiant of that revolutionary ideal, what the Bedford County militia did was representative not just of the disregard for established law, which it was, but also of the regard for the higher law of popular sovereignty.

We can discern, then, two fundamental claims that the Bedford militia made, which would continue to resonate in future pro-lynching discourses. First, there is the claim that the lynchers were driven to a form of "frontier justice" by the absence of proper institutional channels of law. In this case, the added complication, and rationalization, was that these events transpired under conditions of war, and indeed a war meant to establish a nation emerging from under another's power and institutions. The proper institutions of the society, in this case the courts, were not absent per se but undergoing revolutionary changes.[7]

Second, there is the claim of popular sovereignty, that the people were in any case the primal force who consented or not to the making and enforcing of the law. As Edmund Morgan has splendidly shown, the claim of popular sovereignty in early America, and indeed the invention of the "people" on whom it was based, operated as a political fiction advocating deference, not insurgence, and was a political ploy used first by the elite during the colonial and Revolutionary eras, and then later by the yeomanry against paupers and the propertyless.[8] In time, however, the myth of popular sovereignty would become a weapon in the hands of the enfranchised masses.

These, then, were the two major claims that were made by the first, and would be made by later, lynchers—the claim that the institutions of the law were ineffective (through absence or failure), and the claim of popular sovereignty (an authority granted from the original source of governance and thereby the institutions of law). The first would become an argument made especially by those who inhabited the "frontier," either in the West or in their minds. The latter would become an argument made by those who felt that the system of law did not accurately reflect communal values and mores, or failed to mete out appropriate punishments for certain crimes, or was corrupted through an excessive dependence on formal rather than substantial justice.[9]

The second moment in the history of American lynching occurred on July 4, 1835, at the Independence Day barbecue in Vicksburg, Mississippi, when a fight threatened to break out between an officer of the corps of Vicksburg volunteers and a gambler named Cabler. After the fight was averted, Cabler went to his rooms and returned to the barbecue armed with a loaded pistol, a large knife, and a dagger. The crowd decided to punish him for his impudence. The reporter covering the story stated that the "crowd of respectable citizens" took Cabler out to the woods, tied him to a tree, whipped him, tarred and feathered him, and then gave him forty-eight hours to leave Vicksburg. Fearing that the rest of the gamblers in town would avenge this action, the citizens met in the courthouse that night and drafted a public notice demanding all gamblers leave Vicksburg within twenty-four hours. The next day, after the notices were posted, many of the gamblers quickly and peaceably left town. The day following, however, turned violent when a mob of Vicksburg citizens and militia burst into a gambling house and were met with gunfire that killed one of the citizens. After a renewed attack on the house, the mob captured the five residents of the house and lynched them by hanging from the town scaffold.[10]

The Vicksburg lynching had a tremendous national impact, as it inspired the nation to consider the meaning of what struck many as a new wave of lawlessness and what struck others as a wave of democratic energy. Newspapers made claims that "riots and mobs have become so fashionable [and] we have heard much of 'Judge Lynch,' 'Lynch's Law' &c. &c. in connection with them." When they expressed fears that lynching ("this popular code") would "soon supersede all other laws, and the necessity of any further legislation," they were articulating a fear that Jacksonian democratic mores, or what they termed "mobocracy," threatened the social order in a way that no other form of popular or foreign insurgency had hitherto done.[11] What these newspapers feared, other newspapers valued. Some applauded lynching as "a mode of punishment provided for such as become obnoxious in a manner which the law cannot reach."[12]

The newspaper that articulated that defense of lynching was the *Vicksburg Register*, and it exemplified the emergent discourse of lynching that developed around the Vicksburg lynchings. Briefly, we can note four important themes that defined this new discourse of lynching. Two of the themes are essentially the two claims that assumed rudimentary form during the Revolutionary War: the frontier justice claim of the inefficiency of the law as a mechanism for establishing justice and the popular sovereignty claim of the communal support enjoyed by the lynchers as a mandate for their action. The Vicksburg article twice mentions the inability of the law to deal with the situations involving Cabler and the rest of the gamblers. With Cabler, since he had not yet committed any crime, the journalist noted that "to proceed against him at law would have been mere mockery, inasmuch as, not having had the opportunity of consummating his design, no adequate punishment could have been inflicted on him." With the gamblers as a whole, though, the journalist felt that the law required too high a standard of proof. "The laws, however severe in their provision," he wrote, "have never been sufficient to correct a vice which must be established by positive proof, and cannot, like others, be shown from circumstantial testimony." Instead of the sanction of the written law, the journalist felt that the lynchers had the mandate of an agitated and like-minded community. The action received the "unanimous" support of the citizens of Vicksburg, not one of whom had "been heard to utter a syllable of censure against either the act or the manner in which it was performed."[13]

A second set of two themes addresses the specific issues of what we can call citizenship in this community: defining those who aren't and defining those who are. The *Vicksburg Register* referred to those it thought of as "outsiders" simply as "Professional Gamblers, destitute of all sense of moral obligations—unconnected with society by any of its ordinary ties," men who "have made Vicksburg their place of rendezvous," not their residence, not their community, not their home. In the same act of ridding the town of unwanted transients in a communal ritual, the community defines itself, first against those aliens it lynches and then, in the aftermath, against those who would harshly judge the community's act of violence. The *Vicksburg Register* provides a paradigmatic case of this defensive posture: "It is not expected that this act will pass without censure from most who had not an opportunity of knowing and feeling the dire necessity out of which it originated." These sorts of statements define citizenship and belonging in two interrelated ways. First, the actual residents of the town are implicated in the lynch mob, or perhaps interpellated into it; to live here is to know the "dire necessity." Second, those who do not live here, and therefore cannot know that "dire necessity," are rendered outsiders by virtue of not sharing in that knowledge or experience. In its most significant formulation of that insider-outsider rhetoric, the newspaper makes this a case of honor, specifically masculine honor: "We had

borne with their enormities, until to have suffered them any longer would . . .
have proved us destitute of every manly sentiment."[14]

With that rhetorical flourish, the *Vicksburg Register* took the earlier
Revolutionary-era claims that were used to justify lynching—the claims of
frontier justice and popular sovereignty—and added to them the claims of
community and manhood. Those who acted with "manly sentiment" in ridding their community of obnoxious beings were those who understood the
circumstances that required that action, and they were the only ones who
understood. To be a member of a lynch mob, or, what amounts to the same
thing, to defend one, is to be a man, a member of a community, and insularly
impervious to "outside" opinion. In 1835, the "outsiders" were defined as those
not living in Vicksburg; a half-century later, those not living in the South.

The third moment in the history of American lynching that concerns us
here is the development of the San Francisco Vigilance Committee, which
was initially formed in 1851 and then reconstituted in 1856. The main periods
of activity for the committees were between June and September 1851 and
May and August 1856. During those two stretches, each of the committees
hanged four men and banished about thirty more. The 1851 Committee
declared that it was formed primarily to punish criminals whose offenses
were against property and person. In its constitution, the 1851 Committee
stated its purpose as ensuring that "no thief, burglar, incendiary or assassin,
shall escape punishment, either by the quibbles of the law, the insecurity of
prisons, the carelessness or corruption of the police, or a laxity of those who
pretend to administer justice." The 1856 Committee was formed primarily to
punish political graft and election fraud and thus revised its constitution to
make itself responsible for "the protection of the ballot-box, the lives, liberty,
and property of the citizens and residents of San Francisco." The 1856
Committee continued to meet until November 1859, but it punished no one
after August 1856, when it held its final grand review and parade. A week
earlier, it had formed a political party, the People's Party, which would
dominate San Francisco politics for the next decade.[15]

According to their greatest booster, the San Francisco Committees of
Vigilance were "the most perfect and powerful organization hitherto established in any country for the guarding of the public weal" (1851) and "the
largest, most powerful, and efficient popular tribunal known in history"
(1856). Modern historians, less prone to celebration, see the 1856 Committee,
in particular, as "pivotal in the history of American vigilantism" because it
combined the practices of the old vigilante movements (hanging, banishing)
with the new ethnic victims (especially Irish Catholic immigrants). In addition, it marked the shift from "rural frontier disorder" to a concern with the

problems of a "new urban America." Another historian of American lynching notes that the committees helped legitimize "the crowd in the street shortly before the Civil War began."[16] The committees do indeed mark a shift in defining the applicability of frontier extralegal collective violence from rural to urban spaces; they also inspired imitators throughout California and in the newly established rural frontiers east of California. For our purposes here, the committees also mark a distinct development in the evolution of the discourses of lynching.

In between the formation and re-formation of the San Francisco Vigilance Committee, between 1851 and 1856, we can find, I think, a telling shift in how frontier societies defended lynching, a shift that introduced an important new trend in the generation of lynching discourses. First, it is worth noting, briefly, the four general stages that frontier societies went through in their performing and rationalizing of lynchings.[17] In the first stage, frontier societies lynch those accused of crimes against property in the early days of settlement, while the territory still lacks legal and judicial apparatus. In the second stage, primarily homicide or other especially heinous crimes are punished by lynching, sometimes in the absence of the legal apparatus, often despite its presence. In the third stage, vigilante violence becomes a tool for capitalists to dominate particular fields. In what Richard Maxwell Brown calls "the Western Civil War of Incorporation," agents of "the conservative, consolidating authority of modern capitalistic forces," that is, barons of all sorts (oil, steel, cattle), employ vigilante hired gunfighters to intimidate and eliminate local small-scale rivals.[18] Finally, in the last stage, lynching becomes a weapon of terrorism used to control the mobility of particular groups (defined along ethnic, racial, or class lines).

These stages are somewhat sequential, but there is overlap, particularly since the second stage often continues well into the twentieth century. Lynching, then, in frontier societies is not an unchanging ritual but a practice adapted for and rationalized through new ideologies. These lynchers on American frontiers borrowed and expanded on the rationales produced by the early lynchers—that lynching is a form of justice in a barely settled land, that it is a matter of manly honor, that it is an expression of popular sovereignty—and implicitly demonstrated that it was also a strategy for establishing capitalism and white supremacy, that it was, in a word, a word they would not use, a form of terrorism.[19]

The 1851 San Francisco Vigilance Committee justified itself as an example of the second stage (in which courts were too lenient to mete out appropriate punishment for heinous crimes), while the 1856 Committee was an example of the third and fourth stages—the use of collective extralegal violence for capitalist incorporation and violence exercised primarily against Irish Catholic immigrants.[20]

It is particularly in the last two stages of frontier lynching rationales that we find the persistent use of what we can call "cover stories"—that is, public justifications that clearly attempt to hide other discernible motives. Let me be clear. I am not arguing that earlier lynchers did not employ mendacity or indirection in their accounts of why they lynched. The Bedford militia and the civic boosters of Vicksburg employed resonant terms in American political and social life, "consent" and "community," in order to make their actions more palatable to those who might consider other terms like "rights" and "due process" applicable. Their rationales were not hotly debated because the actions they performed did not seem out of line with the rationales they offered for performing them. Those who killed out of a desire to consolidate capitalist enterprise or white supremacy, on the other hand, could not easily employ a term that would raise their actions beyond suspicion. They did employ such phrases—notably, "chivalry" and "law and order"—but the terms and the rationales for which they were shorthand were quickly subject to public skepticism and heated debate because their actions, and the fact that these actions were directed against distinct populations, showed more clearly the fissure between their practice and their justification for it. It is at this point in the history of lynching in America that we find a more robust debate between lynchers who maintain that they perform work that advances irreproachable causes (punishing criminals, especially rapists) and anti-lynching advocates who claim that the lynchers are serving ulterior and much more base motives (upholding capitalist consolidation and white supremacy).

―――――

It is at also this point in American history that we find the emergence of the formative discourse of lynching for the past century and a half, the lynching-for-rape discourse, which arose in the 1870s and 1880s and is either the dominant or only discourse of lynching with which most people are familiar. It emerged from the debate between those who defend lynching as an act of chivalry (to protect white women and punish black rapists) and those who debunk that claim (by showing the infrequency with which rape was the allegation and revealing the terrorist-racist practice of lynching for what it is). This discourse quickly became the dominant one about what lynchings mean. On one side were arrayed the (largely) Southern pro-lynching advocates— intellectuals, editors, and politicians—who claimed that lynching was performed to protect white womanhood, while on the other staunchly stood anti-lynching critics who maintained that the statistics of lynching demonstrably gave the lie to that claim. The case for lynching for rape was most forcefully made by its innumerable advocates in the last decades of the nineteenth century and the first decade of the twentieth, while the case against it was begun by Frederick Douglass and Ida B. Wells in the 1890s and then resumed by the National Association for the Advancement of Colored People (NAACP) and the Association of Southern Women for the Prevention of Lynching (ASWPL) in the 1910s to the 1940s. In our own day, it retains a kind of folkloric presence; it is the assumed scenario when a black politician like Clarence Thomas or Kwame Kilpatrick claims to be "lynched" for his politics.

We can see the process by which the discourse becomes formed by examining a couple of significant early moments in that debate. Consider, first, an August 1906 editorial of the *Atlanta Georgian*. In a piece entitled "An Appeal to Negro Leaders, to Stop the 'Reign of Terror' for Southern White Women," John Temple Graves begins by referring to what he calls the "state of constant siege and danger" faced by white women. He then proceeds to a logical exposition of lynching that follows largely traditional patterns. First, he notes that black rapists were lynched by a justified white community: "Every one of the fiends who has been apprehended has been dealt with swiftly and sternly by an outraged society that could not and did not wait for the slow processes of the law. Every rapist that has been caught has been shot or hanged without hesitation and without remorse." Then, in another conventional rhetorical gesture in the pro-lynching discourse, Graves notes that lynching does not deter future rapists since "killing, shoting [sic], burning has ceased to terrify them."[21] This editorial, and the Atlanta newspapers' inflammatory coverage of a series of false rape charges, inspired the Atlanta race riot in September 1906. Graves was mobilizing a sensibility that had been galvanized by the mature lynching-for-rape discourse.

It was precisely this kind of pro-lynching discourse that had moved Ida B. Wells to respond in the 1890s, once she came to the knowledge that it was indeed a discourse. Wells notes in her autobiography that she, like "many another person who had read of lynching in the South," had "accepted the idea" that a community's "unreasoning anger over the terrible crime of rape led to the lynching; that perhaps the brute deserved death anyhow and the mob was justified in taking his life." It was only when her friend Thomas Moss and his business associates Calvin McDowell and Lee Stewart were lynched in Memphis in 1892 that she recognized that the lynching-for-rape discourse was a cover story meant to mask the actual motivations for lynching, which were to terrorize black communities and to punish and prevent black success and mobility. As a cover story, it had indeed proven compelling. Even someone as experienced in the ways white supremacy masked its program as was Frederick Douglass had "begun to believe it true that there was increasing lasciviousness on the part of Negroes."[22]

Wells undertook to expose that story, as did Douglass. Both of them published pamphlets demonstrating that pro-lynching advocates had pursued three rationales for lynching in the wake of the Civil War. At first, from 1865 to 1872, these advocates claimed that vigilante violence against African Americans was necessary to quell the race riots and insurrections that threatened American spaces. The second rationale, emerging during Reconstruction and after the passage of the Fifteenth Amendment, was that such violence was necessary to prevent "Negro domination." The third rationale followed logically once African Americans had been disenfranchised and "eliminated from all participation in state and national elections." That rationale, what Wells calls the "third excuse," was that "Negroes had to be killed to avenge their assaults upon women."[23] By showing how those wreaking vigilante violence against African Americans kept changing their stories to suit the conditions of the times, Douglass and Wells wanted to show that the latest story was just that, a story fabricated as but another rationale for a practice that clearly served an ulterior motive.

Once she had exposed the lynching-for-rape discourse as a cover story, Wells spent the remainder of her 1895 pamphlet, *A Red Record*, dismantling the tenets of that discourse piece by piece. She shows how straitened is the claimed chivalry of lynchers (who will avenge alleged crimes against only white women), how rape is the alleged reason for lynching in a minority of cases, and how the cry of rape itself is frequently employed to protect a white woman from the consequences of a consensual relationship with a black man. She then flings back the charge made by the pro-lynching advocates by claiming that it is not black communities that are on trial but rather the "white man's civilization and the white man's government which are on trial."[24]

Graves and Wells represent the two opposed positions in the debate over the lynching-for-rape discourse. And this discourse, as I said earlier, was clearly the most dominant and important. It is for this reason that Wells and future anti-lynching advocates had to confront and dismantle that discourse by showing its inaccuracies instead of taking an alternative strategy of simply addressing lynching as a form of anti-black terrorism. They had first to persuade readers that the dominant explanation for lynching was wrong before they could offer an explanation they claimed was right. Moreover, these advocates had to take another extraordinary step and extricate themselves from the role that the lynching-for-rape discourse cast them in. According to the advocates of the discourse, rape is what black men are predisposed to committing, what white women are thereby vulnerable to having committed on their bodies, and what white men chivalrously avenge in lynching. This renders white women beholden to white men and fearful of black men; it renders the violence done to black men justifiable; and it retains for white men the power of controlling their women (through fear and chivalry) and their former slaves (through fear and violence).[25]

Most insidiously, the advocates of the lynching-for-rape discourse cast black women as the originating cause of black men's lasciviousness. Black women, in this discourse, provide for their men what Philip A. Bruce calls "corrupting sexual influences." It is an infection that earlier writers had used to defend white slaveholders who found themselves seduced by the slave women they owned. The "heaviest part of the white racial burden," notes Myrta Lockett Avary in an almost paradigmatic case, "was the African woman, of strong sexual instincts and devoid of a sexual conscience, at the white man's door, in the white man's dwelling." Black women were doing to black men after slavery what they had done to white men during slavery. The "average plantation negro does not consider rape to be a very heinous crime," Bruce concludes, because he is "so accustomed to the wantonness of the women of his own race."[26] Black men are made insatiable because black women are insatiable.

The lynching-for-rape discourse became an almost unassailable constellation of ideas that worked to motivate lynchers, derail their critics, and assign particular roles to every segment of the society. Those forces that arraigned themselves against lynching attempted to undo this discourse, to reveal its false logic, but first they had to challenge the particular roles that defined those critics. It is worth noting that black women's anti-lynching groups had to be committed to defending black women's sexual reputation as well as criticizing lynching. White women's groups, like the ASWPL, made part of their mission the critique of the logic of chivalry and denounced "the mob as a false protector of Southern womanhood."[27] It was the peculiar power of the lynching-for-rape discourse—because it did create roles for all social actors—to demand of its critics that they first challenge their imputed role before they could challenge lynching as a practice.

———

It is important for us to remind ourselves of just how dominant the lynching-for-rape discourse was because it helps us better understand how it obscured other discourses. For the purposes of this study, that discourse obscured two competing concepts that would prove important for those who generate the complicity and end-of-lynching discourses.

Let us return one last time to Graves and Wells to see how the germ of those concepts is indeed hidden in the lynching-for-rape discourse—concepts that we find it difficult to discern and identify because we tend to be overwhelmed by the major tenets of the dominant discourse. After Graves concludes that lynching has so far proved inadequate to deterring rape, he takes up the problem in two distinct ways. First, he suggests that the South needs a "new form of punishment whose very spectacular method and terror will eliminate the foulest criminal instincts of our time." He notes that he has proposed two methods in the past: "personal mutilation of the rapist as a deterrent force" and "some new and mysterious mode of punishment—the passing over a slender bridge into a dark chamber where in utter darkness and in utter mystery the assailant of woman's virtue would meet a fate which his friends would never know and which he himself would never come back to make them understand." Lynching had become too spectacular, it seems, and he suggested modifying it to incorporate more mystery, in the manner of the sheeted original Ku Klux Klan, it would appear.

Second, he levels the charge of the black community's complicity in the crime of rape. He arraigns "the leaders—the teachers, the preachers, the bishops and the editors of the negro race as particeps criminis and co-criminals with the rapist when they fail to co-operate fully and freely with the white race in the swift punishment of this awful crime." Graves concludes with a favorite rhetorical strategy of pro-lynching advocates like Thomas Nelson Page, that is, making all black people ultimately responsible for lynchings because they do not expose and punish alleged black rapists themselves. They "are themselves guilty in part of the crimes which we revenge," he intones, "the crimes which make lynching possible."[28]

Wells, too, had in fact raised precisely the same issues. In writing about the lynching of Henry Smith in Paris, Texas, in 1893, Wells intimated that there was something insidiously novel about this lynching. The "white Christian people" of this town "and the communities thereabout," Wells wrote, "had deliberately determined to set aside all forms of law and inaugurate an entirely new form of punishment for the murder."[29] That "entirely new form" was the spectacle lynching, the public, communal ritual of torture, dismemberment, and hanging or burning. These are the lynchings where thousands attended, where newspapers and radios announced the event, where photographs were taken of the body and parts of the body became souvenirs.[30]

And Wells had anticipated Graves, and forced him to make the charge he made against black communities, with her own charge that white civilization was on trial, and, even more forcefully, with her more precise charge that press, pulpit, and politician were guilty of endorsing lynching by remaining "silent with a silence which means encouragement." Those who acquiesce in that way, she concludes, are ultimately "particeps criminis, accomplices, accessories before and after the fact, equally guilty with the actual law-breakers."[31]

For our purposes, then, we note that both Graves and Wells insist on two seemingly unrelated points. The first point concerns what we can call transformation, that lynchings, in other words, were events that were changing and could be changed in very particular, determined ways. Wells noticed that the spectacle lynching that replaced the earlier forms of lynching was something horribly new, that lynchings were undergoing a transformation that made the practice more public, more a mass media event, and more filled with a particular kind of ritualized violence. Graves, too, acknowledged that lynchings had been and could be subject to transformation. Indeed, he sought to have that form of spectacle lynching be replaced with something even more horribly new that would be less public, less a mass media event, and more filled with mystery. The second point concerns complicity, that is, how we can understand the widespread responsibility for lynching (or rape).

The questions implied in these two topics—transformation and complicity—are nothing less than what constitutes a lynching and what parameters define and identify those responsible for a lynching. We will see in the course of this book the way these two concepts evolve and effloresce in the complicity models and the end-of-lynching discourse. Complicity would remain the legal and ethical principle that the advocates of the complicity models urged as the most robust way to understand what a lynching was and meant. The concept of transformation, on the other hand, became a point of contention between advocates and critics of the end-of-lynching discourse, since the debates between them focused on whether a lynching could still be called a lynching when its formal properties seemed to change (when some new form of violence was "inaugurated," to use Wells's formulation, or some "new . . . mode" was employed, to use Graves's). Both Graves and Wells were making a case about the historical evolution of lynching. Lynching, they maintained, was not a practice that consisted of one set of formal properties that defined it. Rather, lynching—like the discourses that defended and critiqued it—was evolving, and could be best understood as a series of different practices that were engineered to respond to particular historical and social conditions. The debates in the twentieth century would coalesce around the affirmation or denial of transformation, of change, of historical evolution in the practice of lynching. The concept that would emerge as the resonant one in those debates would be denial.

————

These two concepts in the discussion of lynching—transformation (or denial) and complicity—have largely been lost or rendered moot because the other concerns around the combustible combination of sex and race have displaced them. It is my hope in this study to return them to the discussion by tracing the ways that these concepts were important to commentators on lynching. What I am tracing in this study is not a lineage per se, not a clearly marked tradition handed down from Wells and Graves to later writers through the first half of the twentieth century who were aware of and commented on the shared ideas of that tradition. Instead, I am tracing the ways these ideas helped later commentators to conceptualize what lynchings were and what they meant once they were no longer understood as and believed to be formally homogenous acts of vengeful chivalry.

In the rest of this study, I delineate the two discourses that take up these concepts, what I identify as the *complicity models* and the *end-of-lynching discourse*. Because these two discourses have different histories and occupy different places in the social history of lynching, I organize the argument of this study to account for those salient differences. As I noted at the beginning of this chapter, these two discourses are both hidden, but they are hidden in different ways. The complicity models can be thought of as providing an alternative discourse that implicitly challenges the hegemonic lynching-for-rape discourse; the complicity models are hidden because they are obscured by the dominant discourse. The end-of-lynching discourse is also hidden, but it is hidden because it is largely the product of a willed strategy of denial; it is both obscure and manages to obscure other discourses of lynching. I proceed, then, by respecting those differences and choosing what I hope is the best strategy for understanding each discourse most fully.

In the first case, I affirm the existence of an alternative discourse that left behind the main argument in the lynching-for-rape discourse—what was the crime that provoked the lynching—and took up an entirely different question about responsibility and belonging. The advocates of the complicity models wanted to understand what it meant to be a member of a mob, to belong to an entity that was undifferentiated (everyone belongs to the same mob) at the same time as it was differentiated (different people perform different actions in the work of the mob). Using the legal and moral concept of complicity as their primary lens, these advocates analyze how it is possible for someone to be complicit in a criminal act performed by an entity to which one belongs (the mob) even though one does not actually perform the criminal act.

The advocates of these models differ in their assessment of how to determine responsibility, how to assess it, and what sphere of social life is best suited to deal with it (court, church, public). They nonetheless share the belief that complicity is the best way to understand indirect action, and that indirect action is a fundamental aspect of lynching in America. That is, these thinkers are not interested only in the agency of the active lynchers—those who light the fire or cinch the rope—but more so in those who aid, abet, and can otherwise be thought of as complicit in the actions of the mob. These models define themselves by a positive assertion (complicity is a rational way to understand lynching) that in many ways is an indirect challenge to the regnant model for understanding lynching (the lynching-for-rape discourse).

In the second case, I describe the emergence of the end-of-lynching discourse, offer some suggestions about its significance, and then offer an argument that is an explicit challenge to it—the argument that the denial of lynching is a strategy that abets the continuation of what it denies. Because the end-of-lynching discourse is not widely known, I spend some time showing how it emerged and what factors may be said to have played a role in its emergence. I then delineate its major tenets and show how it has determined the ways we began to talk about lynchings after 1940 and how we continue to think about them now. I then offer an extended narrative of a specific event and an analysis of the discussion following that event in order to show both that the end-of-lynching discourse operates to limit our thinking and that it does so at a great cost.

The end-of-lynching discourse, like other forms of common sense, requires a sustained dismantling of its unstated tenets in order for us to get at the purpose it served for those who originally produced it and serves for those who continue to believe it. The original debate over that discourse in the 1930s and 1940s is important because it reveals the different ways we can think about continuity and discontinuity, and about the key question that motivated the complicity discourse—*when* is a lynching? What formal properties or motives or practices constitute that act? That debate, we will see, coalesced into a manifest discourse by the 1940s that continues to play an inordinately influential role in our contemporary thinking about lynching as a practice, and lynching as a historical episode in the national history.

The reader can see two notable differences in my treatment of the two discourses. My argument is implicit in the first section of the book and mostly drawn on those who have gone relatively unrecognized in producing an important, though submerged, strain of thinking about lynching. My argument about the end-of-lynching discourse, though, is both explicit and mostly mine. The first two chapters will feel more like historical explications, as I tease out the premises and noteworthy implications of particular intellectual positions. The last two chapters will feel more like advocacy, as I affirm what I think to be dangers to our society's holding on to certain discursive and intellectual habits.

That, then, is the general trajectory of this book. In less abstract terms, here is what I do as I examine three lynching events in the twentieth century.

In chapter 1, I examine how three individuals—differently situated in time, in relationship to the event, and in outlook—respond to a particular lynching in Coatesville, Pennsylvania, in 1911. Each of these individuals proposes a complicity model—a way of thinking about lynching that implicates a wider range of actors than the law permits. The major questions these individuals ask and answer have to do with how we can account for the members of a mob who watch a crime being committed. In the end, they expand our notion of responsibility at the same time as they expand the definition and duration of a lynching itself.

In chapter 2, I examine three responses to another lynching, in Marion, Indiana, in 1930. In this case, I examine how the idea of complicity expands our focus from the mob itself to the photograph of the mob. These responses raise questions about responsibility, but these questions are now focused on the ways we can understand responsibility in the more concrete details of lynching photographs, and what this expanded sense of responsibility can tell us about the enlarged definition and duration of lynching.

In chapters 3 and 4, I examine the rise and prominence in our contemporary culture of the end-of-lynching discourse. I wish to demonstrate how it frames and controls debates over events that bear a resemblance to lynchings, how it governs our thinking about lynching, and how it has largely misserved our attempts to understand lynchings more comprehensively. After showing how it emerged and became dominant, I demonstrate what role it continues to play by looking at a lynching in Jasper, Texas, in 1998. I examine the public and popular discussion of this event to show in what ways we are still operating under the terms and within the tenets provided by the end-of-lynching discourse. The end-of-lynching discourse works insidiously and by denial. It argues that lynchings were a thing of the past, downplays anything resembling a lynching, and works to lessen the publicity previously granted to lynchings. Its success depends on changing the topic of discussion through denial. I argue for our return to that expanded notion of what constitutes responsibility and what defines a lynching that was the hallmark of the complicity models.

———

The two concepts that predominate in this explication of these two discourses—complicity and denial—are intimately related. If we understand complicity as the state of being involved in an event performed by someone else but for which we are somehow responsible, and denial as the state of refusing or being unable to see or accept an event, then we could say that complicity and denial are distinct but related states of being or attitudes.

To be complicit in something frequently requires that we deny, in some crucial ways, our role in the performance of that event. To be in denial, in the face of evidence that shows our denial unwarranted, is to be complicit in the continuation of the thing whose existence we deny.

In an engaging and illuminating essay on what he calls the "moral imagination," David Bromwich explores how a range of thinkers from Edmund Burke to Abraham Lincoln to Mahatma Gandhi conceive of the complementary relationships between self and other (what Burke called "those whom we are used to consider as strangers") and between individual responsibility and an impersonal social order ("an empire, a Union, an economy") that "absolves us before the fact"—in other words, a system that makes us appear to ourselves to be less responsible because of its existence. The concept that connects these two relationships comes to be complicity, which, Bromwich writes, is the result of "thoughtless choices" and thereby "abet[s] our blindness to the actual harm we do" in not contesting the system. In our contemporary life, he concludes, this belief in "the modern state and society" has the deplorable tendency to "subdue the individual to a point that leaves every person both impotent and exonerated."[32] The complicity models take up these same questions in order to ponder the possibility and meaning of individual responsibility in the midst of expanding collectives or systems (mob, community, society, state). How, for instance, they ask, can someone be an individual citizen of the collective state at the same time as being an individual member of a collective lynch mob (an entity that implicitly denies the state's control over certain instances of law and punishment)? What ways of thinking about responsibility will permit us to comprehend that apparent contradiction?

On the other hand, complicity and denial also have a profoundly antagonistic relationship. As we will see, the advocates of the complicity models emphasize connections and continuity. For them, a lynching needs to be understood as a more expansive event whose performance involves a wide range of actors playing different but equally involved roles. Instead of seeing a lynching as a set of discrete actions—the capture of the victim, the torture of the victim, the killing of the victim—they insist on seeing it as a complete event, each of whose parts is intimately connected to the others in one grand performance. Likewise, instead of seeing the mob that performs a lynching as constituted of discrete kinds of actors—those who kill, those who assist, those who watch—the complicity advocates insist on seeing the relationship of those actors to each other, as they all participate in the performance of one action. In other words, as might be expected from those who orient their understanding of an action through the concept of complicity, the complicity advocates see continuity where their opponents see atomized individuals or discrete actions.

Denial, too, requires the same stance as that of the opponents of the complicity models, that of seeing or insisting on discontinuity. In the case of the end-of-lynching discourse, such denial requires seeing a rupture between a time when lynchings occurred and a time when they ended. There is an illusion of continuity in that account as they promote and follow a traditional narrative of the rise, decline, and end of lynching, but it is illusory insofar as they ignore the historical transformations of lynching that preceded what they designate as the rise and those that followed what they define as the end of the practice. Instead of tracing the connections that might make more meaningful the transition from one set of practices to another, the advocates of the end-of-lynching discourse insist on firm historical markers that they invest with social meaning.

In this book, my sympathy is with the advocates of the complicity models who see rather than deny connections and continuity. Indeed, the concept of complicity is important because it represents an attempt to understand action— the consummation of an event—as something continuous and connected.

The two kinds of connections I am arguing for in this book, then, are local and historical. First, I think it important to recognize the logic of the complicity models when they demonstrate how specific local events make sense only when viewed as more expansive performances that involve a wide range of actors. Lynchings are what they are because they are preeminently just those sorts of expansive performances. Second, I think it important to recognize what Wells and Graves and many others noted about the history of lynching—that lynching is a practice that has formally and strategically evolved over time. We will better understand what an event might be if we think of it as part of a continuous historical pattern than if we deny that possibility from the outset. We learn more about lynchings when we contest the idea that these events are isolated crimes and random events unconnected to the social and historical experience of the communities and this nation where they occur. There is great value in affirming and great danger in denying continuities, connections, and historical flows in the local manifestations and the national history of lynchings.

CHAPTER 1

THE ACCOUNTANT AND
THE OPERA HOUSE

When Albert Johnson, a nineteen-year-old accountant for Duluth Street Railway, heard that there was a lynching afoot on June 15, 1920, in Duluth, Minnesota, he, like thousands of others, went out of curiosity to see what would happen. After he saw the mob attack the jail and remove the three African American men from the building, Johnson spied a vantage from which he could watch the lynching. He climbed a light pole on First Street and waited, perched near the top of the pole and gripping the arm to which the extended light was attached. To his horror, he saw that the mob formed directly under the pole he had chosen. As the lynchers tossed Johnson the rope to cinch over the pole arm, the surrounding mob below howled in delight at the prospect of a triple lynching. Johnson felt his heart catch, his bowels moisten, and his fingers become thick and numb. The roar of the thousands who cheered as he cinched the rope that would become a noose caused his whole body to shudder.[1]

In that moment, did Johnson's legal or ethical condition change? Did he become a lyncher, an active participant in an event he had intended to attend only as a curious spectator? Would the law deem him guilty of a particular crime—lynching, or accessory to murder, or accomplice to murder? Did he in his own moral vision or that of his contemporaries commit an act that now placed him in a different ethical status? These are the kinds of questions the complicity model advocates asked about the function and existential status of the spectators in the lynch mob. Johnson's case is particularly useful for the purposes of understanding the dynamic of a lynch mob precisely because of its ambiguity.

In order better to understand that dynamic, we can consider the makeup of a lynch mob. First, as a caveat, we need to recognize that the dynamics of a lynch mob are difficult to discern because there are many different kinds of mobs and many different roles within these different lynchings. Another way

THE ACCOUNTANT AND THE OPERA HOUSE

of putting it is to say that while lynching follows a generally recognizable script, these scripts change over time and differ within the same historical epoch. Given that, we can nonetheless still discern general categories or roles that help us understand the dynamics of a lynch mob, especially the kind of mob that committed and witnessed spectacle lynchings from the last decade of the nineteenth to the third decade of the twentieth century.

Philip Dray has broken down into five general categories the essential makeup of the standard lynch mob; the five roles occupy different places in an expanding circle of responsibility. First, at the center of the lynch mob, there is "a cell of highly motivated perpetrators" who gather the implements of destruction (rope, gasoline), struggle with the police forces in securing the victim, drive the automobiles, and begin the rituals of destroying a human life. Second, just beyond the central cell of active participants, there is a "ring of cheerleaders," people who either are motivated by a grudge against the victim or have some investment in seeing the alleged crime answered. Third, occupying the next circle of the mob is "the gentleman of some authority or social standing" who gives legitimacy to the lynching and often directs the events through his exhortations. The fourth circle of participants is made up of the "crowd of onlookers, passive, alternately frightened and fascinated." Finally, the fifth circle of participants are those who do not actually show up for the lynching, the elite or "the better people" who express the community's sometimes ambivalent acceptance of the lynching and bring the affair to a close with their rote commentary.[2]

Our focus here is on the fourth circle, the spectators. They are the ones to whom it seems most difficult to assign responsibility. The first three circles are relatively unambiguous in most legal schemes. Those members of the innermost circle would certainly be guilty of murder; those in the second and third circles would equally be guilty as accomplices or accessories before the fact (and, by hiding the identities of the active lynchers, they become accessories after the fact). That leaves us, then, with the spectators, innocent bystanders, the onlookers who are not agents of the action in any discernible way. It is their status—legally, ethically, and existentially—that the complicity model advocates wanted to discuss and understand.

The case of the accountant on the light pole demonstrates the fluidity of the roles, the permeability of the circles. Johnson, after all, could be said to have moved from the fourth to the first circle in the act of unwillingly assisting the process of the lynching. What does this fluidity of movement between roles tell us about the makeup, dynamic, and meaning of the mob in American lynchings? The concept that gives us the best purchase on these questions—that will allow us to conceive of the mob as a specific kind of purposeful agent—is complicity.

We will begin our analysis by looking at a particular lynching at the height of the age of spectacle lynching, in 1911, and see how that case inspired considered thinking among jurists and moralists about the kind of responsibility that can be ascribed to or assumed by those who are not actively committing an act. We will look in particular at three responses—that of a judge where the lynching occurred who attempted to prosecute the spectators, that of a moralist who commemorated the first anniversary of the lynching by contemplating the meaning of widespread social responsibility, and that of a pair of cousins whose family was involved in the lynching who meditated on the meaning of inherited responsibility. We will see how each of these respondents stakes out the grounds on which someone may be said to be responsible for the lynching based on a certain kind of "presence"—*physical* (actually attending the lynching), *civic* (being responsible for what happens in the nation of which one is a citizen), or *hereditary* (having an obligation because of familial descent and inheritance).

Each of these respondents provides us with a model for a certain kind of complicity, and each model demonstrates what kind of legal or moral weight the concept of complicity can bear. These models, we must say up front, have not compelled many people in this society in understanding the nature of legal (or moral) responsibility. After assessing the terms and logic of these complicity models, we will then turn to those conventional models that have compelled many in their thinking about what constitutes legal responsibility, especially in the case of a spectator at a lynch mob, and see what issues they raise that the complicity models answer or reject.

The main question these models ask is, What are the possible ways of thinking about the relationship of action (the doing of something) to inaction (the not doing of something) in the case of lynching? Their answer to this question also describes a particular kind of society, one that apportions responsibility in a restricted way in which only certain actors are malefactors, or one that ascribes a widespread social responsibility to a range of actors who occupy a range of positions in any given action. In the end, we want to know how these ways of thinking about complicity better help us understand the dynamics of lynching. If we accept the premises of the complicity models, what can we say lynchings are precisely, and what kind of society is it where they happen?

A Mob on Trial

On the night of Saturday, August 12, 1911, a very intoxicated Zachariah Walker was stopped by a member of the coal and iron police working for Worth

Brothers Steel Company, the largest employer in Coatesville, Pennsylvania. After a vocal confrontation, Walker shot and killed the company policeman, Edgar Rice, in an act of apparent self-defense. Following an extensive all-night manhunt, on Sunday afternoon Walker was tracked to a nearby field where he had been hiding in the branches of a cherry tree. Seeing no escape possible, he attempted to kill himself but succeeded only in shattering his jawbone and falling from the tree. Some of those who captured Walker talked of lynching him when they discovered he was still alive, and other Coatesville residents also menacingly spoke of lynching him when he arrived by automobile at the Coatesville jail. Still unconscious, Walker was first placed in the jail and then taken to the hospital, where he underwent surgery to remove the bullet still lodged in his jaw. The police chief left one police officer on guard at the hospital, while the chief himself went to the main gathering place in Coatesville and practically incited a lynching by talking loudly to a crowd of Coatesville citizens about Walker's crime. He concluded his ill-advised discourse by observing, "It would be the devil if somebody should go after that fellow," noting that he himself would certainly not get hurt trying to protect him.[3]

Later that Sunday evening, a crowd of about two thousand gathered in the streets around the hospital. According to the report in the *Montgomery Advertiser*, the "orderly crowd was instantly transformed into a riotous mob" when a masked man mounted the steps of the hospital and taunted the crowd into action by asking, Would the "men of Coatesville" allow a "drunken Negro [to] do up such a white man as Rice?" Members of the mob broke into the hospital, met minimal resistance from the police officer stationed as the guard, and dragged Walker out to the street, still chained to the footboard of the hospital bed. By the time they got him to a field in a nearby farm, the mob had grown to four or five thousand. Several people gathered straw and hay, found kindling, and carried wood to the growing pyre. Just before he was thrown into the fire, Walker spoke his final recorded words, "For God's sake, give a man a chance! I killed Rice in self-defense. Don't give me no crooked death because I'm not white!" Three times Walker attempted to crawl out of the fire, and three times he was returned to it by those in the first circle around the pyre. By 9:30 that Sunday evening, half an hour after he was abducted from the hospital, Walker was dead, although his corpse would continue to burn for several more hours until nothing was left but a charred remnant that would be placed into a small, rectangular wooden box.[4]

Zachariah Walker was one of seventy African Americans lynched in 1911, and his was the eighth and final recorded lynching in the Commonwealth of Pennsylvania.[5] The local press was predictably reticent about the mob violence, while the national media were predictably critical. The *Outlook* excoriated the town of Coatesville as a "blot on civilization," and the *New York Times* proclaimed that "nowhere in the United States was a man ever lynched with less excuse or with an equal heaping up of horror on horror." Walker suffered an unspeakably cruel end, but the *New York Times* exaggerates. Walker's immolation was not unique, and the only uncommon feature was the fact that he was still chained to a piece of the hospital bed. There were no special editions of the local newspaper announcing that there would be a lynching, there were no special excursion trains bringing in people from surrounding communities, the mob that attended the spectacle was not extraordinary in its size or its makeup, and, as much as the torture of someone's being burned alive should sicken us, it was by no means the only or last time it would happen in American history, in that year, or in that summer. In fact, it was not even the only lynching on that day.[6]

What is striking about this case, and the reason it is interesting to us here, has to do with the aftermath of the lynching. There were three different responses to this lynching—a legal court proceeding immediately after it, an ethical meditation on the meaning of atonement on its first anniversary, and a reflective meditation on the meaning of inheritance some eighty years later. These three responses provide us with distinct models for understanding what complicity is and means, especially, but not only, in the case of American lynchings.

Approximately nine people were arrested in the immediate wake of the lynching, which fact alone makes the police investigation in Coatesville more rigorous than the huge majority of lynching investigations. Several others were arrested later after the grand jury issued its final report. In addition, both the district attorney and the primary trial judge spoke out forcefully about their intent to indict and convict the guilty parties, and the grand jury issued a report that boldly censured the local politicians for their lack of foresight and charged the police with involuntary manslaughter for their inaction. Indeed, because of the commitment of the state to pursue the lynchers, the criminal investigation became the most expensive one in Pennsylvania history up to that time. Despite the resources put into the investigation and trials, in spite of the vigorous prosecution by the district attorney (with the aid of the state's attorney general), and notwithstanding the judge's clear sympathy for a broader definition of guilt, the prosecution failed to win a single conviction. The jury returned a verdict of "not guilty" in the first trial after deliberating for less than one hour. Different juries in subsequent trials returned similar verdicts after deliberating thirty minutes in one case, slightly more than an hour in another, less than half an hour in a third, and, finally, with no deliberation at all and while sitting in the courtroom in the mass acquittal of the remaining seven defendants at the prosecution's request.[7] The decisions reached by the Coatesville juries are part of a long history of American juries' exonerating accused lynchers. What makes these cases stand out, though, are the court's attempts to define a standard of responsibility that would encompass those who formed the lynch mob.

Judge William Butler bravely defined a lower standard of legal culpability when he announced in the first meeting of the Court of Oyer and Terminer that he believed that those who sanctioned the action of a lynch mob and those who stood by and did not attempt to prevent the lynching were accomplices to murder. In a startling deviation from earlier judges in lynching trials, Judge Butler proved willing to find guilty of complicity those who were previously considered to be bystanders or spectators. The *Philadelphia Inquirer*'s headline the next day proclaimed: "May Punish All Lynching Mob, Court Declares." Five months later, at a second meeting of the Court of Oyer and Terminer, Judge Butler again insisted on casting a wide net of responsibility in defining guilt in the case of a lynching. When a "human being is wilfully burned to death by other human beings, murder is committed," he informed the grand jury, and those "who are present at such killing, physically aiding the act, or by word encouraging it, and those who, though absent from the killing, have by deed or word voluntarily aided the movement to slay, are all guilty of some degree of murder." In one case, and one case only, Judge Butler himself seemed unwilling to maintain this strict standard of determining guilt. With the prosecution's blessing, he asked the jury to render a verdict of "not guilty" to someone whose only "actual aid" to the lynching, somewhat suspect evidence showed, was to carry wood to the fire.[8] In every other case in which he presided, Judge Butler insisted on giving a bold charge to each jury, asking that they find guilty not only the active participants but also those who provided any kind of aid.

In one case, he told the jury: "It is wholly unimportant to know who played the most prominent part, whose words or acts most contributed to Walker's death. His destruction was the result of the combined words and acts of a number of men and the law holds them all equally responsible for his destruction." All should be found "equally guilty"—those who "originated, suggested, or by words encouraged the lynching" as much as those who "in the end happened to be the ones who actively and actually destroyed Walker." Heedless of the judge's charge, the jury returned a verdict of "not guilty" an hour later. In what would become the penultimate trial of the Coatesville lynchers, the prosecution presented its strongest case. Several witnesses placed the defendant, Norman Price, at the hospital and at the site of the lynching, and the prosecution had a written, signed confession in which Price confessed that he had helped break into the hospital, remove Walker from the bed, and drag him to the fire. Judge Butler again charged the jury not to think of guilt in narrow terms: "Even if the prisoner did not by physical help aid in the crime, he is as guilty as those that did do the actual work, if he aided in encouragement by word." Half an hour later, the jury returned another verdict of "not guilty." Frustrated at the series of miscarriages of justice, Judge Butler denounced the jury's verdict as a "public calamity and against law and order."[9]

After Judge Butler spoke fervently in defining the standard for guilt in the first meeting of the Court of Oyer and Terminer, the district attorney, Robert S. Gawthrop, pledged that he would cast an equally wide net to bring to trial all those involved in the lynching. He told the local newspaper: "We are going to arrest everyone who was in that crowd that went from Coatesville to the hospital and followed the lynchers when they carried Walker down over the hospital lawn and were around the fire when he was burned." The local newspaper's headline prejudicially announced: "Encouraged by Judge Butler's Opinion, D.A. Will Arrest Sympathizers." The prosecution's strategy then was to argue for "equal responsibility," that all those who "planned, encouraged, or participated" in the lynching were guilty of murder or of being an accomplice to murder. As we saw, the strategy failed miserably. For the later trials, the prosecution attempted to pursue charges of "second-degree murder," which, as the judge informed the jury, required proof only of the defendant's complicity rather than actual participation in the murder. The lower charge and lower standard for finding guilt also failed to win any convictions. Recognizing that the state could not win a conviction in these circumstances, at the final trial the prosecution requested that Judge Butler ask the jury to return verdicts of "not guilty" for the remaining defendants so that the outstanding cases could be removed from the court's docket. Fifteen minutes later, all those indicted had been found innocent of the lynching of Zachariah Walker.[10]

———

What happened in the Coatesville trials is not surprising, insofar as we can judge by what happened in other trials of accused lynchers where even those who admitted on the witness stand to participating in some way—as Norman Price did, to entering the hospital and dragging Walker to the site of the burning—had before been and would later continue to be found innocent. One local newspaper could brazenly predict that "no one shall be punished for the Coatesville lynching" because community sentiment, which had solid-ified in the face of national criticism, was against the intrusion of the state legal officers and held that Walker's life was not worth much, and because the newspaper could not imagine a jury buying into Judge Butler's interpretation of what constituted guilt in the crime of lynching. The headline in the other local paper, the *Coatesville Recorder*, stated what the members of the jury and the community from which they were drawn implicitly believed: those who were in attendance at the lynching were not criminals but at best "sympathiz-ers," and Judge Butler's mandate was but an "opinion," not a legal standard that they felt compelled to follow or establish.

There were two strongly opposed sensibilities on display in the Coatesville trials—that of the judge and prosecutor who argued that people were guilty if they encouraged a lynching explicitly by word and implicitly by their pres-ence, and that of the jury and the defense attorneys who maintained that guilt requires actual participation in the act of committing murder. Even those who abducted Walker from the hospital and dragged him to the site where he would be burned were found innocent. We can say that Judge Butler held to a broader, and the juries to a considerably narrower, definition of complicity. It was the juries' sensibility that clearly emerged victorious from these cases, but it is Judge Butler's vigorous attempt to speak for an enlarged human responsibility that strikes me as the most significant thing to come out of these trials.

Judge Butler seems to have got at the heart of the lynching dynamic when he articulated the concept of "equal responsibility." Mob violence in that era of spectacle lynchings depended on the spectatorship of the mob as much as it did on the activities of those who placed the rough noose around the neck or the flammable wood at the feet of the mob's victim. Those who "aided in encouragement by word" were a necessary feature of lynching because they incited the actors to their actions and promoted the sentiment of vigilante justice within the mob. Even those physically "absent from the killing," Butler maintained, were guilty if they had "by deed or word voluntarily aided the movement to slay" because they had helped form the mob. Butler's is a strin-gent legal imperative in that he held people responsible for verbally inciting others to action. In a situation where the act of murder requires a mob to make it meaningful, and where a mob becomes the excuse people use to justify their action or their presence, Butler's imperative seems eminently reasonable for locating moral culpability, no matter that the juries refused to hold to it as a standard for determining legal guilt.

The *Pittsburgh Dispatch* was one of the few newspapers to agree. The edi-tor applauded Judge Butler's directive, claiming that it is "just this failure to

appreciate individual responsibility that made this atrocity possible." If there
"had been no mob of curious spectators to swarm around the hospital and
follow the ringleaders to the commission of the crime, if the actual murderers
had not been encouraged by the sanction of the mob and the courage of
numbers," then the lynching would not have happened. "The ruling of the
Chester judge," the editor concluded, "ought to be brought home to everyone.
Properly digested, it may spare some other community the shock just
experienced by Coatesville."[11]

How, then, can we understand the presuppositions about responsibility in
Judge Butler's directives to the juries? What is he saying about how to ascribe
legal guilt in an American lynching? We could describe Butler's schema as a
legal complicity model in which responsibility radiates outward from those
who commit the act to those who view the act to those in whose name the act
is committed. In such a situation as mob activity, guilt is premised on either
physical presence or contemporary ideological aid. To be there or to encour-
age the action is to be equally guilty of the crime committed. Like a virus, guilt
is insidiously passed from the actors to the spectators to the surrounding
community in whose name the lynching had been performed. Those who
watch sanction, by their very presence, the actions of those who do collective
violence for the sake and prestige of the group. Implicit in this schema is the
idea that guilt inheres to those who by silence or omission permit the act to
happen. What makes one a member of the mob, according to this legal complicity model, is not mere presence but active unwillingness to make an
attempt to prevent the crime. One of the defendants in Coatesville insisted, as
did other members of lynch mobs at other places and other times, that he was
simply part of the "crowd" and that he "couldn't do anything to prevent the
work of the mob."[12] According to the dictates of this model, this defendant
has no excuse for inaction. It is the very failure to attempt to prevent the work
of the mob that makes one a member of the mob. The legal complicity model
of accountability holds to a quite strict code of conduct in that it allows
no intermediate situation of safety, a situation in which one can be an
"innocent" bystander. Since it assumes that unresisting presence at a scene
implies tacit approval of the action witnessed, it also presumes that the
failure to resist (a sin of omission) is a crime nonetheless.

As a principle for interpreting the law, then, Butler's legal model for defining lynch mob complicity did not compel the juries in Coatesville in 1911.
The *New York Times* speculated that this was an unsurprising result given that
the "guilt" for the crime was so "widely shared that only accomplices [were]
available for jurymen." The *Philadelphia Inquirer* agreed to a point, but
also felt that the juries acted on a sense of fairness: "Inasmuch as it was

impracticable to punish all who were participants in the Walker lynching, it was not fair or right to single out and punish the few who had been brought before them."[13] Nor have the larger principles of heightened responsibility behind the legal complicity model yet generated the support of legislators, nor are they likely to do so since American common law, as legal scholar Michael Tonry notes, imposes no "criminal responsibility for harms caused by omissions."[14] (We will return to this point below.)

The legal complicity model implies a moral universe in which individuals are responsible for not becoming implicated in an enterprise carried out in their presence and with their tacit knowledge. Nowhere was the community's approval of lynching more apparent than in those cases where witnesses refused to come forth or name the participants in a lynching. By the logic of the legal complicity model, those in the community who are knowledgeable of and yet remain silent about the identity of the lynchers implicitly support those who committed and watched the lynching. This was the view articulated by Theodore Roosevelt, who contributed an article on the Coatesville lynching to the *Outlook*, in which he argued that not only all the observers in the mob but also all those who refused to testify against the lynchers were now placed "on a level of criminality with their victim."[15]

What makes Judge Butler's directive so stringent (admirably so) is that it requires active dissent for anyone to establish a distance between him- or herself and the crime. There are notable examples of individuals who did just that. In the case of Coatesville, the aviator Al Berry stands out for his courageous attempts to prevent the lynching. When Walker was first captured, one of the captors yelled out: "Let us lynch the Son of a Bitch while we have him here." As the leader of the search team, Berry held the captor at gunpoint and informed the rest of the men that he would shoot any "man that tries to do any lynching." Later, after the mob started forming and threatening to break into the hospital, Berry frantically informed Police Chief Charles E. Umsted of the impending danger. The laid-back Umsted insisted several times that there was no danger, until finally Berry raged out of the office claiming, "I wash my hands of the whole matter." Ironically, Berry would be indicted (and found innocent) of participating in the lynching that he, by the most creditable accounts, prevented at least once and attempted to prevent again.

Compare Berry's staunch stand with that of someone like Mordecai Markward, the assistant chief of the Brandywine Fire Company, who likewise attempted and likewise failed to make Umsted aware of the danger but who also later went to the lynching scene, as he stated on the witness stand, because he was "curious."[16] Berry cannot be implicated in the Coatesville mob because he seems to have done everything he could to prevent the lynching and distance himself from it. Markward's is a little more difficult case to assess, but curiosity seems barely an excuse when we consider that most people in the mob would likewise claim to be there for the same reason, and that what they are curious to witness is a human in the process of being burned alive without benefit of trial. Moreover, what their presence implies (whatever their conscious motive) is the unspoken support of the community in whose name this act of vigilantism is being carried out. Innocence, to be free of infection in the legal complicity model, requires vigilant dissent.

Ida B. Wells gives us an exemplary model of such dissent in the case of the Reverend King of Paris, Texas. As Henry Smith was suffering the most gruesome tortures in this 1893 lynching, the African American minister stood up to the mob of ten thousand people and implored them not to lynch this poor soul, first praying loudly in the midst of the mob and then standing at the foot of the burning scaffold and crying out: "In the name of God . . . I command you to cease this torture." Severely beaten, threatened with lynching, and then forced into exile, King, despite failing to prevent the lynching, nonetheless stands as a paradigm of what a morally upright individual could do in the face of mob violence. No one in Coatesville lived up to that challenge on that August night in 1911, but someone would in 1938. The then–police chief of Coatesville, Ralph Williams, prevented a mob from seizing an African American youth being held in his jail by standing up to the crowd until it dissipated and then rushing the youth to another city's jail.[17] Unlike his predecessor in 1911, Chief Umsted, Williams took seriously his responsibility and stood up to rather than ignoring the potential lawlessness he faced. This is what we expect of those who are elected or appointed to ensure public safety, those who get paid to do the job they are supposed to do.

Why, one wonders, can we not expect at least a similar level of responsibility from citizens who, like King, could form a critical mass and also successfully mobilize sentiment against mob violence? For the advocates of the legal complicity model, it is only our low expectations, legally and morally, that keep citizens from aspiring to more serious attempts at being responsible for what happens in their presence, in their name, with or without their freely given approval. For the legal model, then, what defines complicity in lynching is being part of a mob; that is, mere unresisting presence or contemporary ideological assistance. As we will discuss shortly, this belief goes against the grain of Anglo-American law, based on English common law, that holds that individuals are responsible and guilty only when they engage in the active participation of the crime, with conscious and malicious intent. From that perspective, a mob always contains agents who are guilty and spectators who are not. That was the perspective that was upheld in the Coatesville trials, and that is largely still the standard of legal responsibility upheld in most states. A year after the Coatesville lynching, someone would expand on Judge Butler's legal complicity model, and apply it outside of the courtroom to the ethical condition of being American in the age of lynching.

RESPONSIBILITIES OF STRANGERS

So far, then, we have seen how a judge and a district attorney attempted to argue for a broader definition of responsibility, by showing how all the people in a mob and then in a community can become complicit in a lynching if they do not attempt to prevent, renounce, or help prosecute the crime. Where, though, does that responsibility begin to wane or to stop altogether? In the case of Coatesville, does it stop at the borders of the town—the police chief declared that the actual burning of Walker occurred on land outside the city limits—or does it stop at the boundaries of the county from which the jury pool is drawn? Or does it stop at the state where the county is located? Town boosters in West Chester, the rival town closest to Coatesville in the same county, certainly attempted to distance the town from the lynching and thereby save the reputation of Chester County. The newspapers in other towns in the state did likewise for the sake of the Commonwealth of Pennsylvania. When the *Brooklyn Eagle* condemned the whole state—"All are responsible. The commonwealth as a whole is responsible"—the *Pittsburgh Dispatch* editors responded with dispatch in claiming that while they were "chagrined" that the lynching had occurred "within the borders of our commonwealth," the crime was "so manifestly out of keeping with the spirit of Pennsylvania that we can disown it."[18]

Some, though, attempted not to salvage the reputation of the locale but to implicate the entire country. What the foremost historians of the Coatesville lynching, Dennis B. Downey and Raymond M. Hyser, call the "most damning criticism of Coatesville to appear in print," an article by William Ellis in the *Continent* about ten days after the lynching, concluded its harangue by noting that Coatesville in the end was but a symptom, "merely 'Exhibit A' in a study of American life." So, too, in a much more sympathetic article written on the Coatesville lynching, appearing eighteen months later in a county periodical called the *Cresset Magazine,* a local man named Wayne Morris concluded that "there are potential lynchers in every community in the United States."[19] Nobody went further in this act of implicating all of America, and in the process making complicit all American citizens, than the New York social reformer John Jay Chapman, and with him we see a shift from the ascription of legal responsibility (the basis of the legal complicity model) to the assumption of moral responsibility (what we can call the *ethical complicity model*).

———

Chapman felt "greatly moved" when he read about the Coatesville lynching in the newspapers, no surprise since the graphic accounts would horrify even someone not possessing Chapman's extreme sensitivity. What is surprising, though, is how Chapman chose to respond. On the first anniversary of the lynching, he interrupted his planned vacation to Maine and traveled to Coatesville instead, claiming that his "inner idea forced [him] to do something." After some trouble securing a site and finding advertisement, Chapman held a commemorative prayer meeting to atone for what he called this "dreadful crime." The *Coatesville Record* and the *Daily Local News* respectively published one- and two-sentence announcements of the anniversary event. Two individuals joined Chapman and his New York friend Miss Edith Martin for the meeting, a black woman from Boston and a white man Chapman suspected of being a spy.[20] To his small congregation, Chapman delivered a sermon or address that would be widely reprinted under different titles, a few of which, like the one used in the African American publication *Southern Workman*, emphasized the fact that it was an address on lynching. Many others, however, dwelt on the fact that Chapman was "a penitent at Coatesville," donning "Sackcloth and Ashes," or that he was raising the question of "a nation's responsibility."[21] Chapman's subject was indeed the meaning and dynamics of complicity.

Guilt should be assigned, he argued, not only to the active participants in the lynching ("a few desperate, fiend-minded men") but rather to all Americans who benefited from the institution and the enduring effects of slavery. He begins his sermon by including himself in that number:

> We are met to commemorate the anniversary of one of the most dreadful crimes in history—not for the purpose of condemning it, but to repent of our share in it. . . . [The] whole community, and in a sense our whole people, are really involved in the guilt. [This] great wickedness that happened in Coatesville is not the wickedness of Coatesville nor of to-day. It is the wickedness of all America and of three hundred years—the wickedness of the slave trade. All of us are tinctured by it. No special place, no special persons, are to blame. A nation cannot practice a course of inhuman crime for three hundred years and then suddenly throw off the effects of it. . . . You might call it the paralysis of the nerves about the heart in a people habitually and unconsciously given over to selfish aims.[22]

Going well beyond Judge Butler or any of the others who argued for a broad definition of responsibility for participants, spectators, and reluctant witnesses, Chapman saw that responsibility lay not with only the active agents in the lynching but with all who have historically profited from the benefits of being white. Chapman saw in this an opportunity not zealously to celebrate but rather mournfully to lament the course of American history that created and re-created a white supremacy that depended on and defended vigilante racist justice.

Chapman, though, was not just interested in noting that there was a widespread guilt that had historical sources; he also wanted to show the precise dynamics by which that guilt radiated outward from Coatesville. He begins with the spectators of the Coatesville lynching, those "hundreds of well-dressed American citizens, both from the vicinity and from afar," who stood "like blighted beings, like ghosts about Acheron, waiting for someone or something to determine their destiny for them." Chapman is roused to indignation at the thought of "hundreds of persons watching this awful sight and making no attempt to stay the wickedness, and no one man among them all who was inspired to risk his life in an attempt to stop it, no one man to name the name of Christ, of humanity, of government!" Chapman excoriates these spectators as representatives of "the unconscious soul of this country." His point is that a crisis always requires a response, and that the response always reveals the kind of person at the crisis. No one present tried to save the life of Zachariah Walker; no one responded to that crisis with the moral courage to stand up for justice and to take a stand against barbarity. Instead they watched "in cold dislike," and this, Chapman believed, revealed what was arguably true of all spectators at all lynchings, that the act of watching a lynching was itself as atrocious a deed as the lynching itself. "For to look at the agony of a fellow-being and remain aloof," he exclaims, "means death in the heart of the onlooker."[23]

Yet for Chapman, it is not only the physically present spectators in Coatesville who are the onlookers, but all Americans everywhere. The process, he notes, is initiated by the media. When "the next morning the newspapers spread the news . . . the whole country seemed to be helplessly watching this awful murder . . . and the whole of our people seemed to be looking on." All Americans are onlookers, then, but it is not only because they have read the news report or seen the photograph of the event. Rather, all are implicated by the same inaction shown by the Coatesville spectators. The true spectacle is that of the inert crowd, local and national. "That spectacle," Chapman laments, "has been in my mind." To those who would assign moral culpability only to the actors and not to the so-called innocent bystanders, and therefore claim that it is not theirs to express guilt ("someone may say that you and I cannot repent because we did not do the act"), Chapman responds: "But we are involved in it. We are still looking on."[24] For Chapman, this was the essence of complicity, and it was an attitude whose psychic costs he felt to be considerable. Locally in Coatesville, nationally in America, a mass citizenry was able to watch suffering without attempting to allay it, able to view injustice without agitating against it. And for Chapman the figure most representative of the guilt of complicity was the lynching spectator. "We are still looking on."

At the heart of Chapman's ethical complicity model is the belief that individuals ought to have an especially heightened sense of responsibility.[25] Even more than in the legal complicity model, in which responsibility radiates outward from the obvious actors to the less obviously implicated observers, Chapman's ethical complicity model rests on the premise that we are implicated, even more than by our presence at an event, by our relationship to that event through history. "This whole matter has been an historic episode," he perorates, "but it is a part, not only of our national history, but of the personal history of each one of us."[26] It is part of national history in that the lynching had its origins in slavery and the slave trade—those historical institutions that created an ethos in which the lives of people of African descent were worth less spiritually because they were calculably worth an amount materially. It is part of our personal history in that we are products of that national history, reflectors of its values, betrayers of its promises. For "each one of us," as he puts it, our personal history is defined by our relationship to that national history. Each one of us defines our personal history by either challenging or accepting those values (like white supremacy) that betray the promises in our national history.

We can say that Chapman's model replaces the legal complicity model's insistence on physical presence with what we can call civic presence. In the legal model, being in a mob and not struggling to stop its action constitutes approval of its work. In the ethical model, being an uncritical beneficiary of the past and not situating oneself as a conscientious resister to the deleterious ways of thinking formed by that history is the same thing. Chapman's model depends on a particular kind of consciousness, aware of the past and becoming more aware of it and its depth of influence on the present. As he put it, in America slavery had been "the great disease," and the Civil War that ended it had been "the climax" of that disease; the period from Reconstruction through the Progressive Era "began the cure, and in the process of cure comes now the knowledge of what the evil was." Our knowledge is dynamic, not static; with each atrocity that demonstrates the depth of the original disease we come to know better the profound evil that the disease had actually been, and residually remains. Each personal act in such a rigorous moral scheme either helps or sets back the recuperation. Chapman's statement of explanation introducing his Coatesville address—"I felt as if the whole country would be different if any one man did something in penance"—is a statement of his own belief in the power of atonement, but also a declaration of the intimate responsibility "each one of us" has to make ourselves more conscious of the past and act in accordance with healing its illness.[27] Individual penance for the "whole country" is the obverse side of the relationship of personal to national history. Just as each of our acts either uncritically reflects or critically challenges the ills of our past, so does each act of atonement make more possible, bring closer to realization, that era in which "each one of us" knows the dreariness of the past, and acts with that knowledge.

For Chapman, then, atonement in one sense is traditional and an acknowledgment of the human need for intercession—a prayer of forgiveness so that "our hearts may be turned to God through whom mercy may flow into us." But atonement in Chapman's model is also dramatically untraditional and a declaration of human power and responsibility—it is the development of a capacity to search out the past and assume a stance toward it, to know that our actions can be responsible or irresponsible in eradicating the sickness of a national history. That responsibility, for Chapman, extends beyond the self. His model stipulates that even the most vigilant and progressive soul is implicated in the actions of his fellow beings.

It is important to remember that Chapman was addressing precisely those people who had committed this crime—that is why he went to Coatesville ("this town where the crime occurred") to deliver the sermon.[28] In other words, he was seeking atonement for those who either committed or watched the lynching, people we might consider unable to share with Chapman the sense that the person being hanged or immolated was a "fellow-being." Inured to watching and denying black suffering, exposed to popular texts scientifically proving the absence of black pain, the beneficiaries of pervasive practices of black exploitation, these were people who did not question the national history that gave them a sense of racial superiority or the mob violence that retained it for them. It is precisely this indifference for Chapman that deadens the heart and soul. And it is precisely that indifference that he wishes to remove through his act of penance—a penance that is both a prayer for divine forgiveness and an expression of human knowledge.

He did not expect the knowledge he uttered on that occasion to have immediate effect. Just as contemporary events, like the Coatesville lynching, make one retrospectively aware of the profound illness of the past (slavery), so too does knowledge produced on that day, on that anniversary, await later understanding and fruition. As he prophetically put it, "I am saying things which will some day be thought of."[29]

Those things would come to be thought of, in particularly insightful ways, in the 1920s and 1930s, as the anti-lynching movement gained traction and started to sway popular opinion. One key element in that movement, particularly by white anti-lynching advocates and groups, was the recognition of the widespread and shared complicity of white Americans in all lynchings. As the Association of Southern Women for the Prevention of Lynching put it in its publication, "lynching survived only because of the tacit collaboration of the whole white community." The organization's leader, Jessie Daniel Ames, asked at one ASWPL conference: "What group benefits most by the cheap and subservient labor guaranteed by a system of white supremacy and enforced in the final analysis by lynching?" Her answer implicated the women who formed the ASWPL and herself: "We ourselves profit most by cheap labor."[30] As another white woman, Lily Hammond, daughter of slaveholders, the wife of the president of Paine College, and a leading voice of the Augusta, Georgia, branch of the Women's Home Missionary Society of the Methodist Episcopal Church, put it: while the "savage" minority perform lynchings, "we who could prevent it, permit them."[31] The reason the ASWPL was particularly attuned to the ways complicity worked was that the organization was in fundamental ways centered on the idea of complicity, since it consisted of white women who wished to expose the "falsity of the claim that lynching is necessary to their protection." In other words, here was a group of white women who repudiated the ways that white women in general had been made complicit in lynchings, on the pretext of Southern chivalry.

INHERITING THE PAST

About eighty-five years after Chapman's anniversary commemoration of the Coatesville lynching, two of the descendants of the owner of the Worth Brothers Steel Company, the town of Coatesville's largest employer at the time of the lynching, and the employer of many of the steel mill workers who participated in the lynching of Walker, started to consider their relationship to that historical moment. Two cousins, Lark and Robert Worth, began to ponder their own sense of responsibility for what happened in the city that housed their great-great-grandfather's factory eight and a half decades earlier. That ancestor, William Penn Worth, had taken over the Worth Brothers Steel Company in 1874 (from his father, Shesbazzar Bentley Worth, who had purchased and begun remodeling an existing ironworks in 1852). In the wake of the lynching, he did not return from the family vacation on the New Jersey shore (until a week later), and he continued to distance himself from the whole affair. He did not assist the court proceedings against his employees charged with the lynching, did nothing to help prosecute the lynchers, and fired nobody for the crime. His great-great-grandson speculates that William Worth probably "wished the scandal would just blow over, the sooner the better." He notes that the Worth family "took the same attitude" for the next eight decades.[32]

The two cousins who broke that silence—"uneasy about continuing the family policy of turning our backs on what had happened"—and challenged that family attitude did so in different ways. Lark Worth felt that the "family's failure to speak out about the lynching," in 1911 and thereafter, was morally equivalent to the "silence that frustrated justice during the trials in 1912." Those Coatesville citizens who refused to testify or, as jury members, find guilty their fellow citizens (and perhaps fellow lynchers) had rendered it impossible to try the individuals charged with the crime, as we saw above. For Lark Worth, echoing Chapman, the Worth family's silence helped "maintain the cruelties that slavery made possible." She proposed what her cousin Robert calls a "public family atonement." In initiating the process, Lark Worth sent letters to twenty-five relatives. She told her family that the lynching was still a living symbol of racial inequities for Coatesville's black community, and she wanted to see about the possibility of issuing a family apology and creating the grounds for reconciliation between black and white Coatesville residents.

Sympathetic to his cousin's efforts, Robert Worth began to examine what it means to be a beneficiary of a family's fortune. He recognized that the "extended Worth family still lives indirectly on the profits from those mills"—from his grandparents who enjoyed a "large estate in Delaware's 'chateau country,' in a mansion staffed with maids and cooks" to himself with his childhood "on Park Avenue and . . . education at expensive private schools." Robert Worth asked himself hard questions about the nature of guilt by association: "Are we responsible for the misdeeds of our ancestors?" If so, "when does the statute of limitations run out? And are we more responsible if those ancestors have left us money?"[33]

The Worth cousins' effort to understand the nature of complicity by attempting to end the silence about their family's role in the Coatesville affair is akin to Chapman's in one sense—the desire to offer a public act of atonement—but it is quite different in its motivations and the logic behind it. Unlike Chapman's act of atonement, which was meant to demonstrate the ways each of our actions can be a reflection or rejection of certain strains in American history, a reflection or rejection of white supremacy, for instance, the Worth family's apology is premised on the idea that a family has a responsibility for its ancestors' actions (and inactions) and that a public expression attesting to the failure of those ancestors' actions works to promote renewed reconciliation for the rupture that the actions might have caused. Two things stand out here. First, the form of atonement, the public apology, is symbolic, not in the demeaning sense that it is immaterial or trivial, but rather in the sense that it is a staging of a ritual interaction in which representatives (of the offender and offended) stand in for the original actors. Second, those who feel responsible are direct descendants of the original actors, and they feel responsible as a result of their familial connection to the event. In what we can call the *filial complicity model*, then, it is existential status (descent) that constitutes responsibility—just as physical presence and civic presence had done in the legal complicity and ethical complicity models, respectively.

————

The public apology for past events has become almost endemic. With increasing frequency, and all over the world, we witness people taking on themselves blame for historical events they did not take part in and which mostly happened before they were born. We are living in what I have elsewhere called a "guilted age," an epoch of public atonement. The great-grandsons of slavemasters apologize for the sins of their ancestors; leaders of churches ask forgiveness for actions as far-ranging as the slave trade and the Reformation, and even for inaction in events like the Holocaust and historical trends like the oppression of women.[34] Politician, prince, and pontiff apologize for what earlier occupants of their offices have done to groups within or beyond their borders. There are many ways to explain this movement of people to assume responsibility for crimes they have not actually committed. For some, the impetus is religious, as it was for so many who felt a millennial urge in preparation for the jubilee year of 2000; for others, it is political, a strategic form of interdenominational, interracial, or international negotiations, an attempt to atone for the past in order to create reconciliation in the present.

Many engaging debates have emerged out of these public acts of atonement. Some are critical of the idea of apologizing for past atrocities because they think an admission of historical guilt will open the way to demands for reparation or other kinds of restitution, while others are critical because they fear it is an attempt to preempt or prevent just such claims. Some feel that reconciliation between the beneficiaries and the victims of history is impossible without such acknowledgment, while others firmly believe that apologizing for such large-scale horrors cheapens the historical events. The debate that strikes me as most stimulating, and relevant for us here, concerns the concept of responsibility in these symbolic actions. What does it mean to take on responsibility for crimes one has not committed? For some, it is admittedly a facile gesture that has little or no meaning. For others, though, it has represented an action that respects historical continuity and takes seriously the corporate identity that comes with belonging to a church, group, nation—or, in this case, family.[35]

The extended Worth family responded negatively to Lark's proposal for a collective apology. Some offered predictably rote excuses—the company had been sold long ago, Walker deserved to be lynched, some of their best friends were black, they had donated money to the NAACP, and one even suggested that the lynching never happened but was staged as a political maneuver. In the end, they refused to acknowledge that the family had "any connection with the lynching at all." Others offered more considered objections to the idea of apologizing for something they felt they had not actively engaged in doing. How, they asked, "does one go about apologizing for something other people did eighty-five years ago?" The illogic in the apology, to these family members, was both the lag in time (eighty-five years) and the fact that the people apologizing were not the actors in the event for which they were apologizing; those were "other people." Others felt that "collective penitence" belonged to institutions like religions or governments, the former because that is the usual setting for collective confession and forgiveness, and the latter because that is the site of collective representation. Under those conditions, it would be inappropriate for a "family" to offer a "formal apology."[36]

There were also objections about the logistics or staging of such an apology. Who would apologize, to whom, and for what? When Lark Worth proposed creating a coalition of local religious congregations and then approaching Coatesville's "black community," members of her family wanted to know: "What would we tell them? We're sorry our great-grandfather closed his eyes to racial injustice? We're sorry we now live in all-white suburbs or on the Upper East Side, while you still live on the wrong side of Coatesville?" Finally, one last family member objected that it might prove dangerous to express "liberal self-blame" in a time when there was "racial anger" over economic and political setbacks to such issues as affirmative action, minority scholarships, and inner-city education. "If we were to apologize for the lynching," this Worth relative commented, "we'd just be setting ourselves up as a target. People would come up the hill and burn our house down."[37]

Robert Worth, who recorded his family's objections, and shared some of them, had more substantial objections to his cousin's plan for a public apology. His objections were primarily about appropriateness—what would be appropriate or inappropriate, and what might be more appropriate. He felt that the apology would be inappropriate because it did not meet two conditions necessary for it to be meaningful. First, it was not being offered to those who were directly hurt. A "real apology should be addressed to the people who have been injured, and in this case Zachariah Walker and his family were long dead." Second, it was not being offered in the proper historical and political context. Chapman's sermon was appropriate "because in 1912 white Americans needed to be reminded of the legacy of slavery." An apology would have been appropriate in the 1960s because it, like the civil rights movement generally, Robert Worth contended, would have forced "whites to take an honest look at the consequences of their racism." But by the 1980s, "the rhetoric had begun to sound forced." An apology now "would no longer mean much," and "might seem more like self-indulgence than like real remorse."[38] It would be untimely.

What would be more appropriate, then, was something else. Believing that "Coatesville's worst problem [was] no longer racism" but rather the "by-products of racism (poverty, and the attendant drugs, crime, and despair)," Robert Worth felt that "economic development" was now more meaningful than an apology. This was a strategy to which the Worth family had much less resistance. His cousin Lark Worth put aside her "proposed apology" and began instead to work on raising funds for a "cultural center on Coatesville's Main Street." What Robert Worth called "a more private form of reparation" struck him as a "more practical way to do something for the town."[39] It was more "private" in the sense that it was reparations on a small-scale (one family's work), and also in that it did not involve a public admission or apology or other demonstrable statement of complicity.

Robert Worth ends his account, entitled "Legacy of a Lynching," with two images. The first is of a group called Faith at Work, a coalition of black and white ministers who seek "racial reconciliation in the Coatesville area." According to Paul Johnson, a retired African American Chester County district judge who works informally with Faith at Work, the group has made some progress; he also notes that they studiously "avoid discussing the lynching" in order to prevent the pain it would unavoidably incite. The second is of Worth's final visit to the scene of the lynching. Standing among the "grove of tall oak trees," Worth feels no ghosts lingering in the air here, where the lynching happened, but he cannot "shake the feeling that the real legacy of the lynching, if there was one, was elsewhere." He drives back to town, through the East End, where "a group of young boys surrounded the car trying to sell us drugs," and then to Main Street, where in front of the police station stand "a black teenager in handcuffs and a white police officer, his arms crossed, looking the other way."[40]

It is unclear whether these two deliberately chosen images perfectly reflect or perfectly undermine Robert Worth's primary message. In one part of town we see the by-products of racism—poverty, drugs, criminality, and despair— while in another we have an interracial coalition of religious leaders thinking about how to create a better interracial climate by not talking about the lynching. Is the silence about the lynching related to the by-products of racism? Is the silence the cause, the unaddressed festering wound in this community? Or is it simply the most appropriate strategy to follow in order to get anything done, the family secret no one should talk about?

What is clear in Robert Worth's engaging account of the Worth family's struggle to understand the nature of their complicity in their ancestor's inaction is that the apology Lark Worth first proposed genuinely distressed nearly every one of her family. It turns out to be more palatable for them to give money than to express contrition, and perhaps that is because they felt their inheritance to be the primary source of their guilt. Robert Worth consistently emphasized the heightened responsibility that might come with being the financial beneficiary of that Worth ancestor. But the crime in that case is not the lynching but the exploitation of the employees in the Worth factory, which was noted in at least one contemporary account of Coatesville in the aftermath of the lynching. Albert Nock's 1913 article in the *American Magazine* sardonically pointed out that the Quaker owners of the Coatesville steel mills who refused to manufacture products "for any purpose connected with war" felt no compunction about paying their employees a barely living wage and promoting conditions of living "worse than one can find in the countries from which the 'foreigners' have emigrated."[41] Even when Robert Worth tries to formulate possible apologies, he is drawn into the discourse of economic inequity: "We're sorry we now live in all-white suburbs or on the Upper East Side, while you still live on the wrong side of Coatesville?" Perhaps one sense of guilt (inheriting wealth from exploitation) trumps another (having an ancestor who did nothing about a lynching)? Perhaps inheriting ill-gained wealth feels more like an action for which one can be held responsible or hold oneself responsible than being descended from someone somewhat indirectly tied to a lynch mob?

Whatever the case may be, at least some members of the Worth family were sufficiently motivated by a felt inherited complicity to attempt to do something. Lark Worth prompted her family to think about their responsibility for past and present conditions, about their obligations for wealth gained through active means and guilt implied through an ancestor's inaction; and she prompted them to delve into and reveal to public scrutiny what had been a family secret. The effort to apologize and the subsequent debate over the apology, in other words, produced considerable reflection about the nature of complicity.

THREE MODELS ASSESSED

What, then, can we make of these three models for comprehending the nature and extent of complicity—the legal, ethical, and filial models? The legal model, as we saw, appropriately emerged in a courtroom since it is primarily designed to designate guilt, to define how one can be assigned responsibility for being within a comprehensive circle of differently situated actors. *All* who attend a lynching are actors, according to the legal model, and one's presence at a lynching is itself prima facie evidence of some kind of action—from assisting through actual performance of deeds, like collecting firewood, to aiding and abetting through curiosity, thus supporting those who perform the deed itself. The legal model, as we saw, did not prove successful, at least not in that (or any other) courtroom in American jurisprudence.

The other two models—ethical and filial—emerged in the public sphere outside the courtroom, not in a realm governed by the state but in spaces where civil society sets the rules for discourse. It is especially notable that there should emerge a moral sensibility in which individuals take on responsibility for events well beyond their control, especially in light of a society's legal order that does not apportion blameworthiness for acts of omission. The ethical model set the highest standards for responsibility, making each action by any citizen either an act of regressive complicity with or progressive challenge to the major trajectories of national history. In Chapman's version of it, everybody had to possess a heightened sense of responsibility for action and inaction, for doing what promoted or delayed racial justice in a land at the root of whose history was an enormous system of racial injustice. For Chapman, guilt or, better, responsibility inhered in citizenship; all who performed, witnessed, read about, or in some other way came to know of what happened in Coatesville were obligated to own up to their measure of responsibility for its happening. Whereas Chapman expanded the boundaries of responsibility *spatially* to all in America in 1912, the filial complicity model expands the boundaries *temporally*, posing the question of whether or not there is either inherited guilt or a statute of limitations on such guilt.

The three models differ in how they apportion responsibility. The legal model makes one responsible for being in a particular physical space (the mob, or where the lynching occurs); the ethical model makes one responsible for being a citizen in a particular national historical moment; the filial model makes one responsible on the basis of familial descent (and the "family" here can be expanded to include "nation"). One, then, is about shared space, one about shared history, and one about shared descent.

All three models in significant ways failed of their purposes. The courts in Coatesville did not return any sentences of guilt for those brought up on charges of complicity. Only two individuals attended Chapman's sermon in Coatesville. And the Worth family in the end debated the proposed apology into nullity. The material success of these models is not to be found in realized prosecutions or even heartfelt expressions of contrition. Rather, their success is to be measured only in the quality of the terms they propose for our better understanding of what we do and represent in the face of injustice—when we see it, or in some way when we belong to it.

Lawless Samaritans

Each of the models for understanding complicity in lynching provides a challenge—and is in implicit debate with—the conventional belief that responsibility can only inhere to willed, individual action. The proponents of that belief of a restricted ascription of responsibility provide two rationales for it. First, they maintain that crimes are acts of commission, not omission; in other words, there must be willed action. Second, they maintain that crimes are committed by individuals. Mobs, by their very nature, cannot commit crimes; only specific persons within a mob can.

The first of these arguments for a restricted sphere of responsibility maintains that those who observe a lynching, who come out of morbid curiosity or a desire for excitement, are innocent of any crime. Following the canons of English common law, the lynching apologists claim that such spectators are bystanders, and by definition innocent. We can call this model the *Samaritan argument* (since they maintain that one cannot be legally compelled to be a "good" Samaritan).

The second of these arguments maintains that the actions of a mob are by definition not subject to the same laws as actions of individuals. When a sufficiently large group commits what would otherwise be a crime, it becomes an expression of the will of the community. Sometimes the lynching apologists defend their case by invoking the democratic idea of popular sovereignty—that what is done by a group of actual citizens is as legitimate an act of legislation or criminal trial as what is done by the representatives they elect or juries they select to pass or enforce laws. The popular sovereignty argument has a long and sturdy history in both English and American history. One form that argument took in the course of American lynchings was to insist that it was unfair to try some alleged lynchers, usually the acknowledged mob leaders, and not to try the whole mob. We can call this second model the *Lawless argument.*

———

Many Americans of this generation became aware of the existence of "good Samaritan" laws by watching the final episode of *Seinfeld* in May 1998. The four main characters of the sitcom were placed on trial as a test case for a recent (fictional) Latham County, Massachusetts, law for failing to provide aid to the victim of a robbery. In the wake of the death of Princess Diana, where photographers took pictures of the crash scene instead of offering assistance, some American legislators considered passing laws that would require those who could provide succor to potential victims to do so. At least fifteen European countries have laws that allow prosecutors to indict bystanders who refuse help to someone in need if there is no risk to the bystanders. The French version of that law (dating back to 1941) reads: "Anyone who, by their own actions, if there is no risk to themselves or another, can prevent a crime or physical harm and refuses to help shall be punished by five years' imprisonment and a 500,000 franc fine." Although some states have versions of this law (including Minnesota, Rhode Island, Hawaii, Massachusetts, and Vermont), with much less severe penalties than the French law allows, most do not. In addition, the good Samaritan laws in the states that do have them exempt people from liability for civil damages if they attempt to provide emergency care or assistance, rather than hold them responsible for not responding to the need for emergency care or assistance.[42]

Those who oppose good Samaritan laws argue that the state cannot legislate moral behavior or punish the failure or omission to do good. As Lord Thomas Macaulay put it in 1837, "the penal law must content itself with keeping men from doing positive harm, and must leave to public opinion, and to the teachers of morality and religion, the office of furnishing men with motives for doing positive good."[43] In the less restrained language of Jackie Chiles, the defense attorney on *Seinfeld,* "You don't have to help anybody. That's what this country's all about." People cannot be guilty of not offering aid simply because they find themselves at a scene where it is required. "Bystanders are by definition innocent. That is the nature of bystanding," as Chiles states in his opening remarks. Macaulay reluctantly and Chiles gleefully accept that Anglo-American law, based on English common law, protects individual liberty and self-interest over communal responsibility. They accept what appears to be the sensible argument that one cannot be guilty of what one has not done.[44]

Critics of good Samaritan laws generally use three standard arguments to make the case that the law should punish only positive harm, and not the failure to prevent positive harm through inaction. First, they argue that such laws would enforce benevolence, with the corollary effects of "erasing the distinctions between harm and nonbenefit, and between duty and supererogation." If "charity" or heroic acts were legally compulsory, if doing good to others in circumstances in which they face danger were mandatory and failing to do so punishable, we would occupy a very different legal landscape and moral universe.

Second, the critics make the argument that such laws would create a logistical nightmare. In the classic example used to make the case for these laws, a person sits on the edge of a swimming pool in which a stranger's child is drowning. The good Samaritan law would punish the person who refused to reach out and save the child where there was clearly no risk to him- or herself. The logistical argument states that it would be impossible to define reasonable parameters for these laws. How do we define what activity involves risk for any given person? How do we define what constitutes proximity—if one is not on the edge of the pool but rather thirty yards away, is one as liable? If liable for a child in an accidental emergency in a pool, why not for a starving child on another continent, who faces the same peril and could be saved by an even less risky act of monetary charity?

The third argument is that such laws would produce "undue interference with liberty." Whereas the law prohibiting murder, let's say, is also an interference with one's liberty to kill another, it is clear that laws that compel active duty (you must rescue) as opposed to passive (you must not kill) differ significantly in how they interfere with one's liberty.[45]

Legal philosopher Joel Feinberg has done a compelling job of outlining and then answering these arguments as he makes a robust case for the advantages of having "bad Samaritan" laws.[46] The importance of this debate for our purposes is that the case against the bad Samaritan laws very much resembles the argument made by lynching apologists against complicity in lynchings. Those who go to observe lynchings are not guilty or responsible for the actions performed for their viewing. They are more like innocent bystanders who happen upon an accident than they are like active agents who do the actual deed. Their status depends on the same distinctions in the debate over bad Samaritan laws—between being active and being passive, between the commission of a crime and the omission to prevent one. In the Samaritan argument of the lynching apologists, those who look at a lynching occupy a different legal and moral status than those who perform one precisely because "looking" is akin to being passive or not doing.

The dynamics of lynch mobs are not quite that simple, however. For one thing, the distinction between spectator and participant is not always stark. When the editor-son of Joshua W. Ashleigh, a South Carolina state legislator, wrote about the role he played in the dismemberment of an alleged rapist in Greenville, South Carolina, in 1911, for example, he commented that he "went out to see the fun without the least objection to being a party to help lynch the brute."[47] The shift from looking to acting, from being a spectator to becoming a murderer, was smooth and not particularly troubling for the son who watched and helped as his father led the Greenville mob. We saw this same ambiguity in the case of the accountant on the light pole who went to watch and ended up helping in the lynching in Duluth. That firm distinction, then, between those who passively look and those who actively perform does not quite hold in the practice of American lynching. Even more important, though, in fact crucial, is the question of what precisely "looking" means in a lynching. What lynching apologists cast as a passive omission, anti-lynching advocates represent as an active cause—to look, for them, is to do something, to perform an act, in the lynching. (We will return to this point.)

———

Where the Samaritan model argues that an individual who does not commit an act is innocent, the Lawless argument maintains that an individual who commits an act in which he or she is part of a collective is equally innocent. The Lawless argument is based on the notion of popular sovereignty, that what a "people" do informally is an expression of their political will, even though it might constitute a challenge to the laws passed by the representatives they elected. In other words, the advocates of popular sovereignty eschew some of the basic principles of representative democracy. The people, they argue, never surrender or place in abeyance their democratic rights. An election, say, every two years does not imply that the voters can no longer revoke by their actions what they granted with their ballots. The popular sovereignty argument has been the classic defense of lynching in America and can be traced, in fact, to the Revolutionary origins of the nation itself, as we saw in the introduction.

In what has been an enduring motif in the history of American lynching, those who lynch argue that they do it with the "consent" of and in the name of the "people." In the 1850s, defenders of the San Francisco Vigilance Committee described the masses pursuing vigilante justice as "not a mob, but the *people*, in the highest sense of the term."[48] Half a century later, Tom Watson vehemently defended the lynchers of Leo Frank by postulating that the "people" may delegate but never surrender to their "agents" the power of governance. "When the Sheriff kills," Watson argued, "it is not his act; *it is the act of the People*, performed through their statutory law." When the sheriff fails to act in accordance with what the people want, the lynching that follows is just as legal because its sanction comes from the ultimate source of all law. "The Voice of the People Is the Voice of God," ran the headline for Watson's article.[49]

Wielding such divine power over life and death, the "people" in the Lawless argument simply cannot be subject to the law. When their representatives inexplicably fail to understand the people's power and arrest and indict mob leaders, the advocates of the Lawless argument take up another related argument: it is unfair to try some for the crimes of all. We saw earlier that the *Philadelphia Inquirer* had maintained this argument in the trials for the Coatesville lynching: "Inasmuch as it was impracticable to punish all who were participants in the Walker lynching, it was not fair or right to single out and punish the few who had been brought" to trial.[50] A much more forceful statement of this argument came from the mouths of lynchers themselves.

Some of the members of a 1916 lynch mob in Abbeville, South Carolina, published a report in the *Abbeville Scimitar* in response to the governor's attempt to get a grand jury impaneled in another county because no one in Abbeville County would testify against them. In their statement, they argued that all South Carolinians were complicit in the lynching of Anthony Crawford:

> We are ALL responsible for the conditions that caused Crawford's death. Those involved might have gone too far, but they are white men and Crawford was black. The black must submit to the white or the white will destroy [him]. . . . There were several hundred who participated in this lynching, and nearly ALL the others were well-wishers, therefore to pick out a few to satisfy a newly imported mawkish sentiment, is pitiful and cowardly. Men of Abbeville, the eyes of all white men are upon you. Acquit yourselves as white men. The conditions made by US ALL, make us all responsible, so let's not ask only eight to shoulder the whole burden. Answer a mawkish sentiment generated by hypocrisy and craven fear with the ringing verdict, Not guilty.[51]

The Abbeville lynchers are unusually honest in their declaration of the naked white supremacy that motivates lynchers to act, and in their recognition of the complicity of all "white men" who benefit from the effects of any lynching. Of course, their argument goes in precisely the opposite direction of most arguments about the responsibility of the complicit—namely, that since all are guilty, none is guilty.

The classic statement of the Lawless argument appropriately comes from its namesake, Judge Luke Lawless. After Francis McIntosh, a free black man, was taken from his St. Louis jail cell and burned to death by a mob in April 1836, Judge Lawless counseled the jury on their duties. If they determined that the lynching was performed by "a *small* number of individuals, separate from the mass, and evidently taking upon themselves, as contradistinguished from the multitude, the responsibility for the act," then the jury should "indict them all without a single exception." If, however, the jury found the lynching to be the act of "the many—of the multitude, in the ordinary sense of these words—not the act of numerable and ascertainable malefactors, but of congregated thousands, seized upon and impelled by that mysterious, metaphysical, and almost electric phrenzy, which, in all ages and nations, has hurried on the infuriated multitude to deeds of death and destruction," then the members of the jury must not indict. That act of the multitude, as an expression of communal sentiment, would be beyond the jury's jurisdiction and "beyond the reach of human law."[52]

A year and a half later, a young lawyer from neighboring Illinois noted that the violence of the "multitude" was becoming endemic; indeed, mobs were able with impunity to "burn churches, ravage and rob provision stores, throw printing presses into rivers, shoot editors, and hang and burn obnoxious persons at pleasure." Such a situation, he thought, was a dire threat to the American "political edifice of liberty and equal rights." When there is an "increasing disregard for law," and a "growing disposition to substitute the wild and furious passions" of the mob for the "sober judgment of Courts"— under such conditions, the lawyer perorated, "this Government cannot last." That Illinois lawyer, Abraham Lincoln, was fearful of what could be done in the name of the mob—what he called the "lawless in spirit," the "lawless in practice"[53]—and, we might add, the Lawless in principle.

What is fascinating about the Lawless argument is that its advocates assume the same things about the nature of complicity in lynching as do the anti-lynching advocates. As the Abbeville lynchers state it with remarkable candor and appalling aplomb, the "several hundred who participated in this lynching" and the thousands who were "well-wishers" were "all responsible"— responsible for the act itself and the "conditions" that made the act possible. No anti-lynching advocate could have made a more compelling case for the dynamic of complicity in a lynch mob and in a society whose public opinion permits and encourages lynching. The difference, for the Lawless advocates, was their belief in the concept of popular sovereignty, which for them and the lynchers they defended, as for so many others in American and world history, served as a justification for bold bids for bald power in the name of a fabricated "people."

———

These, then, are the ways of thinking about complicity against which the Coatesville judge, John Jay Chapman, and the Worth cousins arrayed themselves. What is perhaps striking about these two models—the Samaritan and the Lawless—is how very differently they proceed in staking out what constitutes a mob and participation in a mob. Indeed, we can say that there is an informative contradiction between these two models. Each model embodies values that contradict the other—the value of individual will and independence of action in the Samaritan argument, collective will and loss of independent action in the Lawless argument. While individual liberty is held at a premium in one case—the freedom of someone to choose to act or not to act in the case of the Samaritan—it becomes a casualty of the Lawless case where mass activity can trump individual will.

According to the Samaritan argument, one can be a member of the mob as a spectator, by which is meant someone not actively participating in the event but witnessing it. That position of spectator is not possible in the Lawless argument, since to be a member of a mob is to be one of the "congregated," one of the "multitude" acting en masse. If there are spectators, then there must be specific actors (which, according to Lawless, makes those actors guilty); if there are no specific actors, but a multitude acting as one, then there cannot be spectators in the mob.

These contradictions do nonetheless support precisely the same principles. It is possible to attend a lynching and not be guilty. The Samaritan at the lynching is only a spectator; the Lawless at the lynching are part of a mass action for which no individual is responsible. In both models, purposefully, complicity is rendered impossible. Either one does nothing but watch (and therefore is not responsible) or all do something (and therefore no one is responsible).

Such contradictions, particularly in a society's way of thinking about guilt, innocence, and legal responsibility, must reveal something about the society where such disparate values are upheld in the same cause. In the case of defending lynching, in the period we are examining, from the end of the Civil War to the 1940s, the transcendent principle that made seamless the different ways of justifying it was white supremacy. The Abbeville lynchers were brutally honest in acknowledging what was more commonly the unspoken truth in defense of lynchings: "The black must submit to the white or the white will destroy" the black. It was acceptable for people and groups of people to look on black suffering and death as amusement; it was understandable that a group of white people could be driven to an "electric phrenzy" when the pillars of white supremacy were imperiled.

Another way of seeing what such contradictions reveal is to see a society in the process of reconciling two different ways of thinking about social organization. Would this be a society in which individual rights are uppermost—a society in which the individual would be taxed with minimal social obligations that are primarily passive (not to kill, not to steal)—or would this be a society in which the collective matters more and in which there are circumstances in which an individual's actions are considered exclusively as expressions of a collective will?

So far, then, we have seen how a series of people have thought about the dynamic of responsibility in American mob lynchings. The legal model had made all in the mob complicit; the ethical model had made all in the nation responsible; the filial model had made all generational heirs the beneficiaries of guilt as well as wealth. The Samaritan argues that a mob is made up disparate elements—some guilty of acting, most simply spectators; the Lawless argues that a mob is an active collective will of the people and therefore not subject to the laws of the state. The last group of thinkers we will address are those who wanted to understand the kind of society that depended on racial lynchings. They worked from the assumption that a large swathe of individuals and groups were complicit in lynchings—both by performing them and creating the conditions in which they could be performed with impunity— and proceeded to diagnose the social malaise at the heart of a society that permitted and promoted them.

Particeps Criminis

It would be deeply interesting to know what one of the two individuals who attended the Chapman sermon—the African American woman visiting from out of town—might have thought of the address. Her presence raises some interesting questions about complicity. She, like Chapman, was not a resident of Coatesville, and to that extent exemplified his point about how all Americans everywhere were implicated in what happened in Coatesville. But she, unlike Chapman, was black and would probably neither claim nor be ascribed the same measure of responsibility for either the Coatesville lynching or the history of racial injustice that led up to it. Being black, and therefore more likely the victim than the perpetrator of such racial injustices, she would likely have listened to Chapman's diagnosis of the country's process of recovering from its sickness of white supremacy more as an observer than as a patient, more as someone overhearing than addressed by the sermon. She might indeed have been someone who had already thought things Chapman was saying now for others to think of someday. And if she was a reader of black publications, she would have known that African American intellectuals were the first and most consistent to make the argument for complicity in lynchings.

Indeed, the Reverend Reverdy C. Ransom of the Bethel African Methodist Episcopal Church of New York City had anticipated John Jay Chapman's statement of the widespread guilt for lynchings when he sermonized that the responsibility for the lynching of Zachariah Walker was not the "cold-blooded mob of Coatesville, but American public opinion."[54] This was a point repeated by African American intellectuals before and after the Walker lynching. Usually these intellectuals condemned the press and pulpit as complicit for either inciting lynchings or refusing to criticize lynchers. In some cases, though, that criticism was leveled at specific individuals.

In 1905, for instance, Kelly Miller, a dean at Howard University, indicted Thomas Dixon, the author of poisonously racist novels like *The Clansman* and *The Leopard's Spots*, which became the basis of D. W. Griffith's 1915 film *Birth of a Nation*, on precisely the grounds that his writing emboldened, inspired, and led to lynchings. "You preside at every cross road lynching of a helpless victim," Miller addressed Dixon; "wherever the midnight murderer rides with rope and torch, in quest of the blood of his black brother, you ride by his side." Wherever "women and children, drunk with ghoulish glee, dance around the funeral pyre and mock the death groans of their fellow man and fight for ghastly souvenirs, you have your part in the inspiration of it all."[55] Here, Miller finds complicity in those who are not present but make lynchings possible and, some would say, inevitable through their propaganda, and the popular opinion they form and mobilize.

For three or four decades, beginning when mass spectacle lynchings first arose in the 1890s, African American intellectuals diagnosed what this new phenomenon in American social life revealed about the nation's politics, its society, and its civilization. In each case, these intellectuals made the case for a wider and expanded concept of complicity, locating responsibility for lynchings not where they happened but where they were permitted to happen.

By the early to mid-1920s, the NAACP had begun to diagnose even more closely just what sources gave rise to lynchings. As it did so, it began to focus on the nature of complicity—the complicity of those who had power to effect change and chose not to, and the complicity of those who watched and thereby allowed lynchings. We can see this change in how the NAACP's campaign differed during and after the Senate vote on the Dyer Anti-Lynching Bill. On November 23, 1922, the NAACP ran a full-page advertisement in the *New York Times* (paid for in part by the Anti-Lynching Crusaders) that urged citizens to telegraph their senators and urge them to vote in support of the bill (which had been passed in the House on January 26, 1922, by a vote of 230–119). The advertisement was called "The Shame of America" and rehearsed the case against lynching that the NAACP had been making for the past decade: noting the numbers of African Americans lynched, the alleged crimes they committed (including the low number of alleged rapes), and then detailing the ways that the Anti-Lynching Bill would be the "remedy" for lynching in America. That was the NAACP strategy before the Senate vote— to shame Americans into seeing the barbarism of a civilization that would allow such atrocities. The strategy was markedly different right after the vote. On December 13, 1922, nine days after the Republican senators abandoned the Dyer Anti-Lynching Bill in the face of the Democratic senators' filibuster, James Weldon Johnson issued an "Open Letter to Every Senator of the United States," in which he noted that four lynchings had occurred in those nine days. "This outbreak of barbarism, anarchy, and bestiality and blood of the victims," he wrote, "rest upon the heads of those Southern senators who have obstructed even discussion of the measure designed to remedy this very condition," and "the responsibility rests equally with the Republican majority who surrendered with hardly a struggle to the lynching tactics of the Democrats."[56]

Ascribing "responsibility" to the senators of both parties, Johnson expanded the notion of guilt for American lynching beyond the lynch mob that did the deeds to those who did not perform them but who refused to create laws to prosecute the lynchers more successfully. The "lynching tactics of the Democrats" were supported and buttressed by the cowardliness of the Republicans, in much the same way that those who lynched were supported by those who formed the crowd watching the lynching.

It was highly appropriate for Johnson to ascribe responsibility to the senators who killed the Dyer Anti-Lynching Bill since that bill itself contained an important clause—that a county where a lynching took place would be required to pay the lynching victim's survivors a sum up to $10,000—which implied, as Christopher Waldrep and Dora Apel have noted, that the community would be held liable for the actions of its residents. This notion of "collective responsibility" fit well with at least one prevailing definition of lynching—that provided by James Cutler in 1905, that lynching was an act performed by those who enjoyed the favorable "public opinion of the community behind them."[57] The NAACP argument that widespread complicity made lynchings possible would be one that other anti-lynching activists would adopt, but it was an argument whose roots we can trace to the origins of anti-lynching activism in the early 1890s.

In 1892, Frederick Douglass dissected the various actors in any lynch mob in order properly to designate the "responsibility for the lynch law prevalent in the South." He starts with the obvious, the lynchers, and notes that the "men who break open the jails and with bloody hands destroy human life are not alone responsible." They are "simply the hangmen, not the court, judge, or jury. They simply obey the public sentiment of the South—the sentiment created by wealth and respectability, by the press and the pulpit." Douglass then turns to the question of regional responsibility in order to deny that the "South alone [is] responsible for this burning shame and menace to our free institutions." The "finger of scorn at the North," he insists, "is correlated to the dagger of the assassin at the South." The guilt of the North, he concludes, is the guilt of omission, the guilt of complicit silence. Until "the voice of the North shall be heard in emphatic condemnation and withering reproach against these continued ruthless mob law murders," he argues, "it will remain equally involved with the South in this common crime."[58] For Douglass, then, lynching was a crime performed equally by those who acted and those who formed opinion and those who stood silently by; it was "common" in that responsibility for it was commonly shared.

Nobody made as compelling and mordant a case for the complicity of white society in lynchings as the greatest of all anti-lynching advocates, Ida B. Wells, who made the charge of complicity a significant part of her anti-lynching campaign in the 1890s. She continually demonstrated how police officers gave up black prisoners to voracious lynch mobs, and how public officials often participated in lynchings. Both the press and the pulpit were equally guilty since "in the main either by silence or open apology, [they] have condoned and encouraged this state of anarchy." Wells went a step further in defining the quality of guilt of those who condone lynching through their own inaction. Those capable of renouncing the crime of lynching, but who choose not to do so, she wrote, make themselves guilty of endorsing it by their silence.

> Men who stand high in the esteem of the public for christian character, for moral and physical courage, for devotion to the principles of equal and exact justice to all, and for great sagacity, stand as cowards who fear to open their mouths before this great outrage. They do not see that by their tacit encouragement, their silent acquiescence, the black shadow of lawlessness in the form of lynch law is spreading wings over the whole country.

Such people, she concludes, "are particeps criminis, accomplices, accessories before and after the fact, equally guilty with the actual law-breakers."[59]

As was so often the case, Wells was decades ahead of her time when it came to offering compelling dissections of what lynchings were and meant. She saw early on what others would recognize later, the central importance of the concept of complicity for an understanding of the dynamics of lynching in America. She did not overstate the case when she maintained that lynching— in which all were involved and accomplices "before and after the fact"— put what she called "the white man's civilization and the white man's government . . . on trial."[60]

These, then, are the diagnoses of American society provided by African American intellectuals who early and profoundly saw the dangers of Lawless Samaritans, the justifications and rationales of those who stood by and did nothing, those at the edge of the mob and those at the center of the society, those who failed to prevent or resist, failed to legislate against, failed even to protest lynchings. What these intellectuals condemned was not only the actions of those who actively perform lynchings—what W.E.B. Du Bois described as "the writhing, yelling, cruel-eyed demons who break, destroy, maim and lynch and burn at the stake"—but those who watch that work being done, what Du Bois called "this nucleus of ordinary men that continually gives the mob its initial and awful impetus."[61] All the circles of the lynch mob were guilty of the work of lynching. These intellectuals also expanded the responsibility of lynchings to those who govern the society, those who enforce its inadequate laws, and, ultimately, those who believe in the mores and values of a civilization that does not merely countenance but thrives on ritual, racist, mob murders. What Wells claimed in the 1890s—that lynching was a symptom of a "civilization"—would become a routine feature of the anti-lynching campaigns of the 1920s and 1930s, as the NAACP continually asked what kind of civilization burns and maims in this way and drew on psychiatrists like A. A. Brill, who argued that anyone "taking part in or witnessing a lynching cannot remain a civilized person."[62]

CONCLUSION

We can conclude, then, by asking in what ways these models for thinking about complicity in lynchings help us better understand what lynchings are, what they mean, and what work they perform. The central question that those who argue for widespread complicity ask is, What does "looking" mean in a lynching? Only the Samaritan model maintains that looking is an innocent activity. Even the Lawless model considers looking as active and necessary; every member of Judge Lawless's "multitude" plays a role, and the "conditions made by US ALL, make us all responsible," as the Abbeville lynchers confess. Yet the Samaritan model has largely prevailed in how we understand lynching dynamics, with all courts and most scholars of lynching ascribing lower levels of responsibility to the spectators, on the assumption that looking and acting are qualitatively different forms of participation.

What the apologists for the Samaritan model cast as a passive omission, the advocates for the complicity models represent as an active cause—to look, for them, is to do something, to perform an act, in the lynching. Perhaps a novel can help us better understand the anti-lynching advocates' case for the dynamics of looking in a lynching. George Schuyler's 1931 novel *Black No More* is often hailed as the first African American–authored satire and science fiction. The premise of the novel is that all the black people in America have been turned white through a scientific procedure. Schuyler then shows us what happens to America when black people are no longer available as scapegoats to deflect labor and other class conflicts, and what happens when white people are forced to confront their own genealogies and discover, as he puts it in the dedication, "the Black leaves, twigs, limbs or branches on their family trees."

At the end of the novel, two white men whose genealogies prove they have black ancestors are lynched in Happy Hill, Mississippi, a town that had rid itself of all black people not by science but by hanging, shooting, or burning them. The men are lynched by the "True Faith Christ Lovers' Church," described by the narrator as the "most truly Fundamentalist of all the Christian sects in the United States." The mob is not frenzied but instead made up of an orderly and organized set of social actors. The leader of the church, and the lynching, conducts "the ceremonies . . . according to time-honored customs." Those customs involve stripping the two men naked, cutting off their ears and genitals, and then burning them until all that is left of them is "two charred hulks." In the mob are two or three African Americans who have been scientifically turned white and who remember "what their race had suffered in the past, [and] would fain have gone to the assistance of the two men but fear for their own lives restrained them. Even so they were looked at rather sharply by some of the Christ Lovers because they did not appear to be enjoying the spectacle as thoroughly as the rest. Noticing these questioning glances, the whitened Negroes began to yell and prod the burning bodies with sticks and cast stones at them. This exhibition restored them to favor and banished any suspicion that they might not be one-hundred-per-cent Americans."[63]

Schuyler is saying many important things about the social causes and purposes of lynchings in this culminating scene. For one thing, Schuyler is noting that lynchings are social institutions where the membership of one kind of association (church) is indistinguishable from that of another (lynch mob). The point Schuyler is making about the connection between Christian fundamentalists and lynching had been made two years earlier when the NAACP's Walter White argued that the "very violence of the emotions stirred up" by "the Bible-beating, acrobatic, fanatical preachers of hell-fire in the South" had "contributed to release through lynching."[64] In addition, by pointing out how black people had served as a wedge for labor and class issues, and by making the connection between civil society groups (like churches) and lynch mobs, Schuyler is making the point more forcibly made by Oliver Cox that lynching was a "*social institution*" that served the "indispensable social function of providing the ruling class with the means of periodically reaffirming its collective sentiment of white dominance." Lynch mobs, Cox concluded, were not furious and mad masses but rather "composed of people who have been carefully indoctrinated in the primary social institutions of the region," and the purpose of lynchings was precisely to indoctrinate them more deeply into those mores.[65]

Schuyler shared with Cox and White, and other black intellectuals of the era, the understanding that lynchings served particular political purposes, and therefore "spectators" at lynchings were no more passive than were other groups of people being indoctrinated into a given ideology. They were actively being recruited into a mindset they had already demonstrated they potentially possessed because they showed up. Schuyler makes clear this process when he points out the connection between racial violence and the opinion-forming function of civil society, which in this case is to promote a particular kind of racialized patriotism based on those who subscribe to lynching as a ceremonial ritual of racial and national belonging.

In showing us the ways that citizens get goaded into participating in a lynching, precisely because it is a ritual that affirms who is "one-hundred-per-cent American," Schuyler shows us in just what ways those who perform and those who look are equally participants in a larger ritual of coercing belief in white supremacy and American patriotism. This participation, then, which involves the spectators' looking in a particular way—they must "appear to be enjoying the spectacle"—is both coerced and fundamentally important. It is Schuyler's point that the relationship between those who kill and those who look is reciprocal; those who look need someone to kill for there to be a spectacle, and those who kill need spectators for the spectacle they produce to have the political meaning it is intended to have. The final and most significant point Schuyler makes is that the spectators become complicit in the lynching once they are transformed from disapproval to action, and the action in this case is their yelling at, prodding, and casting stones at the perished victims of the lynching, signs, in other words, of their being appreciative spectators.

Implicit in Schuyler's representation of the lynching scene is the idea that a lynching neither starts nor ends with the death of the victim. The minister who prevents the overly enthusiastic mob members from departing from "time-honored custom" in lynching does so because he understands that the lynching is a ceremonial ritual. The mutilation and castration are part of a full process that involves the full congregation. Like other religious rituals, it also involves all the senses: the crowd "whooped with glee," felt the "intense heat" of the pyre, and smelled the burning flesh ("many a nostril was guiltily distended").[66] The spectators, in other words, are not just guilty of looking but also of feeling, smelling, touching, and creating a sound for the full spectacle.

And that very spectacle—what essentially distinguishes a lynching during this era of mob lynchings—is a ceremony that begins with the humiliation of a person and ends with the desecration of a corpse. Those who look at a corpse differ little in their participation in a spectacle lynching from those who prod or poke a corpse, since they are equally creating a spectacle, and together they differ little from those who participate in a lynching by mutilating or burning the victim. A lynching, in other words, is not an accumulation of separate crimes—the one who cuts the ears guilty of assault, the one who collects firewood guilty of aiding and abetting, the person who lights the pyre guilty of murder. It is a complete process in which all are involved—those who cut, kill, look—and all guilty of participating in a lynching.

The point of how every participant in a lynching is involved and guilty is surely nowhere more powerfully demonstrated than in a lynching that took place four months before Zachariah Walker was lynched in Coatesville. In April 1911, Will Porter was taken to the opera house in Livermore, Kentucky, bound hand and foot at the center of the stage, and shot by spectators who purchased the opportunity to fire at Porter from the seats they paid for. According to the NAACP report, which conflicts with the *New York Times* version of the lynching, those who paid for gallery seats were limited to one shot, while orchestra seat occupants were allowed six shots.[67] This case robustly shows how this lynching mob is entirely guilty since it is made up of individuals who paid to attend and with the purchase of admittance erased the difference between spectatorship and participation in the lynching.

The two points I have been stressing here are both evident in this lynching. First, while only one or a few bullets were the actual reason for Porter's death, it is clear that all who fired—when he was alive to kill him, and after to riddle his corpse—were acting toward the same end, that is, to kill a person and desecrate a corpse. As the *Philadelphia Inquirer* editorialized, "every man who fired a bullet into the body of the victim was and is a murderer."[68] Or, more accurately, we would say a "lyncher." Second, while there is no other recorded lynching where the difference between agency and witnessing is so clearly erased, the Livermore lynching offers a compelling demonstration of how closely aligned are those who do and those who look, those who perform and those who watch. It is a stark and resonant example of how actors and witnesses together constitute the complete and true spectacle of lynching.

Complicity, then, is a concept that helps us understand the dynamics of lynching because it dismantles two presuppositions crucial to the Samaritan model of responsibility—the presupposition of an event as localized with determinate and identifiable agents, and the presupposition of an event as autonomous and independent of context. The advocates of the complicity model challenge both premises.

First, they show that a lynching is a happening whose boundaries cannot be firmly determined, either by the time it happens or the actors who make it happen. They argue that a lynching is not like a murder, to which a coroner can put a time of death, but rather like a staged event, a two-hour theater play, say, or an opera, which we can say started at such a time and ended at such a time; but we cannot say the play or opera happened at a precise or approximate time. Given that lynchings operate by this theatrical sense of time and participation, then, we cannot employ the Samaritan concepts of independent agents and innocent bystanders. We have to see that, precisely like the opera house lynching mob, all spectators are active agents whose work is a necessary part of the lynching dynamic.

Second, just as a lynching cannot be assigned a precise time but operates in the indeterminate temporality of theater, so too, according to the advocates of the complicity models, lynchings cannot be seen as independent actions that periodically happen. They are the products of a particular history and a particular ideology. As commentator after commentator noted, there is a continuity from earlier forms of social control over black people, slavery and peonage, to lynchings as what Cox calls "social institutions" that affirm an ideology of white supremacy by terrorizing black communities. These commentators likewise noted that lynchings are the logical culmination of the society's public opinion, propaganda, and mores that promote the notion of popular sovereignty and the belief in the lower value of black life. Lynchings, in other words, are products and causes of an ideology of white supremacy.

What the complicity models help us see, then, is that lynchings in America are intimately connected to the nation's history and its racial ideology. They can be most meaningfully understood as theatrical events that deepen and spread among those Schuyler called "one-hundred-per-cent Americans" what Cox called the nation's "collective sentiment of white dominance." Lynchings, we can say, are the operas of white civilization.

CHAPTER 2

DATE NIGHT IN THE COURTHOUSE SQUARE

If you have seen only one picture of an American lynching, it is likely that it was the one that shows a man in the mob pointing at the two bodies hanging from a maple tree in the courthouse square. It is difficult to think of a lynching photograph that has had a more influential life than that picture, which is used as the frontispiece of this book. Poster-size copies of the photograph hang on the museum walls of the Birmingham Civil Rights Institute, the DuSable Museum in Chicago, the Museum of Tolerance in Los Angeles, and the Black Holocaust Museum in Milwaukee. When the Allen-Littlefield collection of lynching photographs and postcards was mounted in New York, first at the Roth Horowitz Gallery and then the New-York Historical Society, the *New Yorker* and the Associated Press used this photograph in their exhibit notices. The *Village Voice* used it in its review of the book compiled out of the exhibit, *Without Sanctuary: Lynching Photography in America*. It appeared in a feature article in *Ebony* in 1980 and in a *Newsweek* special issue on race in 1988, and *Life* magazine showed it twice in 1994. It is the only picture of a lynching in the *Encyclopedia of Black America*.

The photograph has graced the covers of at least five books. It is on the cover of James Madison's history of the Marion, Indiana, lynching that is the subject of the photograph. It is on the cover of the most recent general history of lynching in America, Philip Dray's *At the Hands of Persons Unknown* (2002), and Dora Apel and Shawn Michelle Smith's study of images of racial violence, *Lynching Photographs* (2007). It is on the front and back cover, respectively, of two memoirs of people connected to Marion, Indiana—James Cameron's *A Time of Terror* (1982) and Cynthia Carr's *Our Town* (2006).

It has also influenced nonprint media. In 1986, the producers of *Eyes on the Prize* used the photograph in the first installment of the documentary that included the story of the lynching of Emmett Till. In 1996, a modified copy of the photograph appeared in the film version of John Grisham's *The Chamber*.

In 1992, the rap group Public Enemy used the photograph as a cover for the CD single "Hazy Shade of Criminal." It is quite likely the photograph that inspired Abel Meeropol to write the poem "Bitter Fruit," which later achieved fame as the Billie Holiday standard "Strange Fruit."[1]

The photograph was taken by Lawrence Beitler, a professional photographer in Marion, where the lynching occurred on the evening of August 7, 1930. The photograph was one of several taken of the lynching scene, but for some reason it is the only one that has survived or at least achieved public notoriety. Beitler took the picture after midnight in the early morning hours of Friday, August 8. By Friday afternoon, not many hours after the sheriff cut down the bodies of the two lynching victims at 5:45 A.M., Beitler was selling fifty-cent copies of the photograph from his studio at 502 South Adams Street. For the next several days, Beitler made and sold prints of the lynching photograph, some inscribed with his studio name and others with the more immediate historical information: "Lynching at Marion, Ind, Aug 1930." An investigator from the Indiana attorney general's office reported that the photographs at the studio were "selling like hot cakes." They were also selling well as postcards in Terre Haute, 140 miles away.[2]

This photograph, then, which began as a memento of a lynching a few hours after the event, has influenced music and the marketing of music; it has appeared on museum walls and book covers, in the pages of newspapers and magazines, in documentaries and films. This photograph has indeed become not only what the ABC news program *Compass* called the "most famous photograph of America's era of lynching" but in fact, as historian James Madison says, "*the* generic lynching photograph."[3]

Lynching photographs have recently evoked a great deal of inquiry from scholars and soul-searching from spectators, especially since the mounting of the Allen-Littlefield exhibit and the publication of *Without Sanctuary*. After all, these photographs demand answers to questions about why they were taken, and what purposes they have served and do serve now in their public display. Those who have written about these images have tended to focus, understandably and profitably, on three key questions dealing with their production, consumption, and historical transformation. How can we account for the emergence of this particular kind of representation, and what other forms of photography preceded and help us make sense of these images? What does it mean to look at these photographs, to take them in, and what might it mean for those of European or of African descent, for those who might feel implicated and those who might feel shamed or bruised? How, finally, can we understand the historical and political dynamics that transformed photographs originally meant to celebrate vigilante justice and the workings of white supremacy into images of social anarchy, racism, and barbarity?

In the first section of this chapter, we will see how some of our contemporaries have answered these questions and thereby given us a fuller appreciation for what these photographs were and did as they were produced, consumed, circulated, and transformed from the 1890s to the 1930s. We will then return to the photograph of the Marion, Indiana, lynching and look in particular at three responses to the Beitler photograph, each of which in some way raises questions about complicity. We will examine first the strategies of framing the photograph that newspaper editors used in their publications to give the resulting images a particular saliency and meaning. We will then turn to the responses of two individuals who are not in the photograph but somehow are still of it—one who was almost lynched and would have been in it, and one who was descended from someone pictured in the mob. These three responses—we can call them the responses of *framers*, *victims*, and *heirs*—will show us different ways of understanding the dynamic of complicity in a lynch mob. In the end, we want to know how we would read this photograph (and, by implication, all lynching photographs) if we think of the people we are viewing in a different legal or moral light than simply spectators. What difference is there in our viewing and understanding of these photographs if we ascribe a particular kind of agency and responsibility to those spectators?

THE PRODUCTION AND CONSUMPTION
OF LYNCHING PHOTOGRAPHS

It is important to acknowledge that lynching photographs are, in many ways, anomalous phenomena. The lynching photograph, as Michael Trotti, points out, constitutes a "glaring exception" in the late-nineteenth-century "age of the photograph," in that it portrayed "gore" and violence in a way that was "socially unacceptable" in the coverage the press gave to other stories of murders and crimes. At the very moment when newspapers faced "new and distinct limitations" on what constituted "appropriate visual matter," the lynching photograph emerged and became "increasingly common" in the South.[4]

One way to understand the origins of lynching photography, and to comprehend how it came to be accepted despite its anomalous subject and form, is by seeing what sorts of analogous forms of photography inspired people to stage, take, and publish those particular images. Amy Louise Wood has recently made a very compelling argument for seeing how lynching photographs sometimes merged and sometimes evoked some earlier photographic forms. The traditional tableau of a lynching photograph—black victim, white mob—suggests two ways of thinking about the elements of the picture. One way is to see how the two elements are separate, each occupying its own sphere, and the merging together of them is what gives the photograph its special meaning. Wood begins by noting how the two elements (victim, mob) differ significantly in that the white mob is self-consciously posing for the photographer, while the black victim is "forced" to pose for this picture. In that juxtaposition, Wood argues, we can see the merging of "two of the most prominent conventions of turn-of-the-century photography: the bourgeois portrait and the criminal mug shot." Woods is here building on a point Shawn Michelle Smith originally made about the dynamic of these three photographic conventions when she argued that the "white middle-class portrait" contained the "shadow image" of both the "criminal mug shot" and the "lynching photograph."[5] If we took out the dead body at the center of the lynching photograph, we would be left with the conventions of portraiture— a shot of a group, like a family, meant to record this particular gathering. If we took out the surrounding mob, we would be left with pictures that look like criminal mug shots—photographs of unsmiling, stoical faces captured in a state of unfreedom.

The second way Wood argues we can appreciate the genealogy of lynching photographs is to see how they evoke hunting photographs. Like those conventional pictures of men standing next to the hanging prey they have presumably killed, lynching photographs show us a group of virile and victorious hunters standing next to the "beast" they have dispatched. As the Reverend John H. Holmes noted in a commentary in the *Crisis*, when he "glanced" at one such picture, the "only thing [he] could think of . . . was a photograph [he] had seen of huntsmen returning with the animal that had been shot, proud of their achievement of marksmanship." In both cases, of hunting and lynching, Holmes concluded, "they stand before the camera in order that the evidence of the story may be sure."[6]

There are important differences between these two ways of seeing lynching photographs—as made of separate elements, as a set tableau with a clearly understood relationship between the hunters and the hunted—but there are even more important shared properties. In both cases, we see images of stable white groups represented in poses suggesting civility or virility. In the case of lynching pictures that evoke hunting photographs, for instance, the images of "white men, immobile and stalwart, surrounding the black corpse projected *only* an ideal of restrained and sturdy manhood." In the case of the photographs recalling the conventions of group portraiture, the posing of the mob shows us "confident, restrained white men."[7] In both cases, the violence of the lynching itself is occluded, hidden, made invisible because the victim is portrayed as either an animal (hunted) or criminal (mug shot), and those who performed the deserved violence are represented as bourgeois subjects sitting for a group portrait.

Wood concludes that in either form, merging of mug shot and portrait or evocation of hunting photograph, these lynching photographs performed two fundamental duties—first, they made "visible to white southerners black depravity set against a united white superiority and civility," and, second, they made "an extraordinary event somewhat familiar" by evoking "other, more typical photographic forms and practices," with which their spectators would have been familiar, namely mug shots, portraiture, and hunting photographs. Lynching photographs, then, "served to normalize and make socially acceptable, even aesthetically acceptable, the utter brutality of a lynching," by showing us that those who perform lynchings are regular people familiar to everyone in the community (family members, hunters) and that those who are lynched are also known types that need to be punished and killed (criminals and wild animals).[8]

That, then, is largely how those images operated in their first manifestations and for their first readers. For the white Americans who produced, purchased, and consumed them, these were photographs of celebration, visually capturing the operation of white supremacy and creating a tangible and permanent record of it. If stories of rape and rumored rape constitute what Jacquelyn Dowd Hall calls "the folk pornography of the Bible Belt," the photographic record of lynchings became their hard-core manifestation. A 1908 Texas postcard was unusually candid about its intent. Under a picture of the five hanging bodies of a Sabine County lynching, there was a poem in tribute to the "Dogwood Tree," which, in the rhyme of the poet, is an "emblem of WHITE SUPREMACY." As Shawn Michelle Smith and Leigh Raiford acutely note, photographs became "memorial souvenirs" that "enabled all lynchers, those who actually participated and those who wished they had, to get closer to the event. To possess a photograph of a lynching, like a photograph of Niagara Falls or of a sideshow, was to be able to say, 'I was there.'" In addition, these circulating postcards "served to extend and redefine the boundaries of white community beyond the localities in which lynchings occurred to a larger 'imagined community.'"[9]

As Wood points out, the composition of the photograph itself embodied that message. "By projecting these images of group cohesion," she notes, "photographs of white mobs and crowds imagined the very solidarity that white supremacist ideology propounded." Wood and Smith and Apel have pointed out that whatever class differences might be apparent in the postures and clothing of the individuals in the mob were obscured by "their common purpose" and, more markedly, by "their sharp distinction from their black victim."[10]

The evidence we have of how some white people responded to these photographs shows us, in many cases, people who did treat their participation as if it were an act of tourism. One man, Joe Meyers, wrote on the back of a postcard on which he had marked his place in the mob to tell his parents, "This is the barbecue we had last Saturday." Another wrote to a friend: "I saw this on my noon hour. I was very much in the bunch."[11] These were the responses of those who did want to imagine themselves as part of that community of white supremacists, who were untroubled by the act of lynching or those who performed it.

Yet there were also those who were horrified by those photographs. One 1906 commentator attested that those who were forced to "look at one of the photographs of a lynching" felt "a sense of abysmal horror"—"not the horror alone or chiefly of the thing itself, the ugly, inanimate center of the tragedy. It is the faces of the spectators that shock our very souls. . . . Good nature, even jollity, seems to be the note of these gatherings. . . . [I]t is not the dead, but the living that terrifies."[12] For some, the photographs could not be rendered acceptable, no matter how much different elements of the photographs might feel familiar. For those early, resistant readers, these images displayed barbarity, not white unity or justice. It is worthwhile for us to remember that there is no simple formula for what kind of response we might expect.

That is as true for black consumption of these photographs as it is for white consumption. Leigh Raiford has written intelligently and insightfully about the tensions and contradictions involved in the consumption of lynching photographs. As is appropriate for a form of representation that served first to celebrate and then to condemn white supremacy, the lynching photograph, as Raiford wisely reminds us, has the potential to reveal and to occlude, to help us understand the dynamics of lynching but also to hide from us the very facts of black existence in the United States. After first demonstrating how lynching photographs were, in the hands of black people, "recast as a call to arms against a seeming never-ending tide of violent coercion, and transformed into tools for the making of a new African American national identity," Raiford insists on asking the difficult question about whether this transformation was possible. Can these photographs of what Shawn Michelle Smith calls "the spectacle of the dead black other" be "made to signify differently?"[13] Raiford's answer to that question is complicated, ambivalent, and, I think, correct.

Raiford begins by dissecting the looking agency, by noting that "black spectatorship" is not a simple phenomenon that is either "complicit or resistant, neither wholly absorptive nor completely oppositional." There are many ways of black looking, many ways of construing and understanding what is seen in those images, and many different political responses that can follow from that understanding. The historical transition of those artifacts from lynching postcards to anti-lynching photographs is not simply a result of a willful black spectatorship that insisted on seeing in those photographs something other than terror or abjectness. Nor, from the other side, did those lynching photographs only terrorize or render abject those black viewers who confronted them.

Having demonstrated that there is no such thing as a preferred or singular response of black spectatorship to lynching photographs, Raiford concludes by diagnosing how "lynching photography . . . represents a crisis of representation." Lynching photography is both a deleterious source and product of American anti-black sensibility, a fundamentally problematic way of "seeing blackness," and simultaneously "a crucial archive in the formation of black visuality and American identity," a means by which anti-lynching activists condemned lynchers, challenged governing bodies, and revealed to the nation the betrayal of its spoken or the fulfillment of its unspeakable racial values.[14]

One final point is worth making about the ways these lynching photographs were understood and promoted by both pro-lynching and anti-lynching advocates. Early in the history of spectacle lynchings, that is, early in the 1890s, white communities began to publish and circulate photograph portraits of white victims, especially if the victims were young girls, alongside lynching photographs. This inflammatory display was meant to show the viewer a stark vision of good and evil, of children whose "innocence and moral worth" was on display next to the lynch victim's guilt and moral worthlessness. These contrasting photographs, as Wood notes, "served as visual justifications for lawless vengeance."[15]

In response, perhaps, anti-lynching advocates also employed supplementary images to produce a quite different understanding of lynching. An example from the 1890s will suffice. Shortly after her friend Tom Moss was lynched in Memphis in 1892, Ida B. Wells commissioned a portrait of herself with Moss's wife and two children. This portrait falls into the category Raiford calls "the political portrait," a photograph of a domestic and private scene intended for "public consumption with political objectives." In this case, the portrait shows us another victim, the "family left behind" after the lynching.[16] Just as pro-lynching advocates used the images of white children to inflame sentiments about black criminality, anti-lynching advocates employed images of broken black families to show the results of white savagery.

We see, then, the ways that lynching photographs have been produced and consumed by those who first created them to celebrate white supremacy, how they have been wrought out of earlier acceptable forms of photography, and how they have elicited and trafficked among other pictorial forms. We see, in other words, that these photographs were required to do a great deal of cultural work—buttressing a racial ideology and justifying a community in the wake of a collective act of lawlessness. Even in the moment when they were most unashamedly used to celebrate lynchings as communal acts, those photographs remained unstable entities, public artifacts that contained all the elements of their own undoing. The death at the very center of those photographs—the corpse that the mob and photographers thought they had contained and fixed—would take on a haunting afterlife when those photographs became subject to a considerably more critical set of editors and readers.

TRANSFORMATION

At a couple of key points in the history of anti-lynching movements in America, those who struggled to bring the facts of lynching to the attention of legislators and to bring lynching itself to an end were confronted with the problem of the photographic record of lynchings. What could they do with these images in order to use them to buttress their political case? In both cases—in the 1890s and in the 1920s—the anti-lynching advocates faced something of a paradox. Here were pictures that had resonated quite differently to quite different constituencies. Many African Americans rightly perceived that a photograph that exhibited the raw assertion of white supremacy was inherently an evil that ought never to be displayed. As we saw, from the earliest years of the anti-lynching campaigns of the 1890s, this had probably been the most common response.

Indeed, these photographs were used to terrorize black people and those who advocated for the end of lynching. In the early 1890s, the anti-lynching governor of Georgia, William J. Northern, "frequently received pictures and fragments of victims to remind him of where the power of life and death in that state ultimately lay." In 1891, the liberal former "carpetbagger" Judge Albion Tourgée, then living in Mayville, New York, received a postcard with a photograph of a lynching and a written incendiary message from Clanton, Alabama. After condemning lynching in public, the New York Unitarian minister John H. Holmes likewise received a postcard with a picture of an Alabama lynching with a note on the back promising that he would be placed on the sender's "regular mailing list" and should expect a postcard once "a month on the average."[17] Circulating postcards of lynching scenes were devices of recruitment for white superiority, gathered voluntarily by the willing and mailed maliciously to the unwilling. For those who believed, there was no sense that these pictures could indicate anything other than the highest stage of white civilization in defense of itself.

That was the situation facing anti-lynching activists in the 1890s as they sought to transform those photographs from icons of white pride to emblems of American shame. When the greatest anti-lynching advocate, Ida B. Wells, published her first book on lynching, *Southern Horrors* (1892), she had no illustrations of lynching scenes in it. When she published *A Red Record* three years later (1895), she included a drawing of the 1893 lynching of C. J. Miller in Bardwell, Kentucky, and reprinted the postcard of the 1891 lynching in Clanton, Alabama, sent to Judge Albion Tourgée. Wells does not comment on the photograph or the message on the back. Perhaps Wells avoided commenting directly on what the photograph represented because she so consistently and explicitly put the question of "civilization" at the heart of her anti-lynching work. Because the gist of her book was to show, as she put it, that lynching put "the white man's civilization and the white man's government . . . on trial," she did not have to comment directly on how these pictures show "white barbarity" instead of "white supremacy." Wells, as usual, was ahead of her time. Only later was there a more widespread sentiment that the photographs of lynching scenes, like lynchings themselves, were no longer causing racial pride but civic embarrassment.[18]

Perhaps part of the reason for this shift in popular opinion has to do with the ways English anti-lynching advocates had begun using these photographs. Judge Tourgée forwarded the postcard of the 1891 Clanton, Alabama, lynching he had been mailed to Catherine Impey, an English Quaker, activist, and founding editor of a political anti-imperialist magazine, *Anti-Caste*. When she in turn published the photograph on the cover of *Anti-Caste* in January 1893, she was criticized for reproducing what many thought was an embellished drawing. When her English critics discovered that it was indeed a photograph of an event, they, like Sir Edward Russell, editor of the *Liverpool Daily Post*, were moved from skepticism to zealous anti-lynching advocacy. Liverpool clergyman the Reverend C. K. Aked likewise used the same Alabama lynching postcard to publicize Ida B. Wells's English lecture tour. When Wells lectured in London at a breakfast meeting with sixteen members of Parliament and their wives, a lynching photograph "went around the beautifully decorated tables" as she spoke.[19]

One especially significant sign of the declining tolerance for the expressive value of photographs of lynching is the federal government's passing a United States Postal Laws and Regulations Amendment in May 1908 that banned the circulation through the federal mails of images and other "matter of a character tending to incite arson, murder, or assassination." On one postcard, with a picture of a July 1908 lynching of four men in Russellville, Kentucky, an individual noted the difficulty of purchasing the photograph. He bought it in a neighboring town where, as he noted, they "were not on sale openly." He concluded his message by referring to the new law that was "passed forbidding these to be sent thru the mail or to be sold anymore." Interestingly, there is no address or postage mark on this card—a sign that such postcards would now be mailed in envelopes (and at different postage rates). When officials from the NAACP discovered postcards of lynching scenes circulating in 1911—and it is telling that these postcards were now printed in Germany—they informed the postmaster general, who declared them "unmailable."[20] The federal law reflected the growing public sentiment against lynchings and the use of photographs of lynchings as a way of articulating white supremacist views. Shortly thereafter, African American editors, intellectuals, and anti-lynching activists played on and fed this public sentiment by employing lynching photographs to protest lynchings.

The major strategy in the transformation of lynching photographs into anti-lynching propaganda involved what Raiford describes as the process of "dismantling and reframing" lynching photographs. Anti-lynching activists would place lynching photographs "within alternative and sympathetic outlets such as pamphlets and the black press" where the readership was primed to understand these images as indictments of mob mentality.[21]

In 1911, a black newspaper, the *Topeka Plaindealer*, reprinted a picture of an Oklahoma lynching so that the "world may see and know what semi-barbarous America is doing." Also in 1911, the NAACP issued a pamphlet, "Opinion on the Reign of Terror," in which two of the three pages contained photographs of lynching scenes and victims. In the *Crisis*, the NAACP editors dismantled the original meaning and produced a new one by placing a lynching photograph on the page opposite an anti-lynching speech. As Wood notes, this strategy of "placement" worked to direct "viewers' interpretation of the image so that they would disidentify" with the white mob in the picture, and also "predetermine viewers' disgust and horror" at the photograph itself.[22] In this case, the photograph is trumped by the moral call of the words on the page.

In 1916, the NAACP seems to have made a more concerted effort to employ photographs in its anti-lynching work. The editors of the *Crisis* published a photograph of the immolated and hanging corpse of Will Stanley in the January issue, printed a realistic drawing "From an actual photograph" of the lynching of five men in Lee County, Georgia, in the April issue, and then, condemning the Waco, Texas, burning of Jesse Washington, issued a supplement to the July issue that contained four lynching photographs in its eight pages. Most disturbing was the decision to have their regular "Our Lynching Culture" article on the same pages devoted to their regular feature of pictures of African American babies and children. Having shown in earlier issues that year the actual victims of lynching, the editors implied that here, if nothing were done, were the potential future victims.[23]

In November 1922, the organization ran a national mainstream newspaper publicity campaign, "The Shame of America," the second version of which, containing photographs of lynching scenes, did not run in the December 14, 1922, issue of the *New York Times Mid-Week Pictorial*, as it was scheduled, only because the Dyer Anti-Lynching Bill had been defeated in the interim.[24] It should be noted that anti-lynching activists during these years did not take lightly, and were sometimes tormented over, their decisions on whether or not to reprint these lynching photographs. The ASWPL avoided the use of photographs and what they deemed other "sensational" material in their anti-lynching campaigns in the 1930s and 1940s. Du Bois was deeply troubled as he set about using one such photograph in 1919. Jacqueline Goldsby shows us how James Weldon Johnson "proceeded cautiously" in using the photographs in the 1920s, while Walter White, who assumed Johnson's post as executive director of the NAACP in 1931, "eagerly" and regularly reprinted those photographs through the 1930s.[25] These images, in other words, could not be dismantled and reframed easily, and the strategy these editors and anti-lynching activists followed was not assured of success. They had legitimate fears that these photographs would continue to terrorize rather than mobilize the constituency they were striving to reach, and reinforce rather than chasten the white supremacist views of those they wished to criticize.

They nonetheless did manage to work a change in discernible American public opinion. Consider two scenes from the United States Senate. On the floor of the Senate in 1907, Senator Ben Tillman justified lynching by evoking the traditional images of the stock characters in the lynching-for-rape discourse—black men whose "breasts [were] pulsating with the desire to sate their passions upon white maidens and wives," and a white woman victim, "her body prostituted, her purity destroyed, her chastity taken from her, and a memory branded on her brain as with a red-hot iron"—and then concluded with a stirring narrative of familial dysfunction: "I have three daughters, but so help me God, I had rather find either one of them killed by a tiger or bear and gather up her bones and bury them, conscious that she had died in the purity of her maidenhood, than to have her crawl to me and tell me the horrid story that she had been robbed of the jewel of her womanhood by a black fiend." In 1937, another Southern Democrat, Senator Bennett Clark of Missouri, displayed two poster photographs of a recent lynching and noted that this action had taken place while the Senate was debating an anti-lynching bill. "This was not a rape case," he perorated.[26]

Here was a striking change, from defending lynching as an act of chivalry to condemning it as a crime of barbarity. Indeed, during the congressional debate over the bill that the Senate was then considering, Representative Hamilton Fish of New York reversed the traditional lynching-for-rape discourse so favored by Southerners by claiming that lynching amounted to a "rape of justice, liberty, civil rights, equal rights, human lives, and the Constitution itself."[27] When Senator Tillman spoke in 1907, he presupposed that his constituents and a good number of his colleagues shared his view that the most significant thing about lynching was the alleged crime that prompted it. When Senator Clark spoke in favor of a federal lynching bill in the same chambers thirty years later, and displayed those photographs, he knew that for most of his constituents and colleagues these images were no longer capable of sustaining those values of chivalry, manliness, and white unity they had originally held.

Indeed, in that same year (1937), in response to a single reader who was troubled by the photographs previously published in the magazine, the editors of the *Crisis* were inspired to create a forum for readers to answer the question: "Do Lynching Pictures Create Race Hatred?" In the following issue, there was unanimity among the correspondents that the publication of lynching photographs was necessary for fighting lynching and for urging passage of an anti-lynching bill. Wood correctly concludes that by the mid-1930s anti-lynching advocates had "successfully erased the white supremacist narrative imprinted in the photographs and, by reframing the images, had replaced it with an antilynching narrative."[28]

As a final striking sign of how photographs of lynching had changed in usage from earlier decades, consider the case of another postcard received by the Reverend John H. Holmes, now the vice president of the NAACP. On the back of this scene of a lynched black man surrounded by fifty white men was the inscription: "The colored voter who votes for a man who acquiesces in, or 'pussy-foots,' on this issue of lynching and lawlessness, is a traitor to the race." Earlier in the century, a postcard mailed by white lynchers to the same Reverend Holmes had been a form of terrorism; now it was a form of political mobilization urging black voters to find out where political candidates stood on the topic of lynching before supporting their candidacy.[29]

What the anti-lynching advocates accomplished, then, was a transformation of how the different components in these photographs could be understood by American readers and spectators. The black body in the center of the photograph—which had been cast as a criminal and an animal—now became a victim, and a victim not only of a crime against an individual, but a victim of a crime against law and order, against the nation, against civilization. As Raiford notes, the activists pursued a campaign that essentially remade "the black male body" into the "body of the entire nation."[30] Drawings in black publications labeled the black body as "democracy" lynched. A representative cartoon in a 1942 issue of the *Chicago Defender* labels the black male body "Lynched American," in between two other hanged bodies, a Lincolnesque figure labeled "National Unity" and a young white woman labeled "Democracy."[31] Cast as "American"—a representative American, indeed—the black male body is only one of the victims of this crime against nation, democracy, and unity. The other component in the photographs—the white mob—was also recast; no longer an orderly group like a family or an organized one like a set of hunters, it was now a savage threat to American civilization.[32]

FRAMERS

I do not wish to suggest that by the 1930s the transformation was complete, or that what lynching photographs meant when they were published was a settled issue. When the *Raleigh News and Observer* published a photograph of the lynching of Oliver Moore, who was lynched in Edgecombe County, North Carolina, on August 20, 1930, for example, what a contemporary called a "storm of criticism" fell on the veteran editor of the paper "for publishing the picture and criticizing the officers and community." Later in the century, from the 1930s to the 1950s, photographers who took pictures of lynchings in order to promote anti-lynching activism faced stiff resistance from lynchers and their sympathizers. Arthur Raper reports that a photographer from the *St. Joseph News-Press* attempting to take a photograph of the mob lynching Raymond Gunn in Maryville, Missouri, on January 12, 1931, had members of the mob seize his camera and destroy the rolls of film inside. In 1959, a *Chicago Defender* photographer had to sneak into a guarded funeral home to take a photograph of the corpse of Mack Charles Parker for publication in the *Defender*, and then he had to elude a police manhunt for him afterward.[33]

This was the situation white and black editors faced in 1930, then, when confronted with the Beitler photograph of the Marion lynching. Lynching photographs had largely changed in meaning but had not entirely shed their original intent of celebrating white supremacy and terrorizing black Americans. Indeed, this particular photograph was selling "like hot cakes" because there was still a market for those who wished to possess the picture and thereby

have material evidence of a scene they either had witnessed or were witnessing in proxy. Those consumers were white, since very few black people
bought the Beitler photograph, and it was only black protests that disrupted
that business. The leader of the Marion branch of the NAACP, Katherine
"Flossie" Bailey, threatened to initiate court proceedings against Lawrence
Beitler for selling the photograph out of his studio before she finally got the
state police to stop him. The Terre Haute branch of the NAACP brought the
sale of the postcards in that city to an end through protests.[34]

This was the challenge newspaper editors and anti-lynching advocates
faced, to give these pictures a different meaning and frame them in such a
way as to force viewers to see in them no source of racial pride but only one
of national shame. As James Madison noted in his definitive study of the
Marion lynching, newspapers across the state and nation made different editorial decisions about whether and how to use the Beitler photograph. Those
newspapers nearest to the lynching site avoided the controversy of showing
scenes of a crime so close to home. The *Marion Chronicle-Tribune* chose not
to display the photograph, as did all three newspapers in the Indiana capital,
because it was "revolting," in the words of the editors of the *Indianapolis
News,* and would cater "only to morbid tastes," in the words of the editors of
the *Indianapolis Times.* Some, however, including newspapers in nearby
Muncie and Anderson, did use the photograph the day after the lynching.[35]

Black publications pursued the strategy earlier editors had used, what
Raiford identifies as "dismantling and reframing" the photographs so that
they convey an oppositional set of sentiments. Toward that end, the editors
made two significant choices. First, they used ironic captions to reorient what
the scene in the photograph represents. Black newspapers and magazines
published the Beitler photograph with captions that assumed rather than
expressed the shame of a nation where such crimes continued to happen. The
photograph appeared in the August 16 issue of the *Chicago Defender* with the
title "American Christianity" as a caption. The *Crisis* ran the photograph in
its October issue with the caption "Civilization in the United States, 1930."[36]
Unlike the anti-lynching publicity campaign of less than a decade earlier,
which had specifically to point out that visual representations of lynching
registered "shame," these publications could now assume an ironic tone to
show the hypocrisy of a nation whose piety and civility were proved false by
the mob actions of its citizens, the inaction of its police, and the silence of
its politicians.

In addition to the captions they appended to the photographs, black editors
made dramatic choices in how to frame and present the pictures. As Madison
notes, the "most frequent and interesting uses" of the Beitler photograph

were to be found in "newspapers catering to African American readers." The *Indianapolis Recorder*, for instance, cropped the photograph to show primarily the bodies of the lynch victims, while the *New York World* cropped it to show only the white crowd beneath.[37] This, again, was a sign of how the separate elements in a photograph of a lynching scene registered by 1930. The sight of hanging black bodies presumed the presence of white mobs, and in the picture of a gathering of smiling white people lurked the menace of lynching. To focus on either was not to exclude the other from sight; the other part (death or mob) was always implied.

By reframing the photograph in these ways—through ironic captions and through the separation of the two major figures in the picture—these anti-lynching advocates were indeed attesting to the change in how lynching photographs had come to register over the past three decades. The anti-lynching movement finally caught up with Wells in recognizing that lynching placed "the white man's civilization . . . on trial." The dead body at the center of the picture was a victim of a failed culture, an uncharitable religion, a nation without law and order. And the group of smiling, pointing, celebrating white people—even without a black body at which to smile, point, celebrate—was seen as inherently dangerous. Where white people gathered together was a place that implicitly endangered black life. The basis of that civilization was destruction, and the basis of that religion was sacrifice—a point anti-lynching advocates had also made when they compared lynching to crucifixion. Indeed, the *Chicago Defender* published a cartoon of three crucifixes on a patch of land called "Marion," the one in the middle named "Justice."[38]

The final point I wish to make about the framers is how they frame the concept of complicity. In the end, what the editors are asking us by their two strategies of providing a disorienting caption and reframing the component features of the photograph is, What is it we are looking at when we look at this photograph? Their answer is that we are looking at people who lynch, at a mob in action. Over and over again, the editors insisted that these photographs were of "mobs"—groups that performed the full theatrical production of lynching we discussed in the last chapter. In 1927, the *Chicago Defender* published a photograph of a mob in which a policeman was visible and mocked the police force for claiming no one in the mob could be identified: "And They Can't Identify This Policeman," ran the headline. In 1936, it put a caption under a photograph of the mob lynching Lint Shaw in Royston, Georgia, that stated, "These Can Be Identified." The *Defender* conceded that even if those pictured were not themselves the lynchers, they nonetheless "must surely possess information which would lead honest officials to arrest and convict the murderers responsible for this human outrage."[39]

In both cases, what the *Defender* editors were defending was the belief that the mobs we see in lynching photographs are lynchers—that is, those who make lynchings possible either through killing, torturing, viewing, or hiding the identities of those who do. The concession they made that these people in the pictures might not be lynchers was nonetheless an accusation that these are people potentially guilty of being accessory after the fact by hiding the identities of the actual lynchers—in other words, they too are complicit.

The editors who framed the Beitler photograph made the same point. The *Defender* noted that "Pictures do not lie" as it printed a photograph that it claimed "shows plainly any number of the guilty persons." The *New York World*, which had cropped the photograph to show only the white crowd, gave it a caption that implicated that crowd: "Spectators and Participants in Killing of Negro Boys." Here was a photograph, the *World* insisted, that reveals "faces of many of the mob." The *Crisis* editors noted in their secondary caption that the lynching had been committed "by party or parties unknown"—parodying the conventional grand jury finding in the cases of lynching by implying that those in the photograph were indeed known and guilty.[40] What these framers insisted on, then, was that lynching photographs were prima facie proof of guilt of those complicit in the lynching. There is no distinction between "spectators and participants"—they are all participants in different ways. There are no "parties unknown"—they are known but hidden by all those complicit, including the police, the grand juries, and the communities where lynchings happened.

The main point that these editors made, then, was that we can understand what we are seeing when we look at a lynching photograph only if we accept that the photograph is not just an index of a historical occurrence, a tangible record of an event that took place. Instead, we have to recognize that the photograph provides evidence of who was responsible because the photograph captured a scene *during* a lynching (since lynchings, as we saw in the complicity models, did not end with the end of life but continued on past the gathering—and photographing—of the mob). These were photographs that indicted in a precise legal sense—here are the guilty—and in a larger moral sense—here is a nation (a civilization, a religion) that permits such actions. What the framers framed, in the end, was the crime of complicity.

Victim

Surely no one was more tormented by the Beitler photograph than James Cameron. On the night Tom Shipp and Abe Smith were lynched, Cameron, then sixteen years of age, was in the same jail and had been accused of the same alleged crimes, the murder of Claude Deeter and the rape of Mary Ball.[41] He watched as Shipp was brutally beaten, almost to death, and then hanged from the jail cell bars, and then as Smith was assaulted and bludgeoned to death before being dragged away to have his body hanged from the maple tree in the courthouse square. Some men returned to retrieve Shipp's body from the jail and string him up next to Smith. Shortly after that, the mob came and dragged Cameron himself out to the square, all the while beating him with their hands or whatever implements came to hand. Once at the base of the maple tree, the mob put Cameron's head into the ready noose and threw the rope over the waiting branch. At that moment, a voice called out: "Take this boy back. He had nothing to do with any raping or killing!" For some unaccountable reason, the mob obeyed and the third lynching was prevented.

According to Cameron, the voice was feminine and sweet and clear, unlike anything he had ever heard. He interviewed hundreds of people who were near the courthouse that evening, and not one of them claimed to have heard the voice that saved his life. He believes the voice issued from some supernatural source, an agent of God, an angel, perhaps. Others in attendance that night who did hear a voice believe that it was that of either the head of the local American Legion, Rex George, or Mary's paternal uncle, Sol Ball.[42] Whatever its source, the voice was obeyed, and one man who would have been lynched from the maple tree in the Marion, Indiana, courthouse survived the ordeal.

Even though he was never in it, the photograph that would have potentially contained his corpse played a deeply significant role in his life. The next day, the policemen who were transporting him to a different jail cell bought a copy of a newspaper with the Beitler photograph on the front page. Looking at his friends "swinging from limbs of the tree" and the "upturned faces, pointing and laughing at the spectacle," Cameron felt a "killing rage" for "every white person in the world." It was a rage he was to spend the rest of his life taming through religious discipline and faith. That same photograph today hangs as a poster in the Black Holocaust Museum that he founded in Milwaukee. He also used the photograph on the cover of the first edition of his memoir about the event, *A Time of Terror* (1982)—a photograph altered somewhat with a third noose drawn between the corpses of Shipp and Smith. Underneath the photograph and acting as a subtitle to the autobiography are the following words: "The true story by the third victim of this lynching in the North who missed his appointment with death."[43]

Whether it was prescience about how this scene would be photographed, or whether it was the experience of having seen earlier photographs of lynching scenes, or whether his recollection has been partially displaced by the

Beitler picture, Cameron recalls responding to the moment of his own lynching as if it were a photograph. At the very moment when the noose was tight-
ening around his neck and the raging mob fell silent in the wake of the voice,
Cameron felt as if he were in a large room "where a photographer had strips
of film negatives hanging from the walls to dry. [He] couldn't tell whether the
images on the film were white or Black, they were simply mobsters captured
on film, surrounding [him] everywhere [he] looked. . . . Then the roomful of
negatives disappeared and [he] found [himself] looking into the faces of
people who had been flat images only a moment ago."

Because there are precious few accounts of someone who survived a
lynching, we have no other evidence we can draw on to understand how
lynch victims felt at the moment of their extreme danger, or how earlier
photographs of lynchings possibly played a role in imagining one's own body
after death. The closest we have is the story Bessie Jones tells of her uncle who
asked the lynch mob to take his picture after he was lynched and send it to his
sister. We have no idea what motivated him to do so, or what he felt the
photograph would represent, whether an expression of outrage or simply a
memento of his having been in the world. We can infer, however, that he
knew he could never see himself in the photograph his sister would see. (His
sister fainted when she received the photograph in the mail.)[44] What strikes
me as fascinating about Cameron's account is that he also imagines himself
in a lynching photograph, but he is still looking out as if he were a seeing
subject and not simply an object to be seen.

That Cameron viewed his own threatened lynching in terms of photography tells us something about how lynching photographs framed the way
some people viewed the world itself, especially the world of tense race relations and always potential white mob violence. It is also an apt symbol for the
transformation of usually benign people into "mobsters." As he looked out
from the prison cell at the gathering mob, Cameron had wondered how
people he had thought of as "my neighbors," customers whose shoes he had
shined, whose lawns he had mowed, whose cars he had washed, boys and girls
with whom he had attended school, could be transformed into a dangerous
mob. Years later, he saw a man he recognized from the mob on a bicycle with
his baby daughter. Cameron found it "difficult to believe that happy-
go-lucky man with that equally happy child, had been capable of doing the
things I knew he had done."[45] The image of negatives in a photographer's
studio helped explain that transformation.

In Cameron's account, then, we find two salient points. First, we can see
how the lynching photograph constitutes a form of imagined victimhood.
We have ample testimony from African American writers who have written

about how lynching accounts more generally and lynching photographs more specifically shaped their sense of the dangerous world they inhabited. When Jacquie Jones, for instance, saw the Beitler photograph in her eleventh-grade history textbook, she found that the picture "changed the way [she] looked at everything from that moment on."[46] She recognized that she too was a potential victim of a crime for which there would be no justice. What Cameron provides us with, then, is a caution against overemphasizing the ways in which dismantled and reframed lynching photographs had become exclusively anti-lynching images. These photographs continued to circulate and affect African American perceptions of danger. Yes, these were photographs that were used to demonstrate American barbarity, but they also always contained a portrait of black death, a figure or figures in the center with whom some continued to identify as they viewed a tableau in which it was easy to imagine a third noose.

A second way of thinking about lynching photographs we get from Cameron's account is a more personal assessment of how these pictures comprise a form of proof of complicity. Here are not only what the newspaper and magazine editors called members of the "mob," but members of the mob whom Cameron had known personally, people he had never believed capable of forming or joining a mob. Cameron's account raises the question of what constitutes a "mob." This was a question that legal officials asked in the aftermath of the Marion lynching. A deputy attorney general for Indiana, Earl Stroup, used what we saw in the last chapter to be the more encompassing definition of a mob. He described the mob as "anybody who is in the crowd, who does not resist any members of the mob." Following the example of the complicity models we traced in the last chapter, he too saw that physical presence constituted membership in a mob; and, also like the complicity models, he noted the polar possibilities of either resisting the mob or being part of it. It was a definition that did not work in Marion in 1930, just as it had failed in Coatesville in 1911. Grant County Deputy Sheriff John Fryer represented the majority when he insisted on distinguishing between "members of the mob" and those he called "sight seeing people."[47]

Cameron's account—which erases that distinction and insists, with other complicity models, on seeing responsibility in physical presence ("mobsters captured on film")—demonstrates the process by which individuals become "mobsters." Many have noted that lynchings are ritualistic events, and, as in all rituals, people assume roles assigned by the dynamic of the event and sanctioned by historical precedent. Whoever they were before (customers and school chums), and whoever they may become after (doting parents), at that moment they put on masks and adopt the role that the ritual demands of them. Instead of the supple and more caring human beings they were in other experiences, they become at that moment, at that truthful crisis, "simply mobsters captured on film."

In the end, a photograph that in so many ways is deeply deceptive, a photograph of a Northern lynching that stands in for all hangings from Southern trees, a photograph, as we will see, staged with corpses of men killed elsewhere, proves the cliché true. Pictures don't lie. Those whom Cameron doubted capable of such atrocities were in fact in attendance.

Heirs

Most Americans, one suspects, did not know that there were such things as lynching postcards or photographs before the mounting of the Allen-Littlefield exhibit at the turn of the twenty-first century. Once those photographs were on public display, though, they quickly inspired feelings of shame, loathing, anger, and guilt. Several commentators, particularly African Americans, feel compelled to express how they felt assaulted by these photographs. Patricia Williams noted in her *Nation* editorial on the exhibition that "this re-viewing of violence, this striving for reflection rather than spectacle, for vision rather than voyeurism, for study rather than exposure" was indeed a "difficult task." Hilton Als, writing the preface to *Without Sanctuary*, the published collection of those exhibited photographs, felt such "pain" and "resentment" at having to look at these pictures that he vowed never to write again from what he calls "this niggerish point of view" that these photographs, and the assignment of writing the preface, demanded of him.[48]

Others, almost all white Americans, wanted to examine what it meant for them to look at photographs whose original purpose was to celebrate, and whose transformed political purpose was to indict, white supremacy. A *New York Times* editorial on the Allen-Littlefield exhibit of lynching photographs noted the irony that "at this exhibition we are a crowd looking at a crowd looking at a lynching. And we are looking at a lynching too. Again and again, a white mob looks back at us." Nonetheless, the editorial insisted, the similarities between those looking then and those looking now are relatively immaterial since those who are viewing the pictures in New York museum spaces look at these pictures in a way "very different from the kind [of viewing] that these photos originally elicited." The difference, presumably, is that the viewers in the museum are not viewing out of morbid fascination or because they are looking for proof of white supremacy.[49]

The recent proliferation of lynching photographs, then, has elicited different kinds of responses from those who share a racial identity with a mob with whom they most fervently do not wish to be identified, and from those who share a racial identity with, and see themselves potentially in, the black body at the center of the picture. Another peculiar response has been the confession of those who see these photographs and are driven to reveal a torrid family secret, as did the *New York Post* writer who in the course of his review of the photograph exhibit remarked on how "ghastly" were the "faces of whites in the crowd," and then revealed that his grandfather had "helped lynch a man." Cynthia Carr, who wrote an insightful review of the catalogue of the exhibit, *Without Sanctuary*, for the *Village Voice*, did not use that occasion to make that kind of confession, although she had written another *Village Voice* article in 1994 on the lynching and her grandfather's membership in the Marion, Indiana, Klan. She recognized that these photographs revealed mobs that had "lost their humanity" in gleefully posing with their victims. These photographs, she concluded, would be "Exhibit A" if there were ever to be "a trial of the white race." The graphic the *Village Voice* used in this review was the Beitler photograph.[50]

It was a photograph Carr had first seen in her childhood home in the hardcover edition of *Alistair Cooke's America* (published in 1973), and it is a photograph she has spent a great deal of time since trying to understand. She tried unsuccessfully to interview the daughter of the photographer (who had given an interview to the *Marion Chronicle-Tribune* in 1988, revealing that her mother had destroyed the negative of her father's photograph in 1940). Carr did manage to interview many people who saw the lynching in Marion, and even the nephew of the African American tree surgeon who purportedly poisoned the lynching tree in the town square. In 2006, she purchased a copy of the Beitler photograph from a flea market in Marion owned by a former Klansman. The photograph had become significant to her by then, because in 2002 she had discovered her grandfather in the photograph when she saw an enlarged detail of the picture on the cover of Dray's *At the Hands of Persons Unknown*.[51]

Carr's memoir is about much more than the discovery of her grandfather in the photograph. She spends a year in Marion interviewing Klansmen and former Klansmen, talking to people who saw the lynching, and reporting in general about how this town remains haunted by the lynching event nearly three-quarters of a century later. She covers the various racial reconciliation ceremonies planned by citizens and commissions in the town, some more general, like the Marion Reconciliation Day on October 19, 2003, and some more specific, such as the church-sponsored Community in Unity service where white ministers stage an apology to the black citizens of Marion for the lynching. But the Beitler photograph hangs over her book like an incubus.

It appears nine times in the course of the book, literally from cover to cover, from the title page inside the front of the book to the back cover on the dust jacket, and seven times within the book itself, each time differently cropped and shaded to highlight particular individuals in the foreground.[52]

She knew that her grandfather had not "participated in the lynching, but [she] felt he was implicated." Aside from what she estimates to be the "twenty-five to fifty killers" who performed the lynching, there were "thousands of witnesses like those in the infamous photograph, and beyond them were the white people at home who condoned it." Her grandfather was implicated, then, in at least two ways. First, he was in the photograph and therefore one of the witnesses. Second, he was also someone who condoned the lynching, who participated, as she puts it, "in the code of silence."[53] Carr's meditation on her grandfather, on his membership in the Klan, on his presence at this lynching, is painfully honest about what it means to discover such troubling things about one's ancestor, about someone she loves so very dearly. She finds herself in a position of having to rethink what reconciliation means (and how it is necessary) in a much more personal way.

When Carr does finally find a copy of the photograph with sufficient detail (on the cover of Dray's book), she responds to the discovery of her grandfather's presence in the picture—and therefore at the site of the lynching—with uncertainty: "I *think* it's him, and I will never know for sure. He's way in the back. He's blurry, but I think that's his hat and his nose and the plane of his face." The only specific comment she makes about her discovery is that she was "relieved that he does not appear to be celebrating." It is, one supposes, a measure of relief. It is something, of course, that she finally found her grandfather, thirty years after she first saw the picture, and "after years of looking" at the Beitler photograph "almost daily" ("admittedly in bad prints and photocopies").[54] After researching and writing a great deal about Marion and lynching and the Marion lynching, Carr saw the image, or at least characters of an image, that revealed to her what she had suspected all along—that her grandfather had been there.

She called only one person about her discovery. She told him about finding her grandfather in the photograph, and he told her that by his "silence," her grandfather had given "approval." She agreed. What she wanted to tell that person, although it is not clear that she said it or said it in these words, was that she had had her eyes opened about what she calls "the white illusion," that curse or blessing of "thinking we're not connected to anything terrible."[55] The person she called, someone she had befriended many years before during her earlier research on the Marion lynching, was James Cameron.

Carr's memoir is called *Our Town*, and the subtitle is "A Heartland Lynching, a Haunted Town, and the Hidden History of White America." The title, of course, is an allusion to Thornton Wilder's play of the same name, although her reference to the "heartland" changes Wilder's New England setting and outlook. Carr emphasizes two points in the naming of her book— the fact that lynching constitutes a legacy of horror and secrecy (the town is "haunted," the history of those who lynch "hidden"), and the fact that lynching is a part of the inheritance of those whose history is hidden (it is "our" town, it is the history of an entire—white—nation). The book contains a compelling tension between smaller and larger kinds of places and responsibilities. It is about local events (this town, this lynching) and also national ones ("white America"). It is about the legacy of her own family that hid this event in a "code of silence," and also about the larger inheritance of being haunted by ghosts created from what she calls "the silence of white people."[56]

Like the Worth cousins, Cynthia Carr feels implicated in what her grandfather may have done and where she ended up finding him—in this iconic photograph. Hers, like theirs, is the perspective of inherited complicity. She identifies two distinct kinds of complicity, one for those who attended the lynching and one for those descended from them.

The first kind of complicity is her grandfather's, whose presence at the lynching makes him responsible in a very particular way. Carr had always known that her grandfather had gone to the courthouse square on the night of the lynching. There was a family story that he had received a phone call from someone who told him that if he walked to the courthouse *"You might see something you don't want to see."* And yet seeing his face in the photograph was more than confirmation of what she had already known. It made public a private family story, and it made painfully clear to her the kind of responsibility that inheres with holding the Klan beliefs her grandfather held and viewing impassively the lynching he viewed. She notes that though she had talked to "two other people who admitted to having a relative in that photo, and seemed untroubled by it, [she] personally found it painful."[57] It was the pain of knowing that her grandfather, like those other Marion community members Cameron saw, was a "mobster captured on film." His complicity was in being physically present where a lynching was taking place, and in believing the ideology of white supremacy that made lynchings inevitable.

The second kind of complicity is hers, a complicity she feels by dint of the heritage she has been given, by fate, as it were, of being born to this particular family, this specific race. Let me be clear, though, that what Carr means by belonging to a race is not simply the result of the ethnic phenotype with which one is born, but rather the obligation of discovering connections.

In her schema, one *becomes* white in America by entering into a "code of silence," by leaving the history "hidden," by not acknowledging how whiteness came to mean what it does. One can escape that kind of whiteness (blind and silent) by recognizing the connections that exist and the ones that were denied. At the end of the book, she says she had "opened [her] eyes" and seen how white people were indeed "connected" to something terrible—a history of oppression and terrorism. That is the recognition of the connections that exist.

The connections denied are, first and foremost, to the people who are not white, the ones oppressed, terrorized, and lynched. Carr's statement on that kind of connectedness requires some background. She tells us that her grandfather deeply revered Eugene Debs, the great American socialist, who had once stayed at the family boardinghouse and bounced her then-toddler grandfather on his knee. Carr is puzzled, then, by these contradictions. Her grandfather revered this politician who stood for unity and equality, and yet her grandfather continued to belong to the Klan, continued to believe in white supremacy, continued to express animosity toward Jews, and continued to hate those he deemed different.

She quotes Debs's eloquent statement of his beliefs at his trial: "Your Honor, years ago I recognized my kinship with all living things and I made up my mind that I was not one bit better than the meanest of the earth. . . . I said then, I say now, that while there is a lower class, I am in it; while there is a criminal element, I am of it; while there is a soul in prison, I am not free." That sentiment, as Carr notes, is the "opposite to the Klan's," to which her grandfather belonged.[58] It is a sentiment of inclusion and sympathy, of recognition of the deep and abiding connections that unite us all beyond the superficial differences that distinguish some of us from others. It is that connection—a connection denied—that Carr emphasizes as she tries to understand what kind of complicity ties one to that "hidden history of white America."

The two kinds of complicity differ in one way—the first is premised on physical presence in a mob, the second on attitudes toward descent. But they do share, at their core, the same fundamental point, which is that connections make and unmake us. Carr noted that "there was a chain of implication," from the past to the present, and that she herself was "linked because of [her] feelings for [her] grandparents and the town." She was, she says, morally obligated to "take responsibility as a descendant of that place." But the more compelling link—what she can undo, even if she cannot change her genetic connection to her family or her historical one to her family's hometown—is the one identified by John Jay Chapman, and that is, in Carr's words, the "curse we bring on ourselves by refusing to look at our histories."[59] It is the curse she undoes, the ghost she exorcises, that her grandfather had not.

DATE NIGHT AT THE COURTHOUSE SQUARE

So far, then, we have seen how this photograph has been subject to quite different responses. In one way, it was a photograph no one wanted to see—not
the black citizens of Marion and other Indiana towns who did not wish to see
the picture circulate in their neighborhoods, not the white citizens of Marion
who did not want to see their town's reputation besmirched, not someone
who was almost captured in that photograph, not someone who found her
grandfather in it. In another way, though, it was a photograph that they all
felt compelled to see and interpret, and all of the major responses we have
traced here—that of editorial framers, potential victim, guilty heir—share a
similar perspective on what they see. And what they see when they look at the
crowd beneath Abe Smith and Tom Shipp is responsible agents of a lynching.
They see a mob performing a lynching.

In other words, they do not make that distinction that the Grant County
deputy sheriff had made between "members of the mob" and "sight seeing
people." They see a mob as the Indiana deputy attorney general had defined
it: "anybody who is in the crowd, who does not resist any members of the
mob." Those who are not actively resistant to the actions of capturing, torturing, murdering, and looking are actively engaged in the performance of
the lynching. Their readings, in other words, are all governed by the tenets of
the complicity models we discussed in the previous chapter. The question we
can answer in conclusion, then, is what difference that perspective makes.
What do we see when we look at this photograph, and others like it, from the
perspective taken and provided by the complicity models?

———

We can begin by examining the law of Indiana to see how it helps us understand what constitutes membership in a mob, and what dynamic informs
complicity in a legal context. According to the law of Indiana at the time the
Marion lynching occurred, a "mob" is defined as "any number of persons
assembled for any unlawful purpose and intending to injure any person by
violence and without authority of law." Any act of violence "exercised by
such mob upon the body of any person shall, when such act results in the
death of the injured person, constitute the crime of lynching." The sentence
of punishment for any convicted member of the mob who "participates in or
actively aids or abets such lynching" is either life imprisonment or death. The
law is certainly clear in defining guilt for those people who occupy the first
three categories we saw Dray identify in the previous chapter. Those in the
first circle are the participants, those in the second are actively aiding, and

those in the third are actively abetting the lynching, that is, providing encouragement or assistance to those actually committing the crime.

Indiana differs from almost every other state, however, in that its code also contains an additional provision that does raise questions about the criminal guilt of spectators. Indiana law holds that "any person who, *being a member of any such mob and present at any such lynching, shall not actively participate in the lynching* shall be deemed guilty of abetting such lynching" (emphasis added). The penalty for this secondary form of "abetting" is a minimum of two and a maximum of twenty-one years' imprisonment.[60]

The ambiguity here concerns the issue of membership in a mob. Is someone a member only if one harbors an "unlawful purpose" and intends to injure, as the first definition of the mob states? Or is someone a member of a mob by mere presence, as the second definition of "abetting" implies? In an imaginary court situation, we can imagine that those who are spectators will obviously claim that they are not members of the mob because they did not harbor any unlawful purpose, they did not intend to hurt anyone, and they did not participate or provide aid or encouragement to the lynchers. Likewise, we can imagine the prosecutor arguing that the spectators are indeed members of the mob because their mere presence constitutes abetting a lynching; the very fact of their being at the site of a lynching, and not the fact of their active involvement or passive spectatorship, itself provides encouragement to the lynchers.

It is not clear if any of these charges were leveled against any of those in attendance at the Marion lynching. In the 1970s, Tom Wise, a Marion police officer, discovered a list of names of people who had been indicted for the Marion lynching, two of whom had actually gone to trial and been hastily acquitted. The prosecutor subsequently dropped the charges against everyone else on the list. Because the trial transcripts had disappeared, it was not possible to see what happened in that courtroom, but Cynthia Carr did interview people in Marion who named the two who had been tried, one of whom was rumored by different interviews to be either a "ringleader" in the lynching or someone relatively innocent and indicted as a "scapegoat."[61]

In the end, nobody served any time for the lynching in Marion, as is tragically true of virtually every lynching in American history. Whatever was promising in the Indiana law that sagely suggested the complicity of those who abet by their very presence at a lynching was not manifest at this opportunity, nor at any other in Indiana history so far as I know.

The only person there in Marion that night who did end up serving time was James Cameron. He was found guilty of "being an accessory before the fact to voluntary manslaughter" and sentenced to "not less than two years or more than twenty-one years," the same sentence for those who would have been found guilty of abetting the lynching.[62] To be an "accessory before the fact" is to be someone who "assists or encourages another to commit a crime but who is not present when the offense is actually committed." The category has been largely replaced in most legal jurisdictions with the category of "accomplice," someone, by definition, complicit in the commission of the crime.[63] Cameron, who had now twice faced death—once under the maple tree in the Grant County courthouse square, and once in the Madison County court where he was charged with a capital offense—was found guilty, ironically, not of committing the crime with which he was charged, but of aiding and abetting it, of being complicit.

The law of Indiana, as passed in 1899, amended in 1901, and codified in 1926 before the 1931 lynching, offered tantalizing possibilities for defining a heightened degree of complicity in mob members who do not actively participate but are present. But its ambiguity also renders the law ineffectual. The key point of ambiguity that the law does not address is when precisely a lynching occurs. Would one be a member of the mob if one is "present" at the moment of death only, as is the case in murder, or is one a member of a mob when he or she watches it trying to break into the jail, or watches it remove the victim, or watches it torture the victim, or participates by watching during the displaying of the corpse? As we saw in the previous chapter, the advocates of the complicity models argue that a lynching cannot reasonably be said to consist only of the actual murder itself; the term has usually been applied to an entire ritual, a goodly portion of which is postmortem. The law in Indiana, then, did support the kind of construction that the deputy attorney general put on it, that a mob could be defined in a more capacious way to include not only those actively killing or torturing but also those who are present.

This returns us, then, to the photograph. The editors of *Without Sanctuary* tell us that Indiana historians and researchers are interviewing citizens of Marion who are old enough to remember the events of August 1930 in order to identify the people in the photograph. The purpose, we are told, is "not to demonize them, but to better understand the factors that produced such a violent and tyrannical era."[64] My motive, likewise, is not to demonize any of the people in this photograph. They are no better or worse than the tens of thousands of people who went to view lynchings in their towns and neighborhoods, and I do not wish to draw special attention to them as more heinous examples of the kind of white supremacy that lynch mobs reinforced by their very presence on the grounds and in the pictures of lynchings. And while my motive is, like the Indiana researchers', to understand better some factors in lynching, mine is also more specifically focused on meditating on the topic of complicity and the ways different intellectuals have approached that very question when they think about lynching and lynching photographs.

The question in 1930 was whether the Beitler photograph captured what the deputy attorney general called a "mob" or what the deputy sheriff called "sight seeing people." For the purposes of focusing our discussion of what we see in the photograph, I will primarily concentrate on the couple in the front, to the left of the hanged bodies, the ones who are, in my title, on a date night at the courthouse square.

Each time I have seen this picture, I have found my attention drawn to this couple. There are reasons they stand out in this crowd. His smile is the most unreserved of anyone's in the picture, and therefore the most obnoxious. They are also the only couple in the photograph. Yet what strikes me most forcefully about them is the insouciance with which the two of them show their affection for each other in this scene. Almost the very first thing I noticed about the picture was his slightly blurred right hand holding her right thumb. There are other hands in this picture that have elicited commentary. Most viewers who comment on this photograph draw our attention to the man with the Hitler mustache who points his finger at Tom Shipp's corpse as if to direct the camera's attention there. There are the hands of the two elder men on the right side of the picture holding cigars. All the other women's hands are folded, except for one who is apparently holding a scarf around her neck. Unlike the hand of the man who points to the lynch victims, who seemingly wants to be seen, the hands of the couple appear caught in a secret embrace. Their holding hands seems such a simple gesture, the kind of physical touching common to people long enough in love to know those signs of when a partner wants a hand to be held but not so long a couple as to forgo public displays of their young love. His hand is blurred, I imagine, because it is moving to touch hers; in the kind of unspoken code of coupling, she has learned to put her hand out when she wants it to be touched and he has learned to reach his out in response. This small gesture speaks volumes.

Earlier commentators on this photograph have likewise felt compelled to discuss this couple. James Madison notes that the man looks like a young husband still wearing his summer business attire, while she could be an expectant mother whose pregnancy is just beginning to show. They look for all the world like a couple taking a commemorative photograph as they "picnic along the Mississinewa River." James Allen points out that the woman whose thumb is being held is holding a piece of cloth in her other hand, presumably from Shipp's bloodied pants that had been cut up and divided among the mob. Considering the links—the young man holding on to the thumb of his date, she holding in her other hand a memento of the lynching, from pants that might have been ripped off as the mob prepared to castrate the victim—Dora Apel insightfully notes that for this young couple "it is as though the myth of the hypersexed black male, now safely controlled, has become an invisible erotic power haunting their relationship."[65]

Cynthia Carr interviewed different people, including the man who was the mayor of Marion at the time of the lynching and an elderly white woman who had attended the lynching, who gave conflicting information about the names of the people in the photograph, including the couple. The mayor named the man in the couple as Phil Boyd and claimed that he was in fact a ringleader in the lynching. According to Kate Barnett, a woman who had left a dance in nearby Kokomo in order to see the hanged bodies, the man was not Phil Boyd but someone who had also attended the dance. In 2004, Carr finally learned the identity of the woman in the couple when she interviewed her daughter, Barbara Andrews. The woman's name was Bernadine Whitlock, and, according to her daughter, she was sixteen at the time of the lynching. The daughter asserted that her mother's presence at the lynching was "an accident," and she could not identify her mother's date.[66]

What, then, can we say of this couple, who are, in a way, a synedoche of the whole mob in the photograph? Is this couple *at* the lynching or are they simply part of a photograph of something well after the lynching is over? Much more important, I think, than *who* this couple may be is *what* they are, what role they play in the script of a total drama of lynching, what purpose they serve to those who perform lynchings with the knowledge that a mob will gather, will observe, will not contest, and will implicitly endorse what is done in the name of communal values. As we saw, the court in Grant County did not make much of an effort to define them by laws that Indiana did have on the books. And historians of lynching have largely done the same. They have agreed with the deputy sheriff who makes a distinction between a mob that lynches and spectators who do not.

Commenting on the photograph of the lynching of Charlie Hale in Lawrenceville, Georgia, in 1911, Amy Louise Wood, for instance, notes that since "the lynching took place at 12:30 A.M. and the body remained in the town square until the next afternoon, the photograph may have been taken the next day, and the men may have been merely onlookers." Likewise, commenting on the photograph of the lynching of Lint Shaw in Royston, Georgia, in 1936, Wood again notes that "the photograph was taken the day after the lynching and the men pictured could very well have been curious spectators."[67] Referring specifically to the Beitler photograph of the Marion lynching, James Madison makes a distinction between a "crowd" and a "mob." There are three elements in the photograph, he notes, "victim, mob, spectators." He later makes that distinction sharper by noting the difference between the "lynch mob" and the "ordinary people in Beitler's photograph." It is true that some in the photograph may have "guilty bloodstains on their clothing" and be members of the mob, he notes, but the majority, the rest, are simply a "crowd of shameless spectators."[68]

As we have seen above, the black press and anti-lynching press insisted on seeing the mob as a mass of responsible agents, those who lynch and those who view that work both having a distinct role and agency in that act. The framers, as we saw, maintained that the people in this picture, far from being "shameless spectators," are part of the lynch mob. The *Chicago Defender* argued that the photograph "shows any number of the guilty persons," and the *New York World*, whose editors showed only the part of the picture containing the white crowd, captioned it "Spectators and Participants in Killing of Negro Boys," perhaps hinting at a difference between "spectators and participants," perhaps hinting at their shared responsibility.

These competing ways of viewing the photographs cannot be reconciled because they presuppose entirely different dynamics in defining lynchings. Wood recognizes that radical difference in a skeptical examination of the caption of an anti-lynching advertisement the NAACP ran after the Senate failed (again) to pass an anti-lynching bill. The caption, she notes, "assumed that to pose for a lynching photograph was to join the mob, a mob that continued to 'act' even after its victim was dead. In this context, the photograph represented a continuous act of violence, one in which the Senate, through its failure to act, participated." That, as we saw in the last chapter, was precisely what James Weldon Johnson not only assumed but stated directly in an open letter to the Senate. Yet Wood, because she does not share that assumption, criticizes the NAACP because the organization, she says, "knew that the men posing for the photograph may have been not members of the mob but merely curious bystanders."[69]

For the NAACP, and for the advocates of the complicity models more generally, there is no meaningful distinction between those who commit the crime of lynching by physically murdering the victims and those who commit the crime of lynching by physically watching the events or witnessing the scene after the lynching. The lynching is performed for them, and they accept it as an expression of values they implicitly believe. They are not innocent bystanders, not curious spectators, not simply there by "accident." They are part of a performance. According to the complicity models, they are not spectators; they are participants *as* spectators. That couple, those who chose to smile publicly at a camera while secretly holding hands, are complicit. They are there, not accidentally, but to serve a purpose.

The answer to the question of what we see when we look at a lynching photograph from the perspective of the complicity models, then, is that we see a lynching. We do not see the aftermath of a lynching; we do not see a group of people posing in front of a scene where a lynching had taken place some time ago. Nor do we see the separate components of the hanging victims and the gazing crowd; they are intimately connected, the victim there because the crowd is there, the crowd there because the victim is. We see, in other words, a lynching—an event that follows a script involving a series of actions including capture, torture, murder, desecration, and photographing.

————

If we accept the arguments we were making in the previous chapter about how to understand a lynching—a) as an event that takes place over time, with different events marking that time, from the torture of a victim to the desecration of a corpse; and b) as an event employing different actors in different roles, from the agents to the spectators of destruction—then we can say that the photographing of a lynching scene is, in many ways, the culmination of the lynching event. To give substance to this suggestion, we need to return to the production and circulation of lynching photographs so that we can appreciate how the moment of their being taken, and the process of their being mailed from community to community, constitutes part of the dynamic of lynching.

In an essay on the 1904 lynching of Paul Reed and Will Cato in Statesboro, Georgia, the contemporary journalist Ray Stannard Baker noted that the mob performing the lynching was not so frenzied and driven to mad action that it did not stop its work of chaining and burning the victims in order to permit the photographer to take pictures of its efforts. At one point in the action, he noted, "the crowd stood back accommodatingly, while a photographer, standing there in the bright sunshine, took pictures of the chained Negroes." Indeed, they not only allowed the photographer to take the picture, but the members of the mob even helped frame it, as they "crowded up behind the stump and got their faces into the photograph." As the work of immolation began, the mob "yelled wildly" and "threw knots and sticks at the writhing" victims, but nonetheless "always left room for the photographer to take more pictures."[70]

This was indeed an "accommodating" mob, but not an unusually accommodating one, because mobs knew that the photographer was not, at this time in the early years of the century, a witness against, but a witness for, the work they were performing. The photograph of the lynching was a device for framing the work of lynching as an act of popular sovereignty and rough justice, as a performance of something communally sanctioned. As Wood notes, in "most photographs, the action of a lynching was stopped for the photographer to snap the picture, suggesting that the photographing was an integrated part of the lynching ritual."[71] It is for this reason, at least, that lynching photographs do not generally look like candid shots but rather like arranged family portraits. These were pictures taken after someone, perhaps the photographer, perhaps the mob, had put everyone in place for the shot. They were, in other words, staged photographs.

It is not only the crowd in these photographs that is staged. Even more so, the victim or victims are staged. On March 29, 1912, for instance, two black men, Frank Whisonant and Joe Brinson, were lynched in Blacksburg, South Carolina, and the lynching photographed. Clearly their necks were broken elsewhere and the "lynching" then staged for the photograph: the beam from which they are hanged is so low as to allow their feet to touch the ground.[72] Of course, the corpse of the lynch victim is always staged in the primary sense that it is made a central prop for the photograph, but it is secondarily staged by being put where the photograph wants to show the lynching (not where the actual death took place).

Let's return now to the Beitler photograph. Of the two victims hanging from the tree, one certainly and the other likely died elsewhere. Thomas Shipp, whose body is the one on the right of the photograph, died when the mob hanged him by his neck from the window bars in the jail. Only afterward did the mob cut Shipp's corpse down from the bars and then hang him again from the limb of the maple tree in the Grant County courthouse square. It is also highly likely that Abe Smith died well before he was hanged from the same maple tree. A witness to the scene who watched as a member of the mob "rammed a crowbar through [Smith's] chest several times" was certain that Smith was dead before the mob reached the courthouse and hanged his body from the tree.[73] In other words, the scene of lynching in the photograph is not the site of the deaths of these two men but rather the site of the display of their deaths. So a photograph that has been cropped in different ways and, apparently, for different effects is itself a picture of a staged scene. What we think happened here on this tree in this courtyard (the murder) did not happen here. Smith and Shipp were killed elsewhere, but their lynching was staged here.

What, then, can we determine from the fact that lynching photographs like Beitler's are staged? Most significantly, I suggest, it demonstrates the way that the lynching photograph is part of the entire production that is a lynching. It is not meant to capture the place or setting where a victim met death, nor to capture the mob in the process of effecting that death. It is meant to show a tableau that represents the lynching, a staged tableau where we see black bodies hanged or burned and white living bodies surrounding the victim as if he were a hunting trophy or a talisman of the potency of white supremacy. The photograph, which lynchers stop their work to permit, where victims are set up in the position that best suits the venue where people want the lynching to be remembered, is not a historical rendering of an event but part of it—the part where the event moves from ritually staged activity to ritual recollection.

The circulation of the photograph—published in the newspaper, or in the form of a postcard sent through the mails—constitutes the continuation of the lynching event, its expansion through space and time from the community where and when it happened to the communities that view with satisfaction or horror its having happened. This seemed to be the way newspapers understood the process. After the photograph of Jesse Washington's lynching in Waco, Texas, in 1916 was published, for instance, the *Houston Chronicle and Herald* commented on how the publishing of the picture will expand it from the "hundreds of whites who participated" and the "thousands who looked on" to the "millions who will read."[74] It is just the same point John Jay Chapman had made much more incisively after the Coatesville lynching: "The next morning the newspapers spread the news . . . until the whole country seemed to be helplessly watching this awful murder . . . and the whole of our people seemed to be looking on."[75]

To reiterate, then, what we see in the photograph, its very content, according to the complicity models, is a lynching in process—and the process is drawn out. Again, this perspective is not widely shared by most contemporary students of lynching because they tend to share the assumptions of American case law that a lynching, like other crimes, is circumscribed in time, action, and agency. It is just that perspective that the anti-lynching advocates and those who proposed what I have been calling the complicity models wanted to challenge by arguing that a lynching is not just a crime (although certainly that) but also a performance, a production, a ritual event that involves and implicates a range of actors, from people who kill to people who watch to people who are photographed. And all of them are involved and implicated—and complicit—in a lynching. That is what we see when we view a lynching photograph. We do not see a couple on a date inadvertently caught in the glare of a photographer's flash; we see people, like all the others there, who are lynching.

Conclusion: Toward the End of Mob Lynching

The Beitler photograph—the most famous and iconographic of the lynching photographs—was also one of the last. In 1930, it captured what was becoming a rare event, a gathering of people around a lynched body. Indeed, the year of the Marion lynching, 1930, was marked by a final spike in the frequency of lynchings, which had been annually declining since the beginning of the century. That spike provoked the Southern Commission on the Study of Lynching to undertake a massive research project in which it produced a case study of each of the twenty-one lynchings that occurred in that year. In his prefatory comments to those case studies, the research and field secretary of the commission, Arthur Raper, followed the example of the advocates of the complicity models and insisted on seeing the mob as differentially but equally responsible for the performance of lynchings.

The mobs of 1930, he wrote, were made up of "lynchers" and "onlookers," or, to employ the terms he used in the case of the Marion lynching, an "active mob" and "onlookers." Yet Raper made that distinction only in order to apportion guilt to all. He maintained that "not one of these so-called onlookers is morally or legally guiltless: Their very presence directly complicated the task of the peace officers, and emboldened the active lynchers by reflecting to them the community's general approval." These "curious onlookers" and "sympathizers who stood by" provided the "active mobbers with a semblance of decency and no small measure of immunity from official interference." Their "very presence," he concluded, makes them "morally and probably legally responsible for the outrage against law." In no way was the community's approval of lynching more apparent than in those cases where witnesses refused to come forth or name the participants in a lynching. Those in the community who are knowledgeable of and yet remain silent about the identity of the lynchers implicitly support those who committed and watched the lynching. In other words, lynchers, spectators, and those who hide the identity of lynchers and spectators all "share in the responsibility for the crime of the mob."[76]

Raper continued his analysis of the social complicity that informs mob lynchings by extending it to the larger society from which lynchers, spectators, and mobs are drawn. A mob, Raper noted, "is a mob, not because of what it does, but because of what it is." And mobs, he continued, "do not come out of nowhere; they are the logical outgrowths of dominant assumptions and prevalent thinking." There were 75,000 Americans who joined a lynch mob in 1930 alone, and while they were members of a mob only on one day in the year they "were most probably mob-minded every day in the year." And by "mob-minded," Raper does not mean that they were capable of becoming unthinking agents of violence but rather that they were in daily as well as spectacular practice socialized to act out the white supremacy that is the reason for lynching. In the end, then, the "mobs of 1930 [that] had about 75,000 members—men and women and children who went out to kill, or to look on sympathetically while others killed"—were complicit in lynching insofar as they killed, watched the killing, read about or saw photographs of the killing, or did not resist, contest, and otherwise challenge the potential "mob-mindedness" of the society they populated.[77]

The most manifest expression of that mob-mindedness—the mass spectacle lynching—that Ida B. Wells saw as inaugurating "an entirely new form" in the early 1890s was coming to an end by the early to mid-1930s. There continued to be gruesome lynchings from the early to the late 1930s. The year 1933 witnessed the dragging, hanging, and burning of George Armwood in Somerset County, Maryland, and the dragging, dismembering, and burning of David Gregory in Hardin County, Texas. The years 1937 and 1938 saw mobs use blowtorches to burn three African Americans to death in Montgomery County, Mississippi, drag the burning corpse of Tom McGehee in Sharkey County, Mississippi, do the same to the corpse of Willie Reed in Decatur County, Georgia, and drag and burn to death John Dukes in Crisp County, Georgia.[78] Nonetheless, there was a difference from the era of spectacle lynchings, as the mobs were indeed smaller and the press coverage more condemnatory. Public opinion was changing, and lynchings were no longer as effective a form of terrorism and spectacle as they had been prior to the Depression.

Anti-lynching activists actively recorded this social transformation in lynchings, noting first the "gradual decline in the number of states involved" and then "a change in mobs and in their methods." Around 1936, "mobs began generally to be more orderly," fewer lynch victims were abducted from police custody, and few victims were accused of criminal offenses at all. According to the ASWPL, 1938 witnessed the last manhunt, and the "last lynchings in which mobs resorted to torture and the burning of the bodies of their victims." Mobs became smaller and more private. The apologists no longer claimed that lynchings were performed to protect white women's chastity or to punish its violation. By 1939, then, the ASWPL claimed, lynchings had "gone underground."[79]

An event that was once proudly staged and publicly promoted was now subterranean and secret. The spectacle lynchings of the Progressive Era, the operas of white civilization, had lost their motive, their production value, and become essentially a defunct form. With that historical change at the end of the 1930s—in the frequency of lynchings, in the forms they now assumed—came, simultaneously, a significant transformation in the ways of thinking about complicity in lynchings.

CHAPTER 3

THE END OF AMERICAN LYNCHING

At the corner of Mulberry and White streets in the Central Texas county seat of Eastland, there is a granite slab that commemorates what the town officials designated as "the last mob lynching in Texas." That lynching took place on November 19, 1929, when a mob hanged a white bank robber, Marshall Ratliff, for shooting a much-loved jailer during an escape attempt from the Eastland jail.[1] A little less than two months after the Eastland lynching, on January 12, 1930, the *New York Times*, in an article entitled "Foresees End of Lynching," hailed the fact that only ten people were lynched in 1929 and predicted that "lynching will be a lost crime by 1940—something for scientists to study and the rest of us to remember with unbelief."[2] And, indeed, by 1940, the ASWPL made just that claim, that lynching was a "lost crime."

These sorts of pronouncements—that lynching has come to an end, that some particular lynching is the "last"—marked a new development in the conversation over lynching in America, a new account of what lynchings were and meant. By 1940, that way of thinking and talking about lynchings began to gain traction. What we are calling the end-of-lynching discourse was defined by three particular developments. First, its adherents proposed that the word and practice of "lynching" needed to be defined in significantly narrower terms. Second, the adherents used that narrower definition to deny that a given event—which might previously have been identified as a lynching—was one. Debates during this period shifted from how to understand the nature of responsibility in a mob event to whether or not a specific event was a lynching. Third, the adherents of the end-of-lynching discourse started to identify just which lynching was indeed the "last" one.

This shift in the conversation about lynching dramatically changed the terms of debate over individual lynchings. The debate prior to the late 1930s, as we saw in the previous two chapters, was between those who insisted on a narrow gambit of guilty actors (the Samaritan model) and those who

95

proposed an expanded range of responsibility (the complicity models). In the complicity models that emerged from the 1890s to the 1930s, from Ida B. Wells to Arthur Raper, the focus was on how to understand the responsibility of individuals in a single collective event. What responsibility could be borne by the spectator, say, of any given lynching? Implicitly, these models, to a greater or lesser extent, also commented on how a society creates the intellectual conditions that promote lynchings, or what Raper called "mob-mindedness." Nonetheless, the primary aim of the complicity models was to determine responsibility within an event. A crucial part of that aim was to redefine the event—the lynching—so that its parameters were considerably broadened. A lynching in the complicity models was an event that began well before and ended well after the actual killing of the victim—and participation in the event ran the gamut from capture, torture, killing, and desecration to spectatorship, both those who look and those who pose while looking.

The debate after 1940 became one between those who insisted on a narrower definition of what constituted a lynching and those who argued for a more capacious and flexible definition. The debate, when it concerned specific historical incidents, often devolved into whether or not that incident was a lynching. In broader terms, the debate was also implicitly about different ways of conceiving of the trajectory of American history. On the one hand, the adherents of the end-of-lynching discourse held that lynchings arose at a specific moment and arose as a result of particular social conditions, then declined as those conditions eroded, and then finally ended when those conditions too came to an end. The opponents of the end-of-lynching discourse maintained that lynchings were part of a larger pattern of vigilante and extralegal violence in American history, and that the changes after the 1930s marked a transformation, not a termination, in that history.

That debate has largely been dominated by the adherents of the end-of-lynching discourse, and their terms and presuppositions are still largely in force today. What I will do in this chapter is examine the evolution and presuppositions of the end-of-lynching discourse, showing how it emerged at a particular moment in the interwar period and became more resonant in what some began to call the beginning of the "American century." After that, we can look at a specific case—through a narrative account of an event and then a demonstration of how the end-of-lynching discourse determined the debate over that event. This case shows how the end-of-lynching discourse is still the dominant mode for our understanding the history of lynching. It determines the terms of discussion over contemporary acts of racial violence, and it controls how we imagine the shape and trajectory of lynching in America. In the end, I wish to show how that discourse has also delimited our understanding of the history of extralegal, collective violence in America, and I wish to argue that our rejecting its tenets will, in fact, help us better appreciate just what that history can reveal about the past and current state of the society.

THE END-OF-LYNCHING DISCOURSE

In order best to understand the strategy, force, and imperatives behind the end-of-lynching discourse, we can begin by seeing the twin processes that marked its evolution—the work of narrowing the definition of lynching, and the compulsion to discover a "last" American lynching. After tracing those processes, we can then speculate on what made those claims of a "last lynching" so pressing for some to make and believe; to see, in other words, in what ways those claims had become entangled in a complex of national beliefs and hopes.

———

As lynchings declined in frequency in the late 1930s, anti-lynching advocates, and Americans more generally, began to ponder what exactly it was that was disappearing. Not all anti-lynching advocates felt that lynching was indeed declining, nor did they all agree about what meaning to assign the fluctuating rates of lynching in the first third of the twentieth century. Those disagreements came to a head in 1940, after a series of acrimonious debates among anti-lynching advocates about whether an event was or was not a lynching. The Tuskegee Institute, the keeper of records, often dismayed the two major political advocacy groups, the ASWPL and the NAACP, by recording or not recording an event as a lynching in its official published tabulations. A summit was called at which the groups formed a definition of lynching that would settle those debates. The summit defined lynching by noting four necessary conditions: "There must be legal evidence that a person has been killed, and that he met his death illegally at the hands of a group acting under the pretext of service to justice, race, or tradition."[3] This summit definition would prevent disagreements among the groups and provide a minimal set of standards for identifying an event as a lynching or not.

The rapprochement did not last long. Two of the agencies that attended and approved the definition at the summit—the NAACP and the ASWPL—ended up contesting it later. The NAACP complained that the definition did not cover enough and permitted some lynchings to be classified as some other kind of crime. The ASWPL retracted its commitment to the summit definition because it covered too much and could be used "to convert into a lynching the death of every Negro at the hands of white persons."[4] Here, then, was a conflict in definitions that had a genuine impact on the organizations in their thinking about their political work. If they could not agree on what constituted a lynching—on what specific event was or was not a lynching—then how could they contest and publicize the event, and how could they expect legislators to pass bills against a practice that they now differed in identifying?

A major reason for the conflict was, to put it a little too simplistically, that the NAACP focused on *motive* while the ASWPL focused on *form*. Each, then, saw a very different phenomenon when they viewed the same historical event. Feeling that lynchings were undergoing a transformation, and that these racial acts of terrorism were now manifest in a variety of different acts, the NAACP argued that lynchings did not require the kind or size of mob that had earlier distinguished lynchings, nor did they require the same sort of communal support they had earlier commanded. What made a lynching a lynching, for the NAACP, was its motive—to terrorize a subject people. The ASWPL, as we saw at the end of the previous chapter, had been tracking each formal change in lynching—mobs becoming more orderly, less likely to abduct victims from the police, less likely to make criminal accusations, and less likely to immolate their victims. These formal changes in the makeup, strategy, and work of the mob, the ASWPL concluded, raised "doubts of the validity of designating as lynchings certain types of murder."[5]

As we saw in the introduction, the end-of-lynching discourse in many ways was premised on dismissing the idea of *transformation*—that lynchings changed in form and dynamic. The ASWPL insisted that because lynchings had changed form, they were no longer lynchings. The debate between the two organizations focused on a metaphor that revealed just what each was striving to say about lynchings. When the NAACP published a pamphlet in 1940 entitled *Lynching Goes Underground*, it was arguing that lynchings had undergone a transformation from being public spectacles to private acts, from mob events to secret ones. When the ASWPL used the same metaphor two years later, it suggested that lynchings had gone underground in a more funereal sense—that they had essentially perished.[6] That debate reached its climax in the 1940s, but it had been percolating through the 1930s as commentators considered what to make of what was apparently a transformation in the practice of lynching.

In 1930, Horace B. Davis called the nation's attention to what he called a "substitute for lynching," by which he meant those "borderline cases" in which African Americans were killed by smaller mobs or pairs of killers. He noted sadly that some who condemn mob lynchings will "frequently be found in sympathizing privately with murder when this has as its object the suppression of 'sassy niggers.'"[7] In 1938, the editor of the *Christian Century* asked whether "lynching appears to be passing only because it is passing under another name." He noted that African Americans were now more openly murdered by conventional means—"by shooting in the back"—instead of being killed by a mob.[8]

Jonathan Daniels used the same phrase as the ASWPL in 1940, noting that "lynchings have gone underground," but he used it to dispute the idea that lynchings were any less frequent. Those killings of African Americans that he describes as "expressions of white group bitterness and not of mere individual murderousness" were now performed in such a way as to keep them "out of the statistics and the newspapers." These lynchings had gone "underground," then, because they had sufficiently changed form so that the statisticians who employed a narrow definition of what constituted a lynching were not recording them as such.[9] Likewise, Henry Wallace noted in a *New Republic* article entitled "Violence and Hope in the South" that lynching was giving way to a new form of violence: "The technique now is quietly to murder a Negro, one man doing the killing instead of a mob."[10]

This strategy had the potential to backfire. The *Rome [Georgia] News-Tribune* commented that this expansion of the definition of lynching should also be applied to the North. Such race riots as occurred in Chicago, Detroit, and Harlem, the editor noted, were essentially lynchings: "A lynching party is none the less a lynching party when it murders Negroes with pistols, shotguns and rifles instead of ropes."[11] In Congress, Senator William Borah argued likewise as he spoke against a federal anti-lynching bill then pending: "What is the distinction in this bill between violence committed by a combination of thugs and violence committed by those who are combined into a mob?"[12]

In a widely read *New Yorker* essay, novelist Rebecca West covered the trial of the lynchers of Willie Earle. It was the only lynching of 1947 at the time of the trial, and West remarked on how this killing was "not a true lynching case," or, rather, "not a pure lynching case." Because of the changed dynamics, she felt that it was "an example of a type of crime which is increasing, while lynching is diminishing." Revisiting the case two years later, West recognized that the crime against Earle did contain many of the traditional characteristics of a lynching: "The man taken from prison was a Negro and the men charged with killing him were white," and Willie Earle had been "beaten and stabbed and shot in the body and head."[13]

We can see, then, how the issue of transformation, the recognition or denial that lynchings were lynchings despite formal changes in the size and procedures of the mob, created a public debate that in many ways anticipated and mirrored the debate between the NAACP and the ASWPL on whether to emphasize form or motive in assessing a particular act as a lynching. That larger public debate eventually devolved into a scripted dispute over whether or not a specific event was a lynching.

Two cases from the 1950s demonstrate the dynamic of the debate clearly enough. In 1955, the governor of Mississippi proclaimed that Emmett Till was not "lynched" but simply a victim of what he called a "straight-out murder." The *Jackson Daily News* insisted that what it called "the kidnap-murder was not a lynching." In 1959, a local circuit judge in Mississippi claimed that what happened when Mack Charles Parker was dragged from his jail cell and killed by a mob of Poplarville police officers and citizens was not a lynching but only a "conspiracy to commit a crime, the crime of murder."[14] These became the standard scripted lines of police forces dealing with what they denied were lynchings. Those opposed to the end-of-lynching discourse challenged these assertions by insisting on naming the crime. The NAACP leaders and the editor of the *Crisis* maintained that Till was the victim of a "lynching-crime." Senator Wayne Morse, Senator Jacob Javits, and NAACP head Roy Wilkins all argued that Parker was lynched in presenting a case for the necessity of anti-lynching legislation.[15]

That scripted and rote debate—one side insisting, one side denying that a lynching had taken place—would in time come to replace the earlier discussions around lynchings, those discussions about the nature of consent, the responsibilities of communities, the sanctity of sexual purity, and even the supremacy of one race. The end-of-lynching discourse changed those earlier discussions by insisting that what they were about (the act of lynching) was itself the issue. "Lynching" became a profoundly contested term, and the end-of-lynching discourse made it as difficult for anti-lynching advocates to ask larger questions about the meaning of the continuation of lynching as the lynching-for-rape discourse had made it difficult for its critics to assert that lynching was about racist terrorism and not the crime of rape.

———

Having narrowed the definition of what was a lynching, and then contested each event called a lynching, the adherents of the end-of-lynching discourse now proceeded to identify one moment in American history when lynchings could be said to end. This desire to proclaim a "last American lynching" was evident well before 1940. As we saw above, journalists were prophesying and civic boosters memorializing it in the late 1920s and early 1930s. Even before that, the desire was evident. In an editorial in 1914, the *Crisis* mocked what appeared to the editors to be an annual "season of rejoicing at the decline of lynchings in the United States." That year's celebration, the *Crisis* mordantly noted, had "been rather long drawn out" and "quite vociferous." That same year, the Tuskegee Institute, which had followed the example of the *Chicago Tribune* and in 1900 began presenting first annual and then semiannual tabulations of lynchings in America, added the new category of "prevented lynchings" to its record. By 1920, for the first time more lynchings were prevented than were committed (although this particular statistic was problematic since "mobs" were often defined on the basis of rumors and sometimes failed less because of their ineptitude than their nonexistence).[16]

As we saw in the last chapter, the ASWPL traced each new development in mob dynamics in the 1930s and declared that each signaled a "last" of some sort—the last manhunt, the last torture, the last immolation. This desire to see no more lynchings in America led some groups and individuals to questionable strategies. We saw how the ASWPL, for instance, wanted to retire the term and expressed annoyance when Tuskegee and the NAACP continued to call those events lynchings. The leader of the ASWPL, Jessie Daniel Ames, then set out to claim a "lynch-free year" in America. She was frustrated at some point each year, every year. So desperate did she become to make that declaration that she curtailed the definition of lynching, challenged those events that the NAACP called lynchings, and then even modified the calendar, having the "year" begin in May.[17]

After 1940, the end-of-lynching discourse began to claim ground in earnest. The "lynch-free" year finally became a reality in 1952, when there was no officially recorded lynching. After a second year without a recorded lynching, the Tuskegee Institute announced that it was discontinuing its annual tabulation of lynchings in America. Tuskegee's final report proclaimed that lynching "as traditionally defined" had ceased to be a "valid index" or "barometer for measuring the status of race relations in the United States." Two things are worth noting about the final report. First, Tuskegee proposed that future reports gauging race relations would instead use criteria such as employment and other economic conditions, political participation, education, legislation, and health. Second, the report concluded that lynchings had largely ended because of "significant changes in the status of the Negro" and because of "the development of other extra-legal means of control, such as bombings, incendiarism, threats and intimidations."[18] The violence meant to act as a form of social control and terrorism, in other words, had become less ritualistic and less collective. Individuals and small groups could throw bombs, perform drive-by shootings, and torch a house. Wholly disregarding the Tuskegee Institute's caution in describing the ways that racial violence had changed shape, not been eliminated, the popular media heralded what the *Washington Post* called, in a January 2, 1954, headline, the "End of Lynching." Optimistically arguing that there was good reason to believe that the states had "wiped out this offense to American civilization," the *Post* writer downplayed the three prevented lynchings the previous year.[19]

A sign of how the end-of-lynching discourse governs our own intellectual moment and our understanding of the trajectory of lynching is the fact that so many contemporary historians who study lynchings seem equally eager to place them firmly in the past. A recent anthology on lynching concludes that with "some confidence, we can anticipate that the killings in the manner described and analyzed here are behind us." In an even more concerted way, these historians exert significant effort in designating some particular lynching as the "last." One writer, for instance, calls the 1931 lynching in Marion, Indiana, "the last classic lynching north of the Mason-Dixon line." One argues that the "last large mob" appeared on October 17, 1942, when a "hundred men" took Howard Wash from jail and hanged him from a bridge. Another identifies the "1942 Texarkana, Texas, mob that tortured to death William Vinson for rape as the last open mob." Yet another argues that the 1942 immolation of Cleo Wright in Sikeston, Missouri, "signaled the beginning of the end" of that kind of mob racial lynching.[20] One calls the 1946 lynching in Walton County, Georgia, the "last mass lynching in America." A recent history of lynching in America refers to the 1964 murders of three civil rights workers in Mississippi as "the last lynching in which a mob acted in collaboration with police and intercepted its victims leaving a jail." Finally, some cite the lynchings in 1981 of Kenneth Rex McElroy (white) in Missouri and Michael Donald (black) in Mobile, Alabama, as the "last."[21]

With the "last" lynching, these writers also often find the death of the social order that sanctioned that form of racial violence. One historian, for example, calls the 1955 lynching of Emmett Till a "virtually final spasm of traditional Southern white violence against blacks," the "nearly last lethal gesture" of a disappearing way of life. Another refers to the 1959 lynching of Mack Charles Parker as "one of the last lynchings of America," the "last—denatured—gasp of a bygone era."[22] This tendency to identify a single lynching as the "last" demonstrates to what extent the end-of-lynching discourse governs how we discuss the recent past, how we wish to place markers along a route to a mature modernity, how we want to see these events as anomalies in our social order, things that belong to a "bygone era."

The end-of-lynching discourse—from its emergence in the 1940s to its almost hegemonic hold in our own day—has an imperative, of course, a reason that its adherents believe in it. Obviously, part of the urge for those who first advocated it, like the leadership of the ASWPL, must have been to see their work come to fruition. After years of hard work at publicizing lynchings, and trying and failing to get federal legislation passed, some of these individuals and groups wished to see their work as effective, and that meant claiming an end to the practice they had identified as the one they wished to eradicate.

Another, and arguably more important, factor was what we can loosely call "patriotism," in this case, the salvaging of the nation's reputation. Part of the strategy of anti-lynching advocates had been to insist that lynching was a national event, a crime that reflected ill on America's reputation. As the *New York Times* reported in 1930, when lynching came to pass it would be something Americans would "remember with unbelief." The *Washington Post* writer called it an "offense to American civilization." Lynching, over the four decades of anti-lynching advocacy, had become conflated with the national identity. Over and over again, anti-lynching advocates claimed that only in America are people burned alive, only in the U.S.A. can we see such terrorism of a racial group, only in this place is lynching a defining feature of social life.

"The United States is the native heath of lynching," wrote Lewis Blair in 1894. Even more to the point, he concluded that lynching constituted "a distinguishing feature of American Evangelical Christian civilization." Writing the first academic book-length study of lynching in 1905, James Cutler traced the history of vigilante activity on other continents before calling it a "fact" that "lynching is a criminal practice which is peculiar to the United States." He, like Blair, saw it as constitutive of the national identity when he concluded that "our country's national crime is lynching." Ida B. Wells had maintained this same point in 1895 when she pointed out that "no other civilized nation stands condemned before the world with a series of crimes so peculiarly national."[23] Indeed, not only did many intellectuals believe lynching to be a distinctively American crime, but some went so far as to suggest that even within America it was uniquely the work of "free-born American citizens," not naturalized Americans, or even "foreigners" or "political anarchists."[24]

For the first half of the twentieth century, anti-lynching advocates would continue to insist, as did the NAACP in 1919, that "the United States has for long been the only advanced nation whose government has tolerated lynching." In 1924, the NAACP referred to lynching as the "Great American Specialty," and in 1934 placed a caption under the picture of a hanged lynch victim: "This is what happens in America—*and no other place on earth!*"[25] Anti-lynching discourse, then, had conflated lynching and national identity so thoroughly that it became difficult to disentangle what "America" could mean as a beacon of democratic freedom from what it did mean as a nation where lynching happened. The desire to see the end of lynching, then, was simultaneously the desire to see America no longer stigmatized or condemned for this peculiar crime, to see it as no longer what Mark Twain mordantly called it, "The United States of Lyncherdom."[26]

Given this intense and enduring connection between the nation and its most shameful practice, it is not surprising, then, that commentators who wanted to salvage the reputation of the nation ended up insisting on the end of the practice. Because lynching had for so long been a barometer of race relations, the decline and end of lynching had come to be desired primarily for what that decline would indicate about the state of the nation. A lynch-free year for the ASWPL meant a year that America had become better and less racist; a decline in lynching meant that we lived in a new era, or at least not in a past or bygone one; the advent of the last American lynching meant that we had matured as a nation, become less barbarous as a people.

An editor for a Tennessee newspaper, John Fort, noted that lynchings were decreasing—and the time was near when "limp figures will no longer hang in public, nor will the distant animal cry of the mob pack swell in the night"—precisely because "lynching is the revival of a condition . . . in primitive society," a "wild orgy of primitive purification" that was being rendered moot by the evolving society and civilization of the South.[27] In 1930, the director of the Commission on Interracial Cooperation noted that the "steady decline in lynchings" led Americans to "hope that we had a new South morally, economically, and politically," although the spike in lynchings in that year had "seriously shaken our confidence."[28] As he considered the state of race relations in 1939, Charles Mangum Jr. traced the decline in lynching to three factors: "the educational work of the Southern Commission on Interracial Coöperation, the condemnation of lynching by influential editors and other persons in public life in the South, and the growing spirit of liberalism in southern thought."[29]

In 1952, the Southern progressive editor Hodding Carter reiterated these points as he criticized what he described as "this unfair and unchanging refusal to recognize what the South itself is doing" in ending lynchings. He dismissed the role that federal anti-lynching legislation could play in reducing and ending lynchings, offering instead the usual catalogue of social forces indicating increased civilization and maturity: "Only reason, education, spiritual appeal and local censure can reduce the one and two and three lynchings a year to none."[30] The end of lynching, then, had come to be invested with a special meaning, indeed nothing less than a reclaiming of regional and national pride. In the words of one representative commentator in 1985: "The end of lynching was a milestone of sorts, an overdue sign of growing maturity and fading barbarism."[31] The end-of-lynching discourse

managed to convey that celebratory tenor, and it began to do it on the eve of
and in tandem with what journalists and optimists were calling the "American
century."

What, then, can we say about the effects of the emergence and continued
vitality of the end-of-lynching discourse? First, it reveals that a particular (and
particularly narrow) definition of lynching has managed to displace other definitions. The definition that emphasizes mob size and community support
was operative and useful for the period between the 1880s and 1930s, but it did
not adequately describe the kinds of lynchings that occurred before and after
those years, lynchings that had different dynamics and consisted of different
types of mobs. And, as we shall see, it is most tellingly a definition that is a
result of focusing exclusively on one kind of lynching during those years.
What was lost in the ascendancy of that particular definition were those definitions that were more attentive to the changing dynamics of lynching in the
course of three centuries in American life, those definitions that saw the practice evolve and be transformed to suit particular conditions and needs. What
was lost was also the flexibility of mind to see beyond strictly formal features.

Second, the complex of beliefs that holds that the end of lynching is a
sign of and has led to the beginning of a mature and civilized society has
created a sensibility requiring lynching to be placed unalterably in the past,
made a museum piece, rendered a relic, an icon of a discredited religion
with no remaining effective power. It has become, in other words, a pro-
scribed subject. David Bradley notes that even to use the word "lynching" is
"to risk being accused of the worst kind of demagoguery."[32] In our own
day, it has become a museum exhibition (the Allen-Littlefield collection of
lynching photographs) rather than a living concern. It is a symbolic statement
of racist harassment (nooses hung outside African American workers'
doors or lockers) rather than a form of material violence. It has become a
metaphor (Clarence Thomas and Kwame Kilpatrick claiming they were lynch
victims for political investigations) rather than a practice. Unlike murder,
which we believe we will always have with us, lynching is a thing of the past.
How can we understand the various manifestations of that desire to render as
unalterably historical this horrendous practice—to place it so much in the
past that we can commemorate it, memorialize it, and make it a metaphor?
What does it reveal about us, this profound wish to claim that this is the "last
American lynching"? And what happens when we are confronted with an
event that challenges those desires, those wishes? We can turn now to one
such event.

JASPER, 1998

John William King and Lawrence Russell Brewer woke up late on Saturday, June 6, 1998. They were sleeping off the effects of the liquor and wine they had stolen from Patrick's Steakhouse the night before. Shawn Allen Berry, their roommate, had woken earlier and gone to work in the theater in the small town of Jasper, Texas. In the early afternoon, King and Brewer went to nearby Newton County to visit the younger brother of their roommate. For the rest of the day, they aimlessly went from place to place in Newton and Jasper counties. People who saw them wandering around Jasper said they saw nothing unusual in their movements. Eventually, King and Brewer ended up at the theater where Berry worked. Berry had had an earlier visitor that afternoon, his girlfriend and the mother of his son, Christie Marcontell, who had come by the theater to see if they could patch up their differences from the argument that had caused him to move out of their apartment and into King's. He told her he was going to go to bed early that night.[33]

That same Saturday, James Byrd Jr. had taken a few breakfast sausages to his eighty-one-year-old friend Grover "Pete" Thomas, as he did every day when he stopped by for a friendly chat or a game of dominoes. The day before he had cut Thomas's lawn, and on Saturday morning he promised to take him to church the next day. In the afternoon, Byrd attended a bridal shower for his niece at his parents' home, a small frame house on Broad Street. He was his usual gregarious self and sat on the porch bouncing his one-year-old granddaughter Tayla Mullins on his knee. Later that day, he went to an anniversary party for his sister-in-law. Famed throughout the town for his melodious voice and renowned for his trumpet and piano expertise, Byrd had entertained friends and relatives by singing at both these gatherings. That night, Byrd went to a party at a friend's house just off North Main Street, on the other side of the highway that divides Jasper east from west, U.S. 96. His friend James Brown drove him to the party; Byrd suffered from a seizure disorder and could not drive himself. Sometimes a friend or an acquaintance or some Jasper resident who had frequently seen the forty-nine-year-old Byrd walking along the road would offer a ride. Otherwise, Byrd uncomplainingly walked to wherever he was going.

Berry did not go to bed early that night, as he had told his girlfriend. He and King and Brewer sat around their apartment drinking beer. King's former girlfriend Keisha Adkins visited them late that night. Around 1:45 A.M., Adkins left the apartment. So too did the three men. They got into Berry's 1982 primer gray Ford pickup truck and headed toward Recreation Road in the northern part of Jasper County to visit a woman Brewer had contacted.

Either the directions were flawed or the men were confused about the address, for they did not find the house. They returned to the apartment, loaded their cooler with beer, and decided to drive around Jasper looking for something interesting and exciting. They had been trying to find a girlfriend for Brewer, who was new to town, and they thought they might find someone as they cruised the streets of Jasper.

For some reason, Byrd was not his usual convivial self at the party. One of his friends said he tried to strike up a conversation with Byrd, but Byrd was unusually glum. He told Brown that he did not need him to drive him home that night, since he had lined up another ride. Brown left the party before Byrd. Either Byrd's ride failed him or he declined it. He left the party in the early hours of that Sunday morning and started walking across town to his home. As he was walking down Martin Luther King Drive at about 2:30 A.M., he received another and final offer of a ride from a Jasper resident. The last time he was seen alive, Byrd was sitting in the bed of a truck as it drove down Martin Luther King Drive, his back against the cab. The truck was a primer gray 1982 Ford pickup.

———

King, Berry, and Brewer had been living together for a short time. The apartment in the Timbers Apartment Complex was rented in King's name, although the landlord had been trying to evict him for the past several weeks. Brewer, who hailed from Sulphur Springs, Texas, and whom King had befriended while they both served time in a Texas prison, had moved in about three weeks earlier. A week later, King's pregnant girlfriend, Kylie Greeney, had left after a fight with King. Then, after his own fight with his girlfriend, Berry had come to stay with King, his childhood friend.[34]

The three men who shared the apartment also shared a criminal record. King and Berry had been arrested for burglary in October 1992. Caught trying to steal what the court records describe as "eight tubes of ground beef, 10 boxes of chicken breast, 40 pounds of shrimp, one box of T-bones and other assorted food items," they were sentenced to ten years for the crime. They served less than four months in a boot camp for young offenders before they were released on shock probation. The experience was enough for Berry, who kept himself out of trouble after that. King, on the other hand, violated the terms of his probation in June 1995 and was sent to the Beto I Unit of the Texas Department of Criminal Justice. There he met Brewer.

Lawrence Brewer had a history of trouble in his thirty-one years. Following a serious drug abuse problem in his late teens, Brewer was first incarcerated for breaking into a house in July 1987. He was sentenced to seven years but was paroled after seven months. In May 1989, he was charged with drug possession and was given a fifteen-year sentence. Again he was paroled, this time after serving two years of the sentence. He violated parole in February 1994 and remained incarcerated until he was paroled one last time in September 1997. Following his release from prison, Brewer went home to his father, a retired infantry soldier. Estranged from each other for the past dozen years, since the young Brewer's drug problems, father and son fought over various things, including Brewer's prison tattoos, which his father called "a sickness." Following a fight with his father and the breakup with his girlfriend, Brewer left Sulphur Springs on a bus bound for Houston. About five months later, he found himself in Jasper looking up his old prison buddy.

When he came back to Jasper after serving his time in jail, William King was a changed man, according to his friends and family. He had acquired a nickname, "Possum," and an extensive collection of tattoos covering 65 percent of his body, most of them explicitly racist. His language too was laced with racist expletives. According to one friend, he cheered a scene in *Schindler's List* when Nazis shot a Jewish prisoner and then lectured his friends that the Holocaust was a fiction. He yelled a racist epithet at his black neighbor's five-year-old daughter. There were clear signs of his transformation before his release from prison. He wrote letters to young girls that were strange mixtures of mild eroticism and hard racism. Writing to one girl he had met at a party when she was thirteen years old, King called her "my beautiful kitten" and "Aryan princess." He stated that he had no desire to leave jail and return to Jasper because it was, he wrote, "a town full of race-traitoring nigger loveing whores." These women, he concluded, were "so fuckin stupid and blind to the pride of their race and heritage that they should be hung on the limb adjacent to their nigger loveing men."[35]

John R. Craig is a friend of the King family and also coauthor of a book on Aryan group activity in America. He noted that King went into prison "a street punk and came out a white supremacist." King had formally switched his religious affiliation from Baptist to Odinism, a Norse-based religion popular among Aryans.[36] Berry had listed his religion on prison forms as Christian Identity, an even more popular form of Aryan spiritual doctrine that holds that the truly chosen people descended from the elect tribes of Israel are American whites, while all others, especially all others of color, were spawned of demonic forces. King's racist views were evident enough that the manager of the apartment complex felt compelled to warn one black man who moved in that King was prejudiced.

Once the three men were all living in the apartment, trouble started. The neighbors complained of blaring music and incessant partying, and frequent and loud fights with girlfriends. The men also returned to their criminal habits. For a job they got clearing brush, they stole a weed trimmer and a chain saw. For their snacks, they stole fifty bags of potato chips from a motel lobby and a dozen cases of beer from a warehouse. For their food, they broke into a restaurant and stole frozen steaks.

King and Brewer also started planning together what they had talked about in prison, forming a white supremacist hate group. King ordered a book on the Silent Brotherhood, an Aryan supremacist group of the mid-eighties based in the Northwest. He already owned and read *The Turner Diaries*, a book written by the Nazi National Alliance leader William Pierce, about the destructive actions of an Aryan cell that overthrows the American government by a series of calculated missions and assassinations of Jews and African Americans. He had stolen from the Jasper High School library a book on the Ku Klux Klan. He had cut out from a copy of *Esquire* magazine an article that contained pictures and information about the lynching of Emmett Till. King had drawn up a constitution for the white supremacist group he was forming, and laid plans for the murder and immolation of a black man to inaugurate the group's founding. In a note he had written in a fellow inmate's prison album, King said he planned to start his group on July 4, 1998, at a "huge Wood gathering, B.B.Q., and bashing." His motives, he concluded, were to "DESTROY, ERASE, IMPROVE." His actions, as he wrote repeatedly in his own writings, were intended to "secure the existence of our people and a future for white children."

———

James Byrd Jr. was not one of "our people," as William King used that phrase, and he would not have any of the "white children" for whose future King was making elaborate plans. Byrd was a black child of black parents and a black parent to black children.

Byrd was born to Stella and James Byrd Sr. His mother was a Sunday school teacher at the Greater New Bethel Baptist Church and his father a retired dry cleaner and a deacon at the same church. The Byrds had six daughters and two sons; James Byrd was the third eldest child and the eldest son. As the eldest boy, his nickname in the family became "Son." Outside of the family, he also acquired the nickname "Toe" when a childhood bicycle accident cost him one of his toes. He was, by all accounts, an extremely social person who enjoyed being with friends. His younger sister Mary Verrett noted that he "was very people-oriented" and was "the kind of person who never wanted to be alone; he would walk up to a group and join right in." He just "enjoyed being with others. He was fun-loving, kind, generous."

The niece's wedding shower at his parents' home that Saturday afternoon was a family reunion of sorts as it marked the first time in a while that Byrd and his six sisters had gathered together. There was a feeling of hopefulness at the gathering, and his sisters sensed that James was starting to get his house in order, both literally and symbolically. Six months earlier, he had moved into his own apartment so that he would not be a financial burden on his aging parents. He had recently acquired a roll-away bed so his son could visit. His sisters had helped him decorate the new place, and one of them had just bought him a dinette set. The one-bedroom apartment, number 77 at the Pineview public housing project, was more than just a place to sleep for James Byrd. It also symbolized his new independence. It was a step toward reclaiming and gaining more control of his life.

Byrd had started out with great promise. Attending all-black J. H. Rowe High School in Jasper, Byrd had done exceedingly well, compiling an excellent academic record. One of his classmates recalled that he was an honor-roll student each and every year. He graduated in 1967, the last year that educational segregation was the norm for Jasper. He chose not to follow his older sisters' example and enroll in college, although his parents encouraged him to do so and his grades would easily have gotten him into a good university. There was some kind of aimlessness to his life, his family and friends felt, what they described as an inability or unwillingness to commit himself to a particular course or career. Despite his powerful intelligence, his recognizable gifts and talents, James, they felt, was not living up to the potential he possessed. As his sister Mary put it, the family told him that he "never used his intellectual potential to the highest capacity."[37] They were not berating him for it but encouraging him to use those talents to make something of himself, to achieve the kinds of accomplishments all agreed he was fully capable of achieving.

Instead of pursuing college training and a stable career, James turned to a life of petty crime and escapist drug use. Two years out of high school, he received his first prison sentence. His crimes were never that serious—minor theft and forgery—but they were symptoms of that aimlessness his family detected in him. They also proved detrimental to his family life.

A few years out of high school, in 1970, Byrd married Thelma Adams. Together they had two daughters, Frances Renee Byrd (later Mullins) and Jamie Byrd, and one son, Ross Payne Byrd. The marriage lasted, on and off, for twenty-three years, until Adams and Byrd formally divorced in 1993.

His parents and his sisters were also disturbed at the way his life was going. They would get upset at him, his sister Mary noted, but primarily because they felt that he was harming himself most of all.

Between 1969 and 1996, Byrd served five sentences for the minor crimes he committed. Since completing his last prison sentence in 1996, Jasper municipal court records report, he had been convicted of public intoxication six times and possession of drug paraphernalia twice. Alcohol became a form of escape, and his friends felt that he was squandering what talents he had on drink. His family worried about his health. One of the deacons at his family's church called him "the black sheep of the family," a peaceful soul who minded his own business but unfortunately spent far too much time drinking and then sleeping off the effects of his alcoholism.

Byrd never fully regained the control of his life that he and his family would have wished. He continued his decline with a prison sentence for theft in 1990, his divorce in 1993, and then his public intoxication in 1996. Yet 1998 seemed to bring promise of reform. He had worked at odd jobs, sold vacuum cleaners door-to-door, and was now living off a government disability check because of a back injury and his seizure disorder. He began the new year by moving into his own apartment. And he took up again with renewed vigor the one passion in his life, music. He played trumpet and piano and had an ear that allowed him to play any song without sheet music. His high school friend Tincy Adams said that Byrd had "the most beautiful voice." His favorite gospel song was "Walk with Me, Lord," and his friends claimed that he could "sing Al Green better than Al Green." It was the secular music of Prince that attracted him most, however, and he even adopted as a nickname the title of his favorite Prince song, "Purple Rain." Already a social person, he exhibited an even greater exuberance in his music. One of the neighbors said she saw him dancing and singing as he was cutting Pete Thomas's lawn that Friday. He was also teaching her fourteen-year-old daughter to play the keyboard.

His family sensed that there was a change in his demeanor, and they encouraged him to continue to reclaim himself. There was still a great deal James Byrd needed to do to make his life better, but he had the support of his family and the love of his siblings and his children. He was looking forward to the visit from his son, an army private, stationed at Fort Benning, Georgia, and scheduled to serve in South Korea in a few months. His elder daughter, Renee Mullins, had until recently also served in the military. His children were doing something with their lives, and he was proud of them. The granddaughter he bounced on his knee on that Saturday afternoon was the newest member of the Byrd family, and James could look around him in that house on Broad Street and see generations of family who wished him well, who wanted him to do his best.

———

There was a cooler full of beer in the back of the truck speeding down Martin Luther King Drive. James Byrd helped himself to a bottle and sat back against the cab of the truck. The truck stopped at a convenience store, and the occupants of the cab asked if he wanted to ride in front. He agreed and moved up into the cab with Shawn Berry, while John King and Lawrence Brewer came back and sat in the bed of the truck. They took a dirt road out of Jasper and then came back toward town. King knocked on the top of the cab and asked Berry to stop the truck. After Berry did so, King and Brewer leapt over the side of the truck bed and suddenly started trying to pull Byrd out of the truck cab. Byrd struggled to stay in the cab. As he pulled him out, King yelled: "Fuck it. Let's kill this nigger." Deeply intoxicated, Byrd was not able to put up much of a struggle as they put him in the truck bed and then threw him off the truck onto the ground. King was stomping on Byrd with his sandaled feet, while Brewer was kicking viciously at Byrd's body.[38] Byrd managed to get up, but they pushed him down again. Brewer got a can of black spray paint from the truck and sprayed Byrd in the face. Byrd begged them to stop. Brewer kicked him very hard in the head, and Byrd went down for the final time. As Byrd lay unconscious, they stripped him of his pants and his underwear.

King and Brewer got a twenty-four-foot tow chain out of the truck and tied Byrd to the back of the vehicle by his ankles. They hopped into the cab and started driving down the dirt road, dragging Byrd behind the truck. After they drove a ways, the chain came undone. They backed the truck to where Byrd lay on the road and reattached him to the chain. They drove to the end of the dirt road, the Tran Road, and then eased onto the paved street, Huff Creek Road. As they drove the truck down the paved street, they swerved from side to side. Byrd's body slammed from one side of the road to the other.[39]

James Byrd did not die while he was being dragged behind the truck for the first mile and a half. He suffered incalculable pain. His hands, his knees, his elbows, heels, and buttocks were all ground to the bone. Every single rib on the right side of his body was broken. Eight of the ribs on his left side were broken. His ankles were cut to the bone by the iron chain. His penis and his testicles were shredded from his body. He was conscious, and he attempted to keep his head off the pavement by using his arms and legs. Only after a mile and a half of this swerving death ride did James Byrd finally die, as his body slammed into a concrete culvert on the side of the road that tore his head and his right arm from the rest of his torso.

At some point, the men stopped the truck and looked at what they had done. A pool of blood formed on the street while they stood above the remains of James Byrd. They drove the truck down Huff Creek Road and stopped one last time in front of a black cemetery. They got out of the truck and took the chain off what was left of James Byrd. They threw the chain in the back of the truck and drove off.

They drove in silence for a while. Then Berry asked King why he did it. King sneered and said he was "starting *The Turner Diaries* early." He left him on the road, he continued, as a statement. "That's what they used to do when a black man got caught messing around with a white woman, in the old days," King announced. For the rest of the drive back to the apartment, King and Brewer talked about their alibi. King said that Adkins would tell the authorities that they had never left the apartment that night. At about four o'clock on Sunday morning, they returned to the apartment and fell asleep.

As they slept in their apartment, the blood of James Byrd seeped into the dirt of the Tran Road, pooled on the pavement of Huff Creek Road, and dried on the bottom of a 1982 primer gray Ford pickup. It was the blood that would lead investigators to the three men sleeping in apartment 214 in the Timbers Apartment Complex. Tracing the blood down the streets where James Byrd had been dragged, they would find in the clearing where Byrd had been beaten senseless a cigarette lighter with King's nickname and Klan symbol on it, a torque wrench set with Berry's name written on it, and beer bottles and cigarettes with all the men's DNA signatures on them. It was the blood on the undercarriage of the truck that led them to Berry. It was the blood they discovered on the clothing and shoes in the hamper that led them to the other two men.

King, Berry, and Brewer were caught primarily because they were incompetent at hiding the trail that led from the scene of the crime to their apartment. They were caught because they were foolish enough to pass notes in their jail cell that informed the authorities about their blood-splattered clothes and shoes. In one note they passed in the Jasper jail, King wrote to Brewer: "I don't think any blood was on my pants or sweat shirt, but I think my sandals may have had some dark brown substance on the bottom." It was the first that the investigators heard about the sandals, which they then found in a clothes hamper in the apartment.[40] King, Berry, and Brewer were caught because the blood they spilled so maliciously on that early Sunday morning would betray them. Like the blood on Lady Macbeth's hands, James Byrd's blood would not wash out, it would not disappear, it would not remain quiet.

That weekend—when James Byrd was grotesquely murdered, when his body was dissolved into eighty-one different parts, when his limbs and head were ripped from his body and strewn across a paved road, when his personal effects, his wallet and his dentures, littered a bloody street in Jasper, Texas—that weekend was the first anniversary of President Bill Clinton's race initiative, the end of the "dialogue on race" the president had called for one year earlier.

———

The town of Jasper is the county seat of Jasper County. The town itself, about 120 miles northeast of Houston, is a timber town with a population of 8,000. About 45 percent of the population is black, 55 percent white. A few years earlier the town had elected its first black mayor, R. C. Horn. The town's economy is timber and tourism, especially bass fishing.

Jasper County has a population of 31,000, about 80 percent white and 18 percent black. The county is poor. The unemployment rates are well above state and national averages. The poverty level is 20 percent. Ten percent of the residents of Jasper County have no car; 5 percent have no phone. Of the 31,000 residents in the county, 1,649 are college graduates, 2,816 dropped out before completing grade nine, and a little over half of the adult population are high school graduates.[41] It is the kind of environment that sociologists say is the perfect breeding ground for white resentment and precisely the kind of place to find the spreading of white supremacist beliefs. According to John R. Craig, a specialist on white supremacist hate groups in Texas, the county has a white militia group that operates on a 200-acre training ground, Camp Pulwell, at Double Bayou, south of Jasper. A Klansman, John Mosier, instructed Aryan supremacists in guerrilla warfare until he was jailed for murder. In the woods nearby, at Mount Enterprise, the Reverend W. N. Otwell leads a Christian Identity compound of one hundred followers. Having taken over a small, independent church in Jasper County, Otwell teaches his disciples how they are God's chosen people while Jews are the offspring of Satan and Africans and Asians are "mud people."[42]

The town has reportedly had a Klan chapter since 1986. The Imperial Wizard of the Knights of the White Kamellia claimed that there has certainly been a Klavern in Jasper County since 1996, but it was not so active that many Jasperites knew of its existence. It was certainly not nearly so plainly on public display as the Klan chapter in Vidor, fifty-five miles south of Jasper, which many describe as the nerve center of white supremacy in East Texas. Vidor had been an all-white town until 1993, when a federal judge had ordered the public housing projects in the town to be integrated.[43] Nor did Jasper have the kind of ill repute some other towns in East Texas had gained because of relatively high-profile racial incidents involving their police. In 1988, in nearby Cleveland, a black man arrested for stealing an ink pen died in his jail cell after struggling with white officers. The officers were all cleared, but the police chief resigned the next year under pressure. In Hemphill, a year earlier, a black Louisiana truck driver was beaten to death in the Sabine County jail. The police chief and one of the two deputies were convicted of murder. That same year in Mount Enterprise, a twenty-four year-old black man was fatally shot in the neck during a high-speed car chase.[44]

Jasper was a quiet town without much crime and with no outstanding record of police harassment of black folk. Many of the residents, both black and white, commented on the relatively peaceful race relations in their town. Many blacks in Jasper did note that they did not receive the same kind of economic and employment opportunities as whites, and that residential segregation was still largely undisturbed, but most also noted that there was not the kind of overt racism they associated with the Klan or Aryan supremacists. One member of the chamber of commerce noted that Jasper simply did not have the kind of racism that the murder of James Byrd required. A lawyer who had represented Klan leaders in the Vidor housing case did note, however, that all East Texas, including Jasper, had a "lot of quiet support for the Klan." And when the sheriff of Jasper County announced at a press conference that Jasper had no Klan activity, many African Americans present hooted aloud. Later, in an interview on CNN's *Burden of Proof*, the sheriff changed his mind and noted that there were some Klan members living in Jasper and other towns in the county, but that in his twenty-five years of law enforcement in Jasper County he had never "seen an organized effort from the Ku Klux Klan."

In the aftermath of the murder of James Byrd, all that changed as the quiet town in the pine forest was cast into the national and international spotlight. Even if the hometown Klan did not reveal itself, other Texan Klaverns were willing to make a showing. Michael Lowe of Waco, the head of the Texas realm of the Knights of the Ku Klux Klan, organized a rally to distance the Klan from the murder of Byrd. Claiming that a couple of people in Jasper had asked the Klan to come to the town, Lowe requested and received permission to hold a rally on Saturday, June 27. The point of the rally, he said, was to let Jasper residents know that the Klan rejected such atrocities. Darrell Flinn, the Imperial Wizard of the Knights of the White Kamellia in Vidor, who helped organize the rally, called the killing a "senseless act" and a "tragedy." The ninety-minute rally drew about twenty Klan members, fifty or so African American militant counter-protesters from the Dallas-based New Black Panther Party and the Houston-based Nation of Islam, about two hundred spectators, about a hundred and fifty law enforcement officials, and over two hundred members of the media.

As sheeted Klansmen waved Confederate flags around the courthouse and yelled "White Power," as armed Panthers marched menacingly around the barricades and responded "Black Power," a small group of thirty local residents and officials from the National Association for the Advancement of Colored People gathered in the chapel of Robinson's Community Funeral Home across the town square and sang "We Shall Overcome."[45] The June 27 gathering was the most recent of the prayer vigils that had been arranged following the murder of Byrd. The Wednesday after the murder, the Reverend Jesse Jackson visited and prayed with the Byrd family. The wake was held on Friday night, the funeral on Saturday morning, and another prayer vigil on Monday evening.

Approximately two hundred people attended the funeral at the Greater New Bethel Baptist Church. Three hundred more stood in an overflow tent outside the church, and five hundred others mourned in the unshaded parking lot as temperatures neared a hundred degrees. Even the funeral became a stage for political statements, as fifteen armed black militants marched through town to proclaim the necessity of black people's defending themselves. As well, members of the Texas Coalition to Abolish the Death Penalty distributed a statement at the funeral placing blame for Byrd's murder on the racist influence of the Texas prison system and on East Texas's long history of racism and violence.

The Byrd family remained gracious through the entire ordeal. James Byrd's sisters, especially Mary Verrett and Clara Taylor, and his daughter Renee Mullins spoke to members of the media to thank the people who supported them. They received the predictable calls from town officials, local leaders, and national politicians. In addition, they received some unexpected support from groups, one of many examples being the Black Clergy of Philadelphia, who, along with other human rights groups in the city, raised funds and held a "Reclamation Sunday" vigil so that they could "reclaim some level of peace and comfort for Byrd's bereaved family and to begin to reclaim some degree of faith and human dignity we, as a nation made up of many different colors, were forced to watch be so viciously attacked by the virulent racial hatred that infests so much of this country."[46] Strangers from as far away as Spain, Germany, and England called to express their condolences. The Byrd family was genuinely touched by the outpouring of sympathy, even as they tried valiantly to carve out a space where they as a family could celebrate the life and mark the passing of their son, brother, uncle, and father.

Elsewhere in Jasper, people who knew James Byrd mourned in their own way. His friend and neighbor James Brown was so distraught that he had not insisted on driving Byrd home from the party that night that he refused to leave his apartment for days. Another neighbor at the Pineview public housing project, Jowanna Parks, who lived next door to Byrd, claimed that his apartment was haunted with his sad spirit and she planned to move away. Essica Bartee, the fourteen-year old daughter of a friend whom Byrd was teaching to play the keyboard, was so frightened by the horror and the loss that she was afraid to sleep alone for weeks. Grover "Pete" Thomas, the eighty-one-year-old friend who knew Byrd from childhood, looked mournfully out over his porch and recalled the sinking feeling he had as he waited for Byrd to come take him to church that Sunday morning as he had promised.[47] James Byrd was not one to break a promise.

———

Although things got quieter in Jasper after the June 27 rally, there were some troubling developments elsewhere. There were attempted copycat crimes as white motorists attempted to drag black Americans behind their vehicles in two other states.[48] The peace in Jasper didn't last long, either, as the nameplate on James Byrd's grave marker was stolen, and the Klan organized another rally. In mid-October, forty-three Klansmen, led by the Reverend Doc James, the Grand Dragon of the American Knights of the Ku Klux Klan of Arkansas, gathered again at the Jasper courthouse. Surrounded by several dozen jeering hecklers and amid some 350 police officers, including FBI agents, Texas Rangers, state game wardens, a mounted horse patrol from Tyler, and dozens of state troopers in riot gear, the Klansmen from as far away as Virginia and Indiana rallied for "white rights" for two hours.

On the legal front, Texas legislators in Austin and federal ones in Washington quickly introduced hate crimes bills to enhance the punishment for hate crimes and to enlarge the definition of those covered by hate crimes legislation. When Matthew Shepard was murdered by two homophobic men in Laramie, Wyoming, in October, the national hate crimes bills then pending in Congress received renewed attention as newspaper editors and political commentators weighed in on the feasibility of enhanced hate crimes legislation. Over the next several months, members of the Byrd family, especially his daughter Renee Mullins, would speak before state legislative committees and House and Senate hearings on hate crimes legislation.

Indeed, over the next several months, the Byrd family continued to work toward maintaining peace in their town. The whole family was honored by the South Texas branch of the Anti-Defamation League on October 27, 1998, for the work they had done in advocating community harmony and cooperation in the wake of their personal tragedy.[49] The family had already established the James Byrd Jr. Family Foundation for Racial Healing, and they were developing plans to build an education center in Jasper to study racism and to promote reconciliation.

The people of Jasper responded to the loss of James Byrd Jr. by becoming introspective about the racial climate of their town. The Mayor's Task Force 2000 Committee sponsored a series of some twenty town hall meetings between July and October 1998. At these meetings, the residents of Jasper confronted a past that many had not known about earlier—a past where white citizens unintentionally slighted their black counterparts, a history where white businesses denied African Americans jobs and where some white businessmen routinely cheated black clients. Several different kinds of resolutions were reached at these town meetings. The community task force implemented strategies to make teachers and public officials more racially sensitive. Aside from these educational programs, though, most of the actions were symbolic. In personal meetings, businessmen who had cheated black customers in the past voluntarily came forth and apologized for their behavior. In more public gatherings, at the town hall meetings Jasper residents would join hands and hold unity prayer vigils on the courthouse lawn. The city government also participated in these symbolic gestures of goodwill when it decided to tear down the fence that divided the white and black sections of the Jasper City Cemetery. Just five days before the start of the first trial, on January 20, 1999, city workers tore down the ancient wrought-iron fence as the Jasper Ministerial Alliance held a small ceremony.[50]

———

In the courts, meanwhile, King, Brewer, and Berry were first indicted on capital murder charges by a grand jury on July 6, 1998. King and Brewer were named in one indictment, and Berry, whom the police felt played a lesser role in the murder, was named in a separate indictment. In the following months, the investigators in the case gathered the physical evidence they needed to connect the three men to the murder. The defendants had minor squabbles with their court-appointed lawyers and requested new legal counsel, which they were denied. Shawn Berry, who attempted to cast himself as a spectator and not an agent in the crime in the affidavit he gave on June 9, admitted to lying about the degree of his involvement. Investigators found physical evidence that showed that Berry was more directly involved in the murder than he had admitted. On October 2, a Jasper grand jury re-indicted the three on capital murder charges. Prosecutors said they would seek the death penalty for all three defendants. On October 30, King, Brewer, and Berry were indicted a third time and granted separate trials, all on capital murder charges. King would be the first to go on trial, and his case was scheduled for January 25, 1999.

In a pretrial hearing on November 24, 1998, William King pled not guilty. His lawyer C. Haden "Sonny" Cribbs Jr. filed a motion requesting a change of venue for the trial, claiming that his client could not receive a fair trial in Jasper. Three weeks later, State District Judge Joe Bob Golden denied the motion. On January 6, 1999, King's lawyers asked to be relieved of the case because their client, who refused to attend a pretrial hearing, was uncooperative and ignored their advice. On January 11, after consulting with King, the judge denied that motion. King, meanwhile, continued to go against his attorneys' advice and seek public venues for his views. Finding himself discouraged because his attorneys did not believe his version of the events, and disagreeing with their strategy of trying to save his life instead of prove his innocence, King had taken his case to the media.

On November 12, 1998, William King wrote a letter to the *Dallas Morning News* reporter Lee Hancock and enclosed a seven-page statement entitled "Logical Reasoning." He first of all countered the story that this crime was a hate crime. Denying that he or Brewer had ever been "members of any confirmed hate crime groups," King argued that his tattoo proclaiming "Aryan Pride" should not be misinterpreted. Likewise, the triangular design embossed on his cigarette lighter (conventionally understood as a Klan symbol) represented nothing more than his belief in "Respect, Loyalty, and Honor." He then set out his story of the events of that June night. According to King, it was Berry who murdered Byrd in a drug deal gone awry. Berry, he argued, had a history of violence and abusive behavior that stemmed from his alleged steroid use. King claimed that after the three men picked Byrd up, Berry dropped Brewer and King off and then drove off to conclude his drug transaction with Byrd. King claimed that he was at home asleep when the murder took place.[51] All the physical evidence that would be presented in his trial contradicted King's version of events. His clothing and shoes were splattered with Byrd's blood. His DNA was on cigarette butts at the place where Byrd was beaten senseless.

Happy with his first effort, King developed a fondness for writing to newspapers. On December 5, King wrote a second letter to Lee Hancock, in which he assured her that he was not depressed or suicidal and informed her of how he was preparing for the trial. On January 27, 1999, King wrote a letter to the editor of the local *Jasper NewsBoy* claiming that he was the "victim of a judicial conspiracy" in a "town plagued with political correctness." He concluded with a quotation from Euripides for the people of Jasper: "My hands are clean; the stain is on my heart." King sent another letter to the editor of *Jasper NewsBoy* on January 29, praising Jasper County Sheriff Billy Rowles for allowing him to see and hold his six-month-old son for the first time.[52]

The trial of John William King began on January 25, 1999. By February 8, the lawyers for the state and the defense selected a jury pool of 50 from the 125 Jasper County residents called to jury duty. On February 10, they had selected the twelve jurors and two alternates who would hear the trial. The jury and alternate pool consisted of six white women, seven white men, and one black man.

Testimony began on February 16, 1999. The prosecution presented its case that King had murdered Byrd as a way of attracting attention to the Aryan supremacy organization he had founded, the Confederate Knights of America's Texas Rebel Soldiers. Using as evidence the handwritten outlines, bylaws, constitution, and recruiting letters found in King's apartment, the prosecution showed that King had formed extensive plans for his hate group. Using the testimony of one of the young women King wrote to from his jail cell, the prosecution demonstrated how deeply King felt animosity against black people and how often he referred to the acts of violence he would inflict on them. The tattoos King was so proud of became part of the prosecution's case also; police experts testified on the meanings of the racist skin art on the slides shown to the jurors. A former prison buddy of King's, ex-convict William Matthew Hoover, also testified in court that King had planned to inaugurate his Texas Rebel Soldiers by murdering a black man. The physical evidence, including blood on his clothing and DNA on cigarette butts, placed King at the scene. The pathologist in the case, Dr. Tommy J. Brown, described to jurors the physical trauma suffered by James Byrd, and emphasized that Byrd was alive and conscious until he was decapitated by the concrete culvert on Huff Creek Road.[53] This last point was important for the prosecution's case that King kidnapped as well as murdered Byrd.

On the final day of the prosecution's case, the lawyers presented to the jury a jailhouse note King had written to Brewer in which he gloated that if the jurors "don't find us guilty of kidnapping but do find us guilty of murder, it will be a simple first degree murder, bro. No death sentence!" He ended the note with "Much Aryan Love, Respect and Honor" and signed off "Seig Heil (Hail Victory)."[54] The prosecutors concluded their case by showing a powerful eleven-minute silent video of the 2.1-mile trail where Byrd was dragged and murdered.

The defense lawyers called three witnesses and took only one hour in presenting their case. They tried to challenge the prosecution's case about the meaning of the tattoos by calling one witness, a prison tattoo artist, John

Mosley, to testify that the tattoos on King's body had little meaning in jail; they were just art and not racist statements. They also tried to make the case that the prison environment fostered and almost made inevitable the racist views held by King. Mosley stated that white prisoners either fought, bribed, or performed sexual favors for black prisoners at the Beto I prison where King was incarcerated. A former roommate of King's, Gilbert Allen Cunningham, and King's former boss at a construction site, Dennis Symmack, testified that King seemed to acquire most of his racist beliefs after he was in prison. In closing arguments, the defense returned to this theme: "He was a normal kid from Jasper. This boy had something happen to him in the penitentiary. He became a racist. He became a hater."[55] They spent the second half of their closing remarks challenging the prosecution arguments that Byrd was kidnapped.

After deliberating for a little under two and a half hours, the jury returned a guilty verdict on February 23, 1999. During the sentencing phase of the trial, the defense called on King's father, who tearfully pled for his son's life, and a former Texas prison system psychologist, Dr. Walter Quijano, who claimed that there was little likelihood that King would ever engage in this kind of violence again. One prosecution witness, Jasper County Deputy Sheriff Joe Sterling, said that King had threatened him with violence while he was in the Jasper jail in January, and informed the jury that a noose made of electrical cords and a makeshift knife had been found in his cell. Another prosecution witness, psychiatrist Dr. Edward Gripon, testified that in his interviews with King he found him remorseless and "heavily invested" in his racist beliefs and felt that King would continue to pose a real threat of violence. On February 25, after just under three hours' deliberation, the jury sentenced King to death.

As if intent on proving the jury right, King smirked and uttered obscenities about the Byrd family outside of the courthouse. Later he released a handwritten statement through his attorney in which he unrepentantly closed with the words of Francis Yockey, one of the authors of Nazi doctrine. His father, Ronald King, on the other hand, made a statement through his priest asking for prayers for the Byrd family and phoned James Byrd Sr. to apologize for his son's behavior.

On the evening of February 25, 1999, the younger King, now inmate number 999295, joined the 444 men on death row in the Ellis Unit in Huntsville, Texas. He was at the time the only white American on death row in Texas for killing a black American. His first appeal for a new trial was denied on April 12, 1999.

————

There were some difficulties in scheduling the second trial. Russell Brewer's lawyers made pretrial motions to have the trial moved from Jasper County.

At first the motion was denied, and then approved. The case was originally scheduled for May 17, 1999, and then rescheduled for May 3, then again to May 17. Even the change of venue hearing was rescheduled from April 19 to April 20 because the first date coincided with the anniversary of the 1995 Oklahoma City bombing and the 1993 Branch Davidian fire in Waco. In the end, the trial was moved to the Brazos County Courthouse in Bryan, Texas, about 150 miles west of Jasper, and scheduled for late August. Jury selection began on August 31, 1999; on September 10, a jury and two alternates of seven white men, five white women, and two Hispanic men was seated. Testimony began on September 13.

As they had done in the case against King, prosecutors again presented physical evidence tying Brewer to the crime scene. They also demonstrated through an analysis of his tattoos and his own prison writings that he was a racist who showed no remorse for his role in the murder.

On the first day of testimony, the prosecution introduced as evidence letters Brewer had written in jail. In these letters, he claimed that he felt "like an eagle" and a "God-damned hero of the day" after the murder of James Byrd. In reference to another prisoner's comments about "rolling a tire" (which is prison lingo for assaulting an African American), Brewer wrote that he "did it." No "longer am I a virgin," he exulted. "It was a rush and I'm still lickin' my lips for more." A prison inmate testified that Brewer had expressed no remorse for the murder of Byrd and stated that he would do it over again.[56] Later, the jurors were presented with the physical evidence, including the DNA found on beer bottles and cigarette butts collected at the scene where Byrd was beaten. The prosecution also entered into evidence a tennis shoe with Brewer's initials on it that was stained with Byrd's blood, and a color photograph of Brewer's bruised and swollen toe from the vicious kicking he had given Byrd.

The defense attorneys, Doug Barlow and Layne Walker, adopted a strategy of casting doubt on the prosecution's physical evidence and presenting an alternative story. They challenged the physical evidence by arguing that it was possible that the materials, the blood and DNA samples used in testing, were contaminated when the investigators collected them. They then put Brewer himself on the stand for four hours. The story Brewer told was essentially the same one as that told by William King in his letter to the *Dallas Morning News* reporter. He claimed that Shawn Berry murdered James Byrd during a steroid drug transaction. He admitted to spray-painting Byrd's face and kicking him, but Brewer claimed that he was trying to break up a fight between King and Byrd. As he was doing so, he testified, he heard Shawn Berry open up his knife and then watched, horrified, as Berry slit Byrd's throat. During cross-examination, Brewer was unable to explain how blood got on his own shoes, nor could he answer prosecution questions about why he expressed worry in his jailhouse notes that the police might find his fingerprints on the logging chain used to drag James Byrd. Indeed, in one note entered as evidence, Brewer wrote to King that they had "a 70 percent chance" of getting away with the crime if they could keep their stories straight. "What's the worst they could possibly do?" he asked. "Pull prints off a 20-foot rusty ass log chain?"[57]

Neither defense strategy worked. The jurors were not swayed by the challenge to the physical evidence, and Brewer's account was riddled with inconsistencies. A pathologist had already testified earlier in the trial that there was no evidence of a knife wound. The final defense strategy, as it had been in the King trial, was to argue that Brewer was not genuinely a racist but someone who adopted a posture of racism to survive the racial war in the Texas prison system. Brewer's attorneys argued that he joined the Confederate Knights of America to protect himself from Hispanic and African American prisoners, hiding from his fellow white inmates the fact that he had a Hispanic ex-wife and child. He assumed the semblance of a white supremacist, he said, so that he could "make it out of there alive."[58]

On September 20, 1999, the jury deliberated for four hours before returning a guilty verdict. During the sentencing phase of the trial, Brewer's father, mother, aunt, and cousin and a family friend tearfully testified on his behalf. The defense attorney showed the jury eleven poster-size color photographs of Brewer growing up, including one of Brewer with his Hispanic ex-wife and another of a much younger Brewer with his arm around a black childhood friend. A psychologist called by the defense testified that Brewer suffered from severe anti-social personality disorder as well as paranoia. He was not a danger and posed no threat of continuing violence, but wanted acceptance, the psychiatrist concluded. The psychiatrist called by the prosecution testified that Brewer's personality disorder led him to blame others for his actions, become self-pitying, and show no remorse. He believed Brewer was entirely capable of future violence.

After fourteen and a half hours of deliberation over two days, on September 23, 1999, the jury in Brazos County sentenced Russell Brewer to death. He became the second white man on Texas's death row convicted of killing an African American.

———

The second trial did not attract nearly the same media attention as did the first. On some days of testimony, almost half the seats in the 140-seat courtroom were empty. Fifty-two media outlets had sought accreditation for the King trial, not many for the Brewer trial. The third trial, the trial of Shawn Allen Berry, began in the media and in many ways was very much about the media.

On September 28, 1999, CBS aired an interview Berry had done with Dan Rather for the news program *60 Minutes II*. The interview had been conducted ten days earlier at the Jasper County jail. Berry's attorney, Joseph C. "Lum" Hawthorn, said that Berry agreed to the interview to improve his image before he went on trial. The interview was part of the defense's overall strategy of distancing Berry from King and Brewer.[59] In the interview, Berry cast himself as an observer rather than an agent in the commission of the crime. He said he tried to stop the other two but became afraid when they threatened his life. Berry's lawyer also insistently repeated to news reporters that Berry was not affiliated with any white supremacist groups. In the opening statements to the prospective jurors, Hawthorn said that "Shawn Berry is not a racist, was not a racist, and has no racist writings, is not a member of any white supremacist groups and has no racial tattoos."[60] Berry, the defense insinuated, was unlike King and Brewer in every way, from the way he adorned his body to the way he thought.

In one way, though, Berry was very much like King and Brewer. All three men had made statements that were later proved false by the physical evidence. King had stated that he and Brewer were in the apartment when Berry was killing James Byrd. The bloodstains on their clothing and shoes and the DNA on items found in the clearing showed otherwise. Brewer had stated that Berry had slit Byrd's throat. There was no evidence of a knife wound. Berry had first stated that he had run away when King and Brewer started beating Byrd. Then, to explain why he had blood splattered on his clothing, he changed his account and stated that he had stayed and tried to intervene and stop the beating.

Given the discrepancies among his various accounts, the prosecution wanted to know what Berry had told Dan Rather in the portions of the interview that did not appear in the segment on the television show. The televised segment comprised about eighteen minutes from the three-hour interview. The prosecutor filed a motion to subpoena Dan Rather to testify in the case. The president of CBS released a statement saying that the network would not cooperate with the prosecution's demands to turn over the unedited portions of the interview that were not broadcast. The case, according to CBS and its lawyers, became one about First Amendment issues since outtakes, the president of CBS claimed, were "broadcast journalism's equivalent of a reporter's notebook, and to turn them over to law enforcement can endanger a journalist's relationship with sources and hamper the ability to report freely and independently." The judge ordered the CBS producer of the segment, Mary Mapes, to appear in court. At the hearing, Judge Joe Bob Golden ordered the producer to give the court a complete transcript of the interview or report to the Jasper County jail. Minutes after the deadline, the Ninth Court of Appeals granted Mapes a temporary stay.

The legal question was whether the materials the court demanded belonged to the producer, who lived in Texas, or to CBS in New York. In New York, Dan Rather was ordered to appear before a state court. In Jasper, after a second temporary stay was denied by the appeals court, Mapes was ordered to submit the transcript or go to jail. The case went first to the Ninth Court of Appeals for consideration, then to the Texas Court of Criminal Appeals in Austin. The Austin court ordered Mapes released on $2,000 bail while the case was considered. Four days later, the Austin court denied Mapes's request to overturn Judge Golden's contempt of court citations and revoked the $2,000 bond. Having gone to the highest court in the state of Texas and exhausted all legal options, Mapes and her attorneys started negotiating with the prosecution in the case. The next day, November 10, 1999, CBS surrendered a copy of the transcript to the court in Jasper and posted the entire document on its Internet site. The president of CBS hailed it as a victory for journalists' rights that the outtakes were not part of the settlement and that Dan Rather did not have to testify in court.[61] An interview that began as a legal strategy to improve the media image of the defendant turned into a legal fight about the rights of the media. In addition, halfway through this affair, Berry's lawyer filed a surprise motion to move the trial from Jasper to another venue. Although he had earlier stated that he was very pleased to be trying this case in Jasper County where the people knew Shawn Berry, Hawthorn claimed that the pretrial publicity had now negatively affected his client's chances for a fair hearing. To judge the merit of the motion, Judge Golden had to wade his way through thousands of pages of newspaper reports and transcripts of radio and television broadcasts. In the end, the trial remained in Jasper.

The trial began in the Jasper County courthouse on October 24, 1999, with 170 prospective jurors. The final jury, all white (seven women and five men, plus two alternates), was seated on November 5. The defense opened by stating that Berry was not like King and Brewer, and that he had no motive to commit "a racial hate crime." The prosecution noted that the clean-cut young man before the court was a liar and had a dangerous side that would be revealed in the course of the trial. In the opening statements, the district attorney, Guy James Gray, pointed out that Berry had given seven different written statements that conflicted with each other and with the account he gave during the CBS interview.[62] The forensic evidence placed him at the scene and indicated that he might have been the most active participant in the beating and murder of Byrd.

When testimony began, the prosecution used the information from the CBS interview to its advantage. Berry had stated in the interview that King was indeed wearing sandals. It was the first solid evidence the prosecution had of that fact. At the trial, the prosecution showed the jury the excerpt from the CBS interview where Berry stated that King had been wearing sandals. With Berry now on record, the prosecution had the investigators testify that sandal prints were found only on the passenger side of the truck when the truck stopped at the place where they reattached the chain to James Byrd's ankles after it had come undone. The other footprints on the passenger side were from the tennis shoes already shown to belong to Russell Brewer. That meant that Berry was the driver of the truck.[63] The prosecutors also emphasized the discrepancies among the statements Berry had made to the police. In his first statement, he had said King drove the truck and Berry himself had run away during the struggle with Byrd. In his next statement, he said that he had driven the truck and that he did not run away. Likewise, he had stated in one report that he knew nothing about the chain, and in another that he had helped King wash the blood off the chain at a car wash. After introducing the rest of the physical evidence, the prosecution rested.

The defense challenged the physical evidence, attempted to downplay earlier reports of Berry's violent side, and insisted that he had never been a racist. To challenge the evidence of the bloodstained clothing, the defense brought in a forensic serologist, Paulette Sutton, who argued that the blood-stains on Berry's pants, shirt, and boots could have come from blood-tinted water at the car wash where he and King had hosed down the chain. Berry's girlfriend took the stand to testify that she had lied in her two police state-ments complaining that Berry had assaulted her. The statements she made to the police, one filed in October 1997 and the other in May 1998, accused Berry of choking her, slamming her into a wall, head-butting her, kicking and slap-ping her, and throwing an ice pick into a wall beside her. She also told police that he had threatened to throw her off a balcony and to burn her face with a lit cigarette. In her court testimony, a smiling Christie Marcontell claimed that she made some things up and characterized the assaults as "mutual com-bat." Berry's attorneys also called on sixteen character witnesses to testify that Berry was not a racist. The witnesses, two of them African American and another of mixed race, claimed that Berry had black friends and that he had wept at the funeral of a black co-worker.[64]

Berry himself took the stand on the last day of testimony. In four hours on the witness stand, he attempted to explain the discrepancies in his changing stories about the night of the murder. He claimed that he lied because he was afraid of what King would do to him. In cross-examination, the prosecution again returned to the CBS interview. Assistant U.S. Attorney Brit Featherston, who assisted District Attorney Gray, grilled Berry and challenged his representation of himself as a stable family man, noting that he had worn a fake wedding ring on television and in court. Gray pointed out that while Berry had used "we" forty-five times in his written statements to the police he began to use the word "they" in his television interview when talking about the night of the murder. His testimony, Gray suggested, was a rehearsed performance.[65]

In the end, the CBS interview hurt Berry's case much more than it helped him. It helped the prosecution to establish that he drove the vehicle. It revealed how often he was willing to change his story. It showed the jury that Berry was a performer, whether he changed his language so that he distanced himself from the crime or wore a fake wedding band to appear more responsible.

The jury deliberated for eight hours on one day and two and a half the next before delivering a guilty verdict on November 18, 1999. That afternoon, after a little more than an hour's further deliberation, they sentenced Shawn Allen Berry to life imprisonment.[66] Under Texas law, he would be eligible for parole in forty years.

―――――

On November 19, 1999, the relatives of James Byrd Jr. gathered at his grave in the Jasper City Cemetery. One sister, Mylinda Washington, stated that the wreath of flowers they were placing on the grave was a "symbol of the healing process, not just for our family but for the Jasper community and the world." Another sister, Clara Taylor, stated that the family felt vindicated and that the legal process had proved that "James Byrd Jr. was and is somebody." A third sister, Louvon Harris, read a poem from the many the family had received from people around the globe. And a niece, Farshanda Boatner, led the family in singing one of James Byrd's favorite songs, "I Believe I Can Fly." The ribbon on the wreath read "Rest in peace" and "Justice for James." This final tribute to the slain son, father, grandfather, uncle, and brother proved yet again what Byrd's eldest daughter, Renee Mullins, had stated a week after the murder in her appearance on Jesse Jackson's CNN show, *Both Sides*: "There was a family behind the name James Byrd Jr." Almost a year and a half after her appearance on the show, two days before this final celebration of James Byrd's life, Mullins had given birth to Byrd's second grandchild. The family said the boy would be nicknamed "Son."[67]

CHAPTER 4

THE LAST AMERICAN
LYNCHING

For most readers, I suspect, the first question they want answered is, Was James Byrd lynched? And the unsurprising and, for most readers, unsatisfying answer is, It depends on the definition. Using the definition provided in "The Lynching Records at Tuskegee Institute"—"no process for establishing the guilt of the accused; the punishment is death, often accompanied by torture and other sadistic acts, applied in many instances to persons charged with offenses which according to the ordinary standards of civilization are of a minor character"—Byrd was not lynched because he was not accused of any offense and his murderers did not even attempt to suggest the pretense of a crime to justify their actions. According to the definition formally arrived at by the anti-lynching advocates' summit in 1940 (the one contested later by some of those groups)—"there must be legal evidence that a person has been killed, and that he met his death illegally at the hands of a group acting under the pretext of service to justice, race, or tradition"—and also according to the federal provisions incorporated into the Civil Rights Act of 1968— violence "by one or more persons, part of an assemblage of three or more persons," whose actions "result in . . . injury . . . to the person of any other individual"—Byrd was lynched.[1] He was lynched by a group of three men who acted in what they believed to be the service of their race and to uphold a tradition of white supremacy.

What is perhaps less obvious and more telling is that our first response is to pose this question about whether or not a lynching occurred. The fact that we ask that question is itself a sign of the dominance of the end-of-lynching discourse. For we do not ask it as a way of establishing an objective fact, as we would do, say, in the case of a murder. In answering whether or not there is a murder, we ascertain whether there was a crime, an agent, an ill motive, and so on. When we ask if there was a lynching, we are instead asking about larger social implications. What would it say about a place, community, nation where a lynching happened? That, as I suggested above, constitutes the twin dynamic of the end-of-lynching discourse—an overt, scripted conversation with one side denying and the other affirming that a lynching has occurred, and a covert fear of what that affirmation might mean. We can turn now to the conversation that followed this event to see how that script played out. The brutal facts of what happened to James Byrd have never been in dispute, even as each of the murderers was found guilty in three separate trials. What was in dispute from the beginning was what to call this event, what name to give this tragedy. And that debate largely followed the terms established by the end-of-lynching discourse.

An Undead Past

Public officials immediately recognized the deep importance of what name they chose. The first report from the Jasper County sheriff was that he did "not believe the crime was racially motivated." The justice of the peace who handled the arraignment and inquest maintained that "it was just a random act of violence." Lurking in the background of these early interviews with the officials in charge of the case was the shadow of a past practice that they certainly did not wish to conjure up. Almost the first word out of the sheriff's office was an explicit denial that Byrd was "lynched."[2] Assuredly the office of the sheriff, Billy Rowles, who by all accounts did a splendid job of managing a potentially explosive situation, did not want to inflame the public by using language likely to do just that. Later, the sheriff and the district attorney consistently felt that they had to prove to the black community that "this was not 1920," as the district attorney put it.[3] What he meant was that he had to show the black community that this was not an era when the police and prosecutor would turn a blind eye to the crimes committed by lynchers, when the phrase "by hands unknown" substituted for justice. What happened instead, however, is that the police repeated another dynamic—which is to deny that an event is a lynching. As we saw, especially after 1940, this dynamic became a key feature of the script created by the end-of-lynching discourse—public officials denying, anti-lynching advocates affirming, that an event is a lynching.

The initial response of the police officials in Jasper, indeed, provides a casebook study of how public officials habitually react to acts of violence that bear the marks of hate crimes. Consider the public officials' comments immediately after the murder of Garnett Johnson Jr. in Elk Creek, Virginia, in July 1997. Following a party with some friends, all white, Johnson, a black man, was burned while he was alive, then beheaded with an ax, and then his decapitated corpse burned again over the site where his head had been buried. Claiming that it was friends and not strangers who committed the crime, arguing that there was insufficient evidence to allege that the murder was "racially motivated," the sheriff and the county prosecutor deemed it not a "hate crime."[4] The NAACP in Virginia had noted that the crime against Garnett Johnson was transparently a hate crime, citing the fact that the murderers had yelled racial obscenities at the charred body of the victim. At pretrial hearings and at the trial, months later, witnesses testified that the two white men made racial slurs just before murdering Johnson, and the prosecution claimed that the two murderers had in fact boasted of plans to "kill a Negro."[5]

This debate is not merely an issue of semantics, obviously, but involves a deeply political question about whose descriptions of social reality are valued—public officials' or minority spokespersons'. The governor of Mississippi in 1955, the Poplarville circuit court judge in 1959, the sheriff and prosecutor in Elk Creek in 1997, the sheriff and justice of the peace in Jasper County in 1998—each immediately denied what was later to be obvious to all, that the crime was in fact racially motivated, or, to be more precise, that the crime was one meant to assert white supremacy and create black terror. There are various reasons police officials make these public denials, but probably the most often invoked is that they do not wish to prejudge the crime, and quite clearly the most prevalent, though often unspoken, reason is that they do not wish to create conditions of public outrage that would perhaps lead to rioting. Assuredly we do not want our police and district attorneys leaping to judgments about any crime, but neither should we wish to have public officials so quickly deny and ignore what are clearly marked as historically defined forms of torture and murder.[6]

———

It is not just public officials but public commentators who are uneasy in their assessment of what happened in Jasper. There have been three books written about the events in Jasper, and in not one of them is what happened to James Byrd called a lynching. In Dina Raston-Temple's 2002 book, the history of lynching in East Texas is invoked by a couple of her interviewees, but there is no effort to connect that history with this event, other than one lyrical paragraph where the rituals of lynching are described and interspersed with a refrain of "Just like James." In Joyce King's 2002 book, it is quickly asserted that the subject is "what has come to be known as 'the dragging.'" The court case is referred to as "the dragging trial," one of those on trial the "dragging defendant," those finding them guilty the "dragging jury." The psychologist

Ricardo Ainslie's 2004 book perhaps comes closest to calling what happened to Byrd a lynching, noting in the beginning of the book that "many would characterize [it] as a modern-day lynching" and then quoting some who do. In the end, though, Ainslie himself refrains from calling it such, finding himself more comfortable with the teasing language of psychoanalysis in the reference to "Byrd's murder" as "uncanny, as though something familiar but ancient had been terribly mislocated into the present." As all three book titles clearly indicate, Jasper, Texas, represents a murder, a dragging, a hate crime—but not a lynching.[7] Now, there is nothing wrong with calling the event any one of those things, since it was all those things. It just seems curious that the term that has historically served to describe precisely what happened to James Byrd was so studiously avoided.

Distinguished scholars of the history of previous lynchings were also loath to call what happened to James Byrd a lynching. Some writers, like Philip Dray, prizewinning author of a comprehensive and informative history of the lynching of African Americans, and Orlando Patterson, Harvard sociologist and author of numerous works on race relations, chose to use euphemism, referring to it as "the lynchlike murder of James Byrd."[8] Others, like Christopher Waldrep, author of the most thorough book on the history and politicization of the use of the word "lynching" in American discourse, invoked a definition that restricted "lynching" to designate only acts of mob violence "openly endorsed by the entire community, or most of it." Employing that definition, he called what happened to Byrd a "hate crime," which more aptly defines an "alienated individual's offense against society," where racial violence under that rubric is the act of a "depraved individual, not a corrupt community." Ultimately, Waldrep concludes, "Americans decided" that the three white supremacists in Jasper "had committed a hate crime, not a lynching."[9]

Maybe "many" Americans made that decision, but during the heated media coverage of that event, it was evident that African American political leaders, those elected like Maxine Waters and William Clay, and unelected like Jesse Jackson, immediately called it a lynching. The Congressional Black Caucus collectively denounced it as a "gruesome lynching." In their stories and editorials, black newspapers like the *Miami Times*, the *Bay State Banner*, the *Baltimore Afro-American, Community Contact*, the *Washington Informer*, and the *Caribbean Today* and African American writers and journalists David Bradley, Dorothy Bruce, Clarence Page, Sheryl McCarthy, Carl Rowan, William Raspberry, Tony White, Lovell Beaulieu, Thomas Novel, Bernhardt Dodson Jr., Karen A. Holness, Brent Staples, and Joseph H. Brown all called the crime a lynching. I could not find any black newspaper reporters or columnists who suggested, as did a report in the *Irish Times*, that "there is

little evidence . . . to justify describing it as a lynching incident, given that it
was isolated and denounced by all local representatives."[10]

———

This argument—that what happened to Byrd was not a lynching because
it did not receive the support of the community—was widespread, and it is
worth examining in more detail. Like dozens of other spokespersons and
journalists, Gail Gans, a hate crimes expert at the national New York offices
of the Anti-Defamation League, noted the basic difference between this and
previous lynchings: the "town in which Emmett Till was killed didn't rise up
and say this isn't us. The town that Mr. Byrd lived and died in did. I think that
shows a big difference."[11] Stanley Crouch likewise claimed that "unlike the
time of Emmett Till, the town itself was outraged by the killing."[12] Orlando
Patterson also maintained that the behavior of the three men who killed Byrd
"was in no way sanctioned by their communities." And that, he concludes, is the
"critical point" of difference between the killing of James Byrd and the historical lynchings of an earlier era when "the ritualized murder of Afro-Americans
had the full tacit or active support of all classes of Euro-Americans."[13] The
point, then, is that what made this event different from earlier ones that we
might call lynchings is that Jasper did not support the act as earlier towns had.

That stark distinction between Jasper and earlier towns, however, is not
historically accurate, at least not entirely. It is certainly true that many
communities did indeed revel in the lynchings that took place within their
borders. The photographs and postcards of lynched victims surrounded by
jubilant mobs assuredly attest to a significant mass support for the lynchings
by those who attended these community rituals and, presumably, were citizens of or lived nearby the towns where the lynchings took place. Newspapers
also frequently celebrated those towns where lynchings occurred, as did one
representative 1903 article that applauded "the work of the mob" as "the highest testimony to the civilization and enlightenment and moral character of
the people."[14] Indeed, in the wake of at least one notable and notorious lynching, that of Henry Smith in Paris, Texas, in 1893, a civic booster published a
pamphlet about the lynching that concludes with an invitation to anyone
who supports the lynching to "come or write to us: for we have thousands of
acres of land at $2 per acre." Not only does this town endorse this lynching;
it uses it for the purposes of recruiting new residents.[15]

Yet there was also a strong counterbalancing trend of towns' and counties'
attempting to salvage their reputations by denouncing the mob violence in
their midst. Such a trend can be traced back to at least the 1850s. In Sabine
County, Missouri, for instance, the local newspaper responded to an 1859

lynching by condemning what it called the "sins of a few misguided men" whose actions would cause "reproach" to "our beautiful county."[16] During the 1870s and 1880s, there was a growing awareness that such lynchings were a violation of state power and thereby constituted a danger to established order. When sixteen African Americans were lynched in Tennessee, the white residents of Gibson County called a mass meeting to express to the nation the county's true "public sentiment" and to show "the world our utter disapprobation and regret" for this crime. In 1884, the local paper of Leadville, Colorado, urged that a mob allow the law to take its course because the town "cannot afford to have a lynching" since the "stigma will rest upon the community for all time." When lynching reached epidemic proportions in the 1890s, places like Graves County, Kentucky, in 1894, and Butler County, Alabama, in 1895, responded to local lynchings by claiming that the crime was committed by a "lawless element" for which the community should not be held responsible. A district court judge in McLennan County, Texas, condemned an 1896 lynching as "the worst stain on the fair name of the county."[17] In 1899, the former governor of Georgia faced a mob and begged them not to "stain the honor of this state" with the lynching they were about to perform; he did not succeed in stopping this lynching, but he made clear the stakes involved and the importance of reputation in an increasingly interdependent nation. What is important to note is that it is resident public officials who are making these pronouncements, like the city solicitor of Wilmington, Delaware, in 1903, who condemned the lynching of George White as "a blot and disgrace on the name of the state."[18] These are citizens of the state, often holding public office, who are denouncing these acts—not outside media venues or nonresident critics.

By the first decades of the twentieth century, as lynching came to be publicly viewed as a barbaric practice rather than a form of necessary frontier justice or chivalry, local newspapers regularly denounced lynchings and condemned lynch mobs. The business elite and the newspaper editors, concerned about their towns' reputation and fearful of economic retributions, responded to lynchings with a public display of outrage. In Georgia, for example, the towns of Monticello and Clarksville held mass meetings in 1915 and 1916 to deplore recent lynchings in their counties, while the press of Atlanta denounced the lynching of Leo Frank in 1915.[19] In Texas, the local Waco newspapers claimed that the "feeling amongst the best people is one of shame" for the 1916 lynching of Jesse Washington, while other newspapers across and outside the state bemoaned the fact that the lynching would come to be what they variously called "the shame of Texas" and a "disgrace to the state of Texas."[20] Following the 1911 lynching of Zachariah Walker in

Coatesville, Pennsylvania, the town council, the Presbyterian church, the fire department, and the Business Men's Association all placed themselves "on record as unanimously condemning the act of outrage and inhuman brutality against law and order."[21]

By the 1920s, in the face of changing public sentiment, communities regularly responded to lynchings with public meetings organized by Rotary Clubs and chambers of commerce. After a wave of negative publicity following a lynching in 1922, the leading citizens of Freestone County, Texas, called a mass meeting at which they elected officers and instructed a resolutions committee to pen a statement for public release to make the case for the self-defined "citizens who believe in the supremacy of the law and who are jealous of the reputation and fair name of Freestone County."[22] Newspapers routinely condemned lynchers as unrepresentative of the town's citizenry. The *Tampa Daily Times*, for example, urged "civilized people" to keep lynchers, characterized as an "unthinking" mob, from bringing "our city and its citizenship into disrepute."[23] Political leaders now regularly preempted the condemnation from beyond the borders of the town, county, and state by producing their own critique. The governor of Georgia responded to a lynching in his state by declaring that "we stand indicted as a people before the world." By the early twentieth century, then, there was what historian Fitzhugh Brundage describes as "an accelerating shift from outright glorification of mob violence to defensive embarrassment."[24]

That embarrassment, of course, was financial as well as moral. At stake in a town's reputation, as a representative Alabama newspaper editor made explicit, is its attractiveness to financial centers as a site of investment. A lynching was bad publicity and a sign of absence of respect for law and order that made investors wary.[25] In Abbeville, South Carolina, for example, the lynching of Anthony Crawford produced a wave of concern nationally. The *New Republic* suggestively noted that lynching was "an expensive luxury"—in other words, an activity that would cost Southern towns and counties the capital as well as the respect of Northern businesses. A group of Abbeville business elites called a meeting and passed resolutions denouncing lawlessness and promising law and order for all citizens regardless of color. It was the sort of tactic necessary to placate both much-needed black Southern laborers and white Northern capitalists, discouraging the one from migrating and the other from disinvesting.[26]

Communities where lynchings occurred faced increasing public scrutiny of their collective civic morals through the thirties, forties, and fifties. The 1946 lynching of four African Americans in Monroe, Georgia, produced an international wave of reaction. The mayor of the town received mail addressed to "The Town Where Four Negroes Were Slain, Georgia." The editor of the local newspaper felt the town had undeservedly become "the target of a hostile press throughout the world." After the 1959 lynching of Mack Charles Parker, the town of Poplarville, Mississippi, felt besieged. The public officials of Poplarville received mail from across the nation criticizing their town. One man echoed widespread sentiments when he wrote, "Frankly, you people are a disgrace." An article in *Look* magazine lambasted the people of Poplarville as self-deceived and fearful while depicting the town itself as a "world-wide symbol of race violence." As the media descended on Poplarville, administrators and residents quickly began to defend their town. Complaining that "the town is getting the brunt end of the publicity," the mayor reported that Poplarville had "the best race relations of any town in the United States," offering as evidence that the black folk to whom he had waved on his way to church the Sunday after the lynching had amicably waved back at him.[27]

A Poplarville student attending the University of Mississippi hoped that "people in the North realize that we don't condone this use of violence," and argued that this lynching was in no way "representative of the sentiments of Mississippians." Even hard-core white supremacists deplored the event. One North Carolina Klan leader stated unequivocally that the "Ku Klux Klan does not advocate violence" or condone mob action of this sort.[28] In response to widespread criticism, Poplarville took the predictable route and waged a media campaign of contradictory defenses—town officials denied that the lynching was a lynching, asserted that they did not condone such lynchings, argued that the alleged crime of rape deserved no less a punishment than that inflicted on Parker, and generally lamented the sullying of their town's good name.

Even the town where Emmett Till had been lynched and the lynchers publicly exonerated—the town our contemporary commentators hold up as the polar opposite of Jasper—was privately concerned about its reputation and sent a committee of white people to tell one of the murderers to leave town (which he did, eventually moving to East Texas). In the aftermath of the Till case, Hodding Carter, the liberal editor of the Greenville *Delta Democrat-Times*, lamented the fact that "Mississippi must now suffer" a soiled reputation for the murder and jury decision "for at least another generation."[29]

It would seem, then, that the argument that we cannot say Byrd was lynched because the three men who killed him did not have the support of the community behind them is at least suspect, since earlier lynchers did not always enjoy that same communal support. Moreover, the definition of lynching employed in that argument is deeply problematic. It was first proposed by James Cutler, who authored the first book-length academic study of lynching in 1905. Cutler defined lynching as "an illegal and summary execution at the hands of a mob, or a number of persons, who have in some degree the public opinion of the community behind them." He emphasized the last point by claiming "it is not too much to say that popular justification is the *sine qua non* of lynching." By "popular justification," Cutler meant "public approval, or supposed favorable public sentiment, behind a lynching."[30]

The Cutler definition is based exclusively on the types of lynching ascendant in the Progressive Era—the large-scale lynchings that arose during the 1890s and began to diminish in frequency by the 1930s. These are the most iconic lynchings—attended by thousands of people, involving ritual acts of torture and dismemberment, and covered graphically in the newspapers. Because of the mass attendance and the news coverage, there does seem to be evidence of "favorable public sentiment." But these are only one type of lynching—the spectacle lynching of the Progressive Era—and by no means the only type. In fact, they were not even the most common type during the Progressive Era. Lynchings during, before, and after had different dynamics and different degrees of community support, which cannot then be the sine qua non of lynchings.

Moreover, lynchers, for a century and a half, from the American Revolution to the interwar period, claimed rather than enjoyed popular support. Edmund Morgan has brilliantly demonstrated that claims of "popular sovereignty"—on which claims of community support rest—are political fictions whose necessary characteristic is precisely "the impossibility of empirical demonstration."[31] The "proof" in such a case, then, is essentially the testimony of the lynchers and their apologists—that is, the channels for propagating and controlling information: newspaper coverage, editorials, sermons, and other informal testimonials from community members.

The Cutler definition, then, applied as it is by those who deny that James Byrd was lynched, proves to be too narrow and less than useful because it attempts to extrapolate a transhistorical definition of lynching from one type of lynching unique to one historical period to cover all lynchings in any historical epoch. As we saw in the introduction, lynchings have undergone considerable transformation from their Revolutionary War origins to their most recent manifestations. The definition that was useful in 1905 was not in 1940 or 1998.

———

We can see, then, the script that we have inherited from the end-of-lynching discourse—the script in which the first and immediate response of law enforcement officials and public intellectuals, of police and pundits, is to

deny that the event is a lynching. Only a few—and primarily minority journalists and civil rights advocates—affirmed that Byrd was lynched, and their
voices were largely drowned out in the overwhelming chorus of those who
insisted that he was not. We can also see in these scripted lines offered by
those denying that Byrd was lynched the second feature of the end-of-lynching
discourse, the motive to affirm that we in this nation are now *not* what
we were. That is why it was important for these commentators to cast mid-
century Mississippi as an icon of the kind of hatred that they could not locate
in the present. Jasper was not like the "town in which Emmett Till was
killed," and we most emphatically do not live in what they call "the time of
Emmett Till."

Two things need to be noted here. First, let me be clear that I do believe
that America in 1998 and 2010 is not the same place as it was in 1890 when
spectacle lynchings arose or the mid-1930s when they declined. Our ways of
thinking about race and racism are different, and our tolerance for outspoken
hatred based on color is considerably straitened. Things, in other words, are
not what they used to be; and they are better than they used to be. Denying
that fact reveals a superficial understanding of what that earlier world was
like. The second point is that we lose the complexity of history if we cast that
earlier time as if it were relentlessly and monolithically in favor of lynchings,
just as we today are relentlessly and monolithically unable to imagine them
happening here and now. We see how earlier towns and counties were
ambivalent about the lynch mobs that emerged in them, and we see how there
is a trajectory in that pattern as communities became more robust and regular in their condemnation of lynching.

Sadly, we need to affirm these two things—that post–civil rights America
is a very different place than it used to be, that earlier towns and communities
did not unequivocally support lynching—because the end-of-lynching discourse has conflated the end of lynching with the onset of a racially tolerant
modernity. And what is lost as a result of that discourse is the opportunity for
more subtle analyses of what racial conditions were like then and are like
now. We also lose the opportunity to understand the meaning of what
happened to James Byrd without resorting to a denial of one kind or the
other—either denying that our nation's racial mores have changed significantly since lynchings were more common, or denying that those racial
mores still move some people to lynch.

It is easy to understand the motivating force behind those who deny that
James Byrd was lynched. It causes grief for us to realize that at the end of the
twentieth century we could have crimes that grotesquely mock what we want
so much to think of as an advanced civilization. The polls that consistently

demonstrate that a large majority of white Americans believe racism to have ended with the passage of civil rights legislation in the mid-1960s tell us how strong a desire there is to believe that we live in a new era, having rid ourselves of the past.[32] A lynching in the 1990s forcibly rips us out of the comforting present and places us in that stark and ugly past. It is a profoundly painful thing to have to acknowledge that the past does not die but lives on to haunt the present. The greatest American writers, like William Faulkner and Toni Morrison, have made that fact the central feature of their narratives about America, and the stories they tell make us uneasy the way ghost stories do— because something dead is not.

Consider this: for fifty years, between 1880 and 1930, an African American person was killed by a lynch mob at the rate of more than one a week, once every 5.44 days to be precise, every week, of every year, for half a century. That calculation is based on the definition of "mob" as containing three or more people, and does not therefore include those African Americans murdered by either individual or paired assassins or black people killed in the anti-black race riots that erupted frequently during those years. How could we possibly expect that this kind of violence, its frequency, magnitude, and focus, would disappear without leaving its mark? A violent heritage, a history of regimented hatred and terrorism, does not go away without leaving a residue in the society that sanctioned it. That is not to say we are condemned to repeating the past, for we are not. But certainly we are in no way free of it, in no way able to claim a new era uninfluenced by a history we would forget, deny, or exculpate rather than acknowledge and understand.

The Uses of Continuity

Having seen what is lost in our commitment to the end-of-lynching discourse, let me suggest what we have to gain by renouncing that discourse. To put it another way, if we did determine that James Byrd had been lynched, what difference would that make? To answer that question, we can return to the principles that guided the complicity model advocates. When they asked how the idea of complicity can help us understand what lynchings are and mean, they insisted that a view that valued continuity would more accurately enable us to understand the dynamics of lynching. Since lynchings were performances that were neither random nor sporadic, but instead followed a ritual pattern and endured in time, conceiving of them as expansive events that involved a wider range of actors playing different roles allowed us to identify what distinguished a lynching from other forms of crime and violence, and also to appreciate better how an entire society abetted that event. Lynchings, they insisted, were neither localized nor autonomous; they were the result of widespread participation and an enduring history.

The end-of-lynching discourse attempted to suggest that that history had a terminal point, a "last American lynching" that we could memorialize, which would, by virtue of its existence and status, implicitly render impossible any future lynchings. The result has been a fair amount of denial over the course of the past six decades, and a persistent attempt to explain away "family resemblances" by misidentifying them as something else. If we instead return to the complicity models' emphasis on continuity, we can then appreciate how lynchings have evolved, how their formal features have changed, and be better able to understand what those transformations mean. If we dispense with the conventional narrative provided by the end-of-lynching discourse (rise, decline, and end of lynching), we can then tell a different and arguably more coherent story.

Toward that end, then, we can take up three related issues. First, if we understand that Byrd was lynched, we are in a better position to understand how lynchings have evolved into what we today call "hate crimes." Second, we will be considerably better able to answer some key questions about certain characteristics of the crime that have been misconstrued because they have been seen as entirely isolated from the earlier practice of lynching. Finally, if we do determine that Byrd was lynched, we will be equipped to understand what transformations there have been in lynchings since the 1930s, and to identify certain features of lynching that seem to have disappeared since then.

———

So, to return to the earlier question, was James Byrd lynched? I would maintain that he was. Like Garnett Johnson, who was burned to death in Virginia in 1997, James Byrd was lynched. When white men burn a black man or drag a black man behind their truck—these are not acts of simple violence but ritually enacted hate crimes that have historically been understood as lynchings.[33] What defines these acts as lynchings, I would suggest, is that they share the intentions and the ritual features of earlier forms of racial violence. Johnson was burned alive as so many earlier African Americans were, his body ritually dismembered as so many others had been. And while hanging and burning were the most common ways of lynching African Americans because they provided a spectacle that a large mob could easily view, automobile dragging was also common, particularly as a way of parading the body of the victim to those unable or unwilling to join the mob.

Indeed, the practice of dragging preceded the invention of the automobile. Robert Lewis was dragged through town by a rope fastened around his neck behind a wagon in Port Jervis, New York, in 1892 before being hanged from a maple tree. Lee Walker was dragged, shot, mutilated, his legs amputated, and then the trunk of his body dragged behind a wagon and finally burned in front of the courthouse in Memphis, Tennessee, in 1893. In 1912, a mob in Gainesville, Georgia, tied the corpse of Rob Edwards to a wagon and dragged it around the courthouse before hanging the body on a telephone pole. In 1921, after William Turner was hanged but before his corpse was burned, his body was tied by rope to the back of an automobile that drove through the streets of Helena, Arkansas, while citizens shot at the moving target from the sidewalks. In 1927, John Carter was riddled with bullets, tied headfirst to an automobile and then dragged through the black community in Little Rock, Arkansas, in a procession of cars twenty-six blocks long. The body of Willie Kirkland was dragged through the streets of Thomasville, Georgia, and then left on the courthouse lawn in 1930. In 1934, after being forced to eat his penis and his testicles, after his stomach was sliced open and his fingers knifed off, after he mercifully died, Claude Neal was likewise dragged behind a car in Marianna, Florida. In 1942, Cleo Wright was dragged behind a car through the black community of Sikeston, Missouri, and then burned alive.[34]

In Texas, dragging has historically been a way of lynching black Americans. Ester King, an activist in the Houston black community, recalls that his grandmother would relate how "the favorite way of lynching" when she was growing up was "to drag Black folks from behind a horse or a wagon or a buggy."[35] In 1916, Jesse Washington was chained to an automobile and dragged through the streets before being immolated in Waco.[36] In 1930, in Honey Grove, George Johnson was "fastened by the feet to the back of a truck" and "dragged for five miles in and out of town, and later burned in front of a Negro church."[37] In Kountze, not far from Jasper, the body of David Gregory was dragged behind a car for thirty-five minutes in the black section of town to terrorize the African American population in 1933.[38] The prosecuting district attorney in the Jasper case, Guy James Gray, recalls being haunted by a story his father told him about a 1930s murder in East Texas when a "black man was tied to the back of a truck and dragged through the town square until he was dead."[39]

James Byrd, then, was a victim of a specific kind of crime that followed a historical pattern and was modeled on American precedents and local practices. James Byrd was the victim of a crime that was directly a product of the beliefs and motives of the white supremacists who wished to perform this event as a celebration of and a recruitment device for their white supremacy. James Byrd was the victim of a lynching.

———

By recognizing a lynching when it happens, we are able to understand better the continuities in a history of violence that we too frequently attempt to deny. When one commentator noted that James Byrd was the victim of a "hate crime" and "not a lynching," he was, as we saw, drawing on a definition of lynching that was inadequate to the task, and also presupposing that a hate crime was an entirely different thing, an event of our time and entirely unrelated to the history of lynchings. That has indeed been the tendency of most media pundits in their commentary on hate crimes legislation. Consider, for instance, Andrew Sullivan's essay in the *New York Times Magazine*, which appeared about a year after Byrd was lynched. Sullivan's argument is essentially that it does not matter how an individual is murdered, or what category of motives inspires the murderers. Sullivan glibly comments that the "distinction between a crime filled with personal hate and a crime filled with group hate is an essentially arbitrary one."[40]

In one way, Sullivan is correct—for the victim of a crime, it matters little whether the perpetrator committed the act because of personal animosity toward the victim or out of a commitment to a particular set of beliefs that rendered this victim worthy of being assaulted or killed because of the victim's group identity. To the victim, the distinction is arbitrary since he or she is hurt or killed without justification. But that is also the only way that the distinction is arbitrary. In every other meaningful way, that distinction is crucial. Criminal acts motivated by someone's hatred against a specified group are not the same as criminal acts spurred on by personal hatred for a specific individual. The former are acts that tell us something about the political climate in which we live, and how contemporary attitudes toward certain groups are products of a long and enduring set of beliefs in the value and worth of certain kinds of identities based on race, sexuality, gender, and so on.

Moreover, if we challenge that foreshortened perspective and think of hate crimes as part of a continuity in the history of American violence, we can see that hate crimes are homologous to lynchings, and, when committed by a group rather than an individual, are indeed lynchings. That history should inform our discussion of contemporary social ills, and should cause us to modify the ways we talk about these issues. *Pace* Sullivan, then, there was nothing arbitrary about five decades of weekly extralegal executions of African Americans from the 1880s to the 1930s. And there is likewise nothing arbitrary in the crimes committed now against individuals who are hurt and killed because of their being identifiably a member of a specific group. Both lynchings and what we now call hate crimes are effectively expressions of a set of beliefs that has historically determined social relations in this nation. They are both acts of terrorism against identifiable groups. And our best hope of curtailing them both is by recognizing the connections rather than denying them. Once the blinkers of the end-of-lynching discourse are removed, we can appreciate the depth of our contemporary problems because we can see and identify the historical trajectory and continuum of which they are a part.

———

A second advantage in recognizing the historical continuities in the history of American violence is that we can more readily identify just what features of lynching have survived in large part unchanged. We have seen that Byrd's lynchers acted on their belief in white supremacy, that they followed a mode of torture and killing that had historical antecedents, and that they concluded their lynching by leaving the corpse in front of a black church as an act of terrorism. Another feature of their crime also clearly belonged to the history and practice of lynching, but it was misconstrued by public officials and public commentators.

In the trial of Lawrence Russell Brewer, the second of the three trials, the court was informed that Byrd's pants and underwear had been pulled down before he was chained to the back of the truck. The prosecuting attorney noted that this constituted "a form of humiliation" and also meant "more torture" since it put the skin directly against the sand on the road.[41] In the *New Republic*, Michael Berryhill is so eager to answer in the affirmative the question he asks in the title of his article—"Did the Texas Penal System Kill James Byrd?"—that he argues that this "kind of racially motivated sexual torture" is to be traced to the sexual fears and anxieties that Brewer and John William King developed in the racial maelstrom of a Texas penitentiary.[42] It seems clear, however, that this anxiety is far more pervasive, and stripping Byrd of his clothing far more meaningful. White lynch mobs did not need to go to prison to acquire the sexual anxiety they acted on when they repeatedly, ritually, emasculated and castrated black men.

What drove King, Brewer, and Shawn Berry to undress James Byrd was not simply the desire to enhance the pain they wished to inflict on him. It was the desire to share with those lynch mobs in that ritual act, a clear demonstration of that enduring white American fascination with black people's sexuality and black men's sexual organs. As Berry reported in his interview with Dan Rather, King reportedly followed up this act by saying, "That's what they used to do when a black man got caught messing around with a white woman, in the old days."[43] It is telling that in this case the criminal who committed the act is more willing to define it as a lynching than are many who decry it.

James Byrd's Body

Another, and for us final, advantage of recognizing the historical continuities is that we are then able to determine what features of lynchings have changed, how they have changed, and what that change reveals. The two major features that we have discussed in the earlier chapters are the spectacle of the mob and the photograph of the spectacle. If Byrd was indeed lynched, as I maintain he was, then what can we say about the absence of these two elements—a spectacle and a photographic record? Before examining where we can find the spectacle and what to make of the absence of a photographic record, we need to recognize some of the major contours in the history of lynching, since that will help explain how those two features—spectacle and photograph—arose and evolved over the course of three centuries of lynching in America.

———

As I noted in the introduction, lynchings have not been identical in form or singular in purpose but have been an evolving practice. They have differed in motive in several ways. As the various frontiers in the new nation were being settled, lynchings served as the precursors of police and judicial apparatus. In those frontiers, lynchings served to punish the most important crimes—against property and against communal values—by killing those who transgressed. These were local affairs and generally served to punish accused criminals. In some cases, in that of the San Francisco Vigilance Committee, for instance, the people lynched were killed as a result of an exaggerated nativist spirit, which also led the committee to expel many others from Australia and Ireland. This same sensibility was evident from the earliest lynchings—of British loyalists and Welsh miners during the Revolutionary War—to some of the most famous in the twentieth century, including the lynching of Leo Frank.

The lynching of African Americans—even when its goal was ultimately an affirmation of white supremacy—was also motivated by different needs during different periods. During slavery, African Americans were more subject to horrible forms of lynching like immolation than were the white alleged criminals caught with them, just as the law in most states punished people of African descent in a harsher measure than people of European descent for the same crimes. The lynchings of the Reconstruction era were more directly intended to terrorize and subjugate the newly enfranchised black population. These lynchings occurred around voting issues and often targeted elected or powerful black leaders. The lynchings from the end of Reconstruction until the Depression were meant to control black laborers, to stabilize the class hierarchy of the South, and to assert white domination in a segregated society. These were the spectacle lynchings that had communal support, media approbation, and massive mob participation. The lynchings of the 1940s through the 1970s were spasms of violence in a dying order, isolated but nonetheless grotesque attempts to prevent the onset of social equality. Performed by smaller bands of loosely organized white supremacists, these lynchings were guerrilla attacks against a civil rights army and part of the "massive resistance" to integration.

While these are all lynchings—from the hanging of cattle rustlers in Wyoming in the late 1880s to the immolation of black farm laborers in Georgia and Mississippi in the 1930s—they clearly differ in their form. Technological developments like trains, newspapers, and cameras made it possible to advertise, transport, and photograph lynchings in a way that had been impossible before the 1890s. So the spectacle lynchings of which there is a photographic record were those that began in the 1890s and tapered off by the 1930s. The photographed mob lynchings ended, as I suggested before, because of changing social, geopolitical, and economic conditions. They also ended because of the activist work of anti-lynching advocates who shamed the nation and its leaders, in part by transforming lynching photographs into anti-lynching propaganda. The kind of spectacle, then, that we think of in classical lynchings is something that occurred in its most spectacular form only during a four-decade period. If we were to try to identify where there was a spectacle in a lynching before the 1890s, we would have to note that such spectacle as there would have been was local, small, and more for the benefit of a posse than a mob. If we were to try to identify where such a spectacle could be found in lynchings after 1940, we would again be forced to find it elsewhere than the actual site of the murder. In the case of the lynching of Michael Donald in 1981, for instance, the United Klans of America published a cartoon of the hanging Donald in their official publication, *The Fiery Cross.*

————

Given this history of the evolving practices and forms of lynching in America, then, what do we look for if we want to understand where we might find the "spectacle" in the lynching of James Byrd? As was the case with Michael Donald, we would look first at the white supremacist organization to which the lynchers claim allegiance. What distinguishes the lynching of Byrd, though, is that the white supremacy in question resides less in specific formal groups and more in an informal and largely virtual network. It is certainly true, as was revealed in the first trial, that William King had drawn elaborate plans to form a white supremacist group, the Texas Rebel Soldiers, and the murder of Byrd, or any African American person who crossed their path at the wrong time, was meant to generate publicity for that group. The constitution of the Texas Rebel Soldiers stipulated that each new recruit would have to murder a black person to gain admission into the group. So, in this way, there is a formal white supremacist group involved in this lynching.

It is more important, though, to realize the connections of this group with the larger white supremacist network. The Texas Rebel Soldiers emerged from a fledgling prison gang called the Confederate Knights of America, whose members swore loyalty to another group, the Ku Klux Klan. One of the tattoos on King's body is of Anton LaVey, the founder of the Church of Satan. One of the books found in his apartment was neo-Nazi National Alliance leader William Pierce's *The Turner Diaries*, and one of his accomplices testified that King initiated the lynching by declaring that he was "starting *The Turner Diaries* early."[44] Another book King had ordered was *The Silent Brotherhood*, a history of Robert Mathews and a small cell group in the Northwest that likewise drew on diverse threads of white supremacist groups while robbing banks and assassinating Jewish radio talk show host Alan Berg in Denver. King, then, was not a devotee of any single church of white supremacy but drew on a range of different groups' systems of beliefs. Indeed, the single most significant feature of his white supremacy is arguably its ecumenical nature.

Given the diverse sources and patchwork quality of King's beliefs, we can best understand this lynching as part of a contemporary trend in terrorist hate crimes, acts committed frequently by what police refer to as "lone wolves." Instead of mobs made up of people belonging to a single group, lynchings and other forms of racist mayhem are carried out by individuals, pairs of men, or small cell groups who act independently while drawing their inspiration and beliefs from the more established hate groups. Books like *The Turner Diaries* and Pierce's other novel, *Hunter*, are narratives of lone killers or small terrorist cell groups who put into practice the beliefs the formal organizations preach and theorize.[45] A sample telephone message sent out by Tom Metzger, the leader of White Aryan Resistance, concluded: "Good hunting, lone wolves." The individuals involved in that form of "leaderless resistance" rely on a network of white supremacist ideologues, but they are usually not, or only tangentially, connected to the actual groups.[46] Theirs is rather a virtual connection, as they are on the list of people who receive these groups' pamphlets and telephone messages, and, most importantly, they are visitors to these groups' websites.

The websites in turn celebrate these lone wolves' predatory acts. Here, I think, is where we can find the "spectacle" of this lynching—that display of white support and the tortured black body that gave lynchings their expressive content as they demonstrated white supremacy and exhibited black powerlessness. The "spectacle" had become transformed from the 1890s, when, in the most memorable tableau of lynching, white people were part of the spectacle as mobs gathered around the hanging or burned body, took pictures to commemorate the event, and then collected and displayed parts of the bodies they mutilated, to the 1980s, when Klan publications produced cartoons of the killings no one had actually seen happen. By the 1990s, the Internet had become the newest technological development that helped transform the lynching spectacle.

There were some rare websites that denounced the murder of Byrd, as did a Klan-related one that dissociated the "White Christian Patriot organization" from what it called "a heinous crime that none of us in the movement would orchestrate, condone, or even permit within our ranks." That website appeared in the week following the murder. By the time William King was tried, found guilty, and sentenced to death eight months later, King had become a hero for the racist right. Web postings by a California neo-Nazi writer, another by an extremist Mississippi lawyer, and one by a former California Klansman who gave the skinhead movement its philosophical core expressed support for King, many calling for the release of the "Jasper three." One tribute page on the Web called James Byrd "subhuman" and included a cartoon of hooded Klansmen dragging black people behind cars.[47]

The Web replaced actual mobs, photographs, and body parts by creating a virtual spectacle and allowing a cyberspace mob of white supremacists to express their support for the cause through their postings. Support also came in less technologically advanced forms. King's lawyer noted that he received "a daily stream of letters and phone calls" applauding King's actions, while the prosecuting attorney received both threatening letters and a request from one writer to give King the enclosed memoirs of the commandant of the Treblinka death camp.[48] But the Web is the primary means by which lone wolves have the support of their pack—and lynchings, even when not seen, become spectacles.

The lynching of James Byrd, then, should provide us with an object lesson in how past practices continue to haunt us in different forms. It is undeniably true that lynchings are extremely rare. What used to be a weekly event has become, recently, an annual one. Garnett Johnson was burned to death in

1997, James Byrd dragged to death in 1998, and H. W. Walker burned to death in 1999.[49] It is also undeniably true that these lynchings were performed by small groups and condemned by the communities where they happened, and the lynchers sentenced by juries of their peers. They are different, then, because they are less frequent and less tolerated. They are different also because they depend less on actual and more on virtual support. We should not, however, downplay the significant amount of support that King received on this occasion, and white supremacy receives in general. Organizations that track extremist white supremacist groups, as do Political Research Associates, the Anti-Defamation League, and the Southern Poverty Law Center, emphasize how these groups are only the tip of the iceberg, as their websites provide information and inspiration for unaffiliated terrorists. At the turn of the century, the Simon Wiesenthal Center alone monitored 2,100 hate sites on the Web. To combat the practices of white supremacy, the hate crimes, the lynchings, and other forms of terrorism spawned by these technologically advanced systems of purveying hatred, we need to value and recognize the continuities in the history of American violence, and to do that we need to dismantle the end-of-lynching discourse.

––––––

While we can find a transformed spectacle of sorts in new media, we cannot find the other element of lynching that the complicity model advocates used to discuss the dynamic of complicity—the lynching photograph. It will seem hardly a surprise that no picture of James Byrd's lynched body has been published anywhere. Indeed, no editor interviewed for a *New York Times* story on newspaper photography had seen a single picture of Byrd's body.[50] It is not likely that anyone other than the police investigators, the lawyers, and the jurors, and maybe some of the spectators in the courtroom, ever saw those dozen or so photographs that the prosecution presented as part of its case and the court accepted as evidence despite defense objections that the pictures were inflammatory. The image of Byrd that remains in the public mind comes from those first photographs published in the *Boston Globe* and *New York Times*, among other places, in which he looks directly into the camera while wearing his Colorado Rockies baseball cap. The most we might get is a picture, such as the one in the *Boston Globe*'s June 12, 1998, front-page story, of dried bloodstains on the Jasper street where Byrd's torso had lain. The inset picture is of Byrd with the Colorado Rockies cap.[51] We see the man; we never see the body.

One reason for the absence of that photographic record is perhaps that photojournalism in the mainstream media had changed dramatically from its heyday in the 1920s and 1930s. As John G. Morris, a former photographer and picture editor for *Life* magazine and the *New York Times*, noted, pictures of the dead came to be frowned on during World War II. *Life*, for instance, had to wait eight months while censors in Washington debated whether it could publish a picture of some American dead on Buna Beach in New Guinea in 1943. That form of censorship did not ease until the Vietnam War, when again graphic pictures of death were allowed. In our own time, a similar form of censorship has returned. David Turnley, a photographer for the *Detroit Free Press*, had to argue and cajole to convince military censors to approve a photograph of an American soldier crying over a body bag during the Persian Gulf War. Even when official censorship was not so overt, as when the *Toronto Star* and *Time* magazine printed a picture of a dead American serviceman dragged through the streets of Mogadishu during the American military presence in Somalia in 1993, it operated covertly because the American public did not accept such graphic representations. A reader of the *New York Times* wrote an angry letter complaining about a photograph of a victim of a Kosovo massacre in October 1998. His brief comment—"This is not something I wish to see alongside my breakfast"—serves well to describe the sensibility of an American reading public that will not tolerate a certain graphic violence in the images they expect in a responsible media. When the *Laramie Daily Boomerang* published a picture of a local university student shot to death in 1994, the readers of the newspaper were outraged. The effect was such that the editor of the *Daily Boomerang* noted that even if he had a photograph of the murdered body of Matthew Shepard, another Laramie student killed in a homophobic crime in 1998, he would not have published it.[52]

Interestingly, perhaps ironically, it is the body of Byrd's lyncher that came to operate the way the body of the lynch victim had previously. John William King's body was part of the evidence in the state's case against him because he had a passion for racist tattoos, a passion that even led him to compose what he titled a "Psalm of the Tattoos" (modeled on the 23rd Psalm) and write a letter to the county prosecutor asking him to send to "Tattoo and Skin Art magazines" copies of the photographs the FBI agents took of his tattoos for the prosecution's case. Prosecutors at the trial showed slides and thirty-three photographs of King's tattoos: a cross with a black man hanging from it, a swastika, Nazi-SS symbols, a woodpecker peeking out from a Ku Klux Klan hood, the Satanic image of the Virgin Mary holding a horned baby Jesus, reproductions of Church of Satan founder Anton LaVey, goat heads, Valentine hearts turned upside down, playing cards showing eights and aces (the traditional dead man's poker hand), a dragon emblazoned with "Beto I" (the Texas prison where King was incarcerated from 1995 to 1997), the slogan

"Aryan Pride," and several allusions to "peckerwoods" (white men in prison), one reading "100 percent loco wood" and another "PWCCA" (acronym for Peckerwood Confederate Coalition of America). Not presented at the trial but reported in an earlier media account was the fact that King had a tattoo of Tinker Bell on his penis.

In a reversal of traditional historical roles, King's body, not Byrd's, became the advertisement for white supremacy; and, to judge by the tribute pages to King on the Internet, it seems to have worked.[53] Those pictures of King's tattooed body were available in the print media and could be downloaded from the Web. Those pictures, the ones of the lyncher, in other words, came to serve the original purpose of lynching photographs—to produce an emblem of white pride in deeds of violence. King was the perpetrator of lynching violence, and his body was littered with images of those who advocated racist violence and images of actual racist violence (the cross with a black man hanging on it). The pictures of King's tattooed torso contain both the image of the lyncher that we used to find in lynching photographs—smiling and proud of his accomplishment—and also, in the tattoos, images of the lynching effect (the dead person at the center of the old lynching photographs).

What can we make, then, of this altered sensibility about the publication of photos of death in photojournalism? How can we understand this transformation in light of what we saw in chapter 2, the ways that photographs of lynching were transformed into anti-lynching photographs by the 1930s? And what might this transformation of our public sensibility tell us about the period *after* the 1930s, the period when there was a public debate over the definition of lynching, when there were political debates over whether an event was or was not a lynching, when, in other words, the end-of-lynching discourse became ascendant? To begin to suggest answers to these questions, we need to turn to one of the last times a photograph of a lynching gained public attention—and that was in 1955 with the lynching of Emmett Till.

———

One of the most remarkable features of the lynching of Emmett Till was the fact that his mother refused to hide the body of her son after he was lynched. When his mutilated and grotesquely decomposed body was found after three days in the Tallahatchie River, the sheriff of Tallahatchie County had wanted to bury Till's remains immediately. After Mamie Till Bradley insisted her son's body be returned to Chicago, the sheriff reluctantly relented and had the mortician order that the casket not be opened. In defiance, Mrs. Bradley opened the casket as soon as it arrived at the Illinois Central terminal and immediately announced that she wanted an open-casket funeral, claiming, she said, that she wanted the world to "see what they did to my boy."[54] On the first day the casket was open for viewing, ten thousand people saw it; on the day of the funeral, at least two thousand milled about outside of the packed church where the services were performed. The body of Emmett Till, badly beaten, the left side of the head crushed in, one eye dangling out of the skull, became a different kind of icon, because of Mrs. Bradley's insistence. Rather than hiding the mangled corpse of the lynch victim, Mrs. Bradley forced the world to look on it, to show the nation just what the gross physical articulation of white supremacy looked like.

There were two notable signs of her success. The first is that the white Southern press criticized Mrs. Bradley's decision to have an open-casket funeral. According to one report, the funeral created an "emotional explosion" in which "thousands of cursing, shrieking, fainting Negroes" responded with anger and horror to the "corpse . . . displayed 'as is.'" The Southern media denounced her decision as "macabre exhibitionism" and cheap political "exploitation."[55]

The second is that African American youths who were exposed to this scene, who heard stories about the funeral or saw the pictures of Emmett Till featured in the black press, were mobilized by this representation. One reader congratulated the *Amsterdam News* for "putting the picture of the murdered Till boy on the front page," and a writer for the *Pittsburgh Courier* predicted that Mrs. Bradley's decision to have an open-casket funeral for her son might "easily become the opening gun in a war on Dixie which can reverberate around the world." The photo-essay feature story on Till's life and death in *Jet* magazine proved especially effective. Representative Charles Diggs felt that the "picture in *Jet* magazine showing Emmett Till's mutilation . . . stimulated a lot of . . . anger on the part of blacks all over the country," while a black sociologist later remarked that "the *Jet* magazine photograph of Emmett Till's grotesque body left an indelible impression on many young Southern blacks" who went on to become "the vanguard of the Southern student movement."[56]

The twelve-year-old Joyce Ladner, later to become a civil rights activist in Mississippi, kept clippings of the case in a scrapbook and responded to the "*Jet* magazine photograph of Emmett Till's grotesque body" with horror that transformed itself into a promise to alter the political and racial terrain where such a crime could happen. The eleven-year-old Cleveland Sellers, later to become an activist and a field director of the Student Nonviolent Coordinating Committee, remembers how the "pictures of the corpse" carried in the "black newspapers and magazines"—showing "terrible gashes and tears in the flesh . . . [giving] the appearance of a ragged, rotting sponge"—created a stir and an opportunity for education about civil rights in his hometown of Denmark, South Carolina.[57]

When eight-year-old Lew Alcindor saw the *Jet* photos, he felt "sick" and "shocked." He also "began thinking of [himself] as a black person for the first time, not just a person." At first, that conception of his blackness was based on a sense of danger, that one "could be hurt or even killed just for being black." Over time, though, that black identity would be based on pride and an activist sensibility, and eventually Alcindor, having renamed himself Kareem Abdul-Jabbar, would produce the book *Black Profiles in Courage.* The thirteen-year-old Muhammad Ali (then Cassius Clay) stood on the street corner looking at pictures of Emmett Till in the black newspapers and magazines, in one picture smiling and happy, in the other his "head . . . swollen and bashed in, his eyes bulging out of their sockets and his mouth twisted and broken." Ali admired Mrs. Bradley, who had "done a bold thing," he felt, in forcing the world to see her son's beaten body. The young Ali responded to the lynching and the acquittal of the lynchers by vandalizing an army recruitment poster and the railroad tracks in Louisville. Fifteen years later, when Ali met Brother Judge Aaron, who had survived a Klan lynching attempt in the 1960s—they had carved the letters "KKK" into his chest and castrated him as a "message" to "smart-alecky . . . niggers like Martin Luther King and Reverend Shuttleworth"—he responded with more political sophistication by dedicating all his future fights to "the unprotected people, to the victims."[58]

What we witness here, I suggest, is yet one more transformation in the visual iconography of lynching. In traditional lynching photographs, the lynched body had earlier been a source of shame because it publicly signified the vulnerability of all black people at the same time as it expressed white supremacist pride. By the 1920s and 1930s, those images had been transformed into anti-lynching photographs that represented national shame, a direct critique of a white supremacy that required such savagery to buttress itself. The photographs of Emmett Till, it seems to me, mark another development. The tableau of the photograph is different. There is no black victim surrounded by a white mob, as had been the case in both lynching and anti-lynching photographs. Instead, we are focused exclusively on the solitary black corpse. This photograph, it is important to note, evokes another tradition of postmortem photography in African American communities, and that is photographs of black funerals. James Vander Zee's *The Harlem Book of the Dead* is likely the most famous collection of such photographs. The photographs of Emmett Till had the effect they had, I suggest, because they constitute a marriage of two distinct traditions—the postmortem celebration of peaceful passing in a black community and the anti-lynching photograph of sudden death at white hands.

Unlike the anti-lynching photographs of the 1920s and 1930s, this photograph was not meant only to shame lynchers and their apologists. It was indeed a condemnation of white supremacy, but it was also a new sort of lynching image meant to galvanize a different constituency through showing the horrors of the practice that produced such mutilation. It was aimed less at white lynchers and their apologists, then, than it was at black spectators who found themselves inspired by it and responded to it by working to change the conditions in which lynchings were possible, by dedicating themselves to collective and individual acts of social transformation.

The photographs of Emmett Till proved to be a charged symbol. The fact that individuals like Ladner, Sellers, Ali, and others who shared that experience of viewing the *Jet* pictures were compelled by the representation of the body itself tells us how important it was to have visual records of what a lynching was and meant, not just to have heard about or read accounts of this grisly horror but to see the pictures of a body so wholly abused and maniacally destroyed that it had to be identified by a ring, so completely damaged by the river water that the trial physician claimed he could not even identify the race of the body. Those pictures proved so potent not simply because visual confirmation is always more compelling than any other kind of proof but because the vision of a body subject to violent rituals helps us comprehend as nothing else can, allows us to feel viscerally as nothing else does, the entire history of a vile practice that culminated in the destruction of that one youthful body. Because of those pictures Mamie Bradley was brave enough to allow and the black press courageous enough to publish, Emmett Till's body became the most potent symbol for a nation trying to emerge from a history of atavistic savagery. As John Edgar Wideman sagely put it, "the murdered boy's picture raised issues of responsibility, accountability."[59]

That moment in 1955—where an anti-lynching photograph established a new tableau for showing the lynching effect, addressed a new community of spectators, and inspired a new generation of activists—was a historic development because it changed the meaning of anti-lynching photographs and demonstrated the possibilities for how images could inspire social movements. Yet it was also a short-lived moment. As we saw in the last chapter, when a *Defender* photographer wanted to take a picture of Mack Charles Parker's recovered body in 1959, the guards and police attempted to prevent him and ran him out of town. Even more significantly, newspapers and magazines were subject to stricter control and became wary of offending censors and an American reading public that quickly became either immune to or revolted by images of death.

After James Byrd was lynched, then, there was little likelihood that a photograph of his remains would ever be published. Instead, we got a running refrain comparing his killing with Till's. The Jasper lynching of James Byrd was routinely referred to in the press as "the nation's worst racist killing since the 1955 lynching of Emmett Till in Mississippi."[60] The connections between the Till and Byrd lynchings are fairly striking. Part of the evidence in the trial against King was that he had an *Esquire* magazine article on the Till lynching in his apartment, suggesting that his actions were premeditated. Emmett Till's mother commented on the Jasper murder on a New York radio talk show; and two weeks after Byrd was murdered she held the hand of James Byrd's father onstage at a Harlem memorial service. There even seemed to be a repetition of historical patterns of discovery. After the trial of Till's lynchers, the newspapers revealed that Till's father had been hanged in 1944 after being charged and convicted of rape and murder while in the army in Italy (he pled not guilty). After the trial in the Jasper case, King's father revealed that his own brother, then a nineteen-year-old marine, had been tried and acquitted for killing a gay man in 1939.[61] Separated by forty-three years were two lynchings, two grieving parents, two families in some freakish way afflicted by a history of hate crimes.

Although these similarities are significant, what is clearly the most salient difference between the two cases, aside from their quite different outcomes, has to do with the representations of the body of the lynch victim. While Till's body was boldly displayed in the black Chicago community during an open-casket funeral and pictures of it circulated in the black press, Byrd's body was almost completely invisible, both in the closed-casket ceremony the family decided to have because the corpse was so torn up and dismembered and in the absence of a photographic record available to the public. The American reading public learned about Emmett Till's life, but they saw his death; that contrast between a vibrant youth and a violent end made a significant difference in their responses. We learned about James Byrd's life, but we were denied the pictures that might have inspired a greater and more productive outrage. In 1955, some courageous Americans could not rest content thinking that they knew something about the short life of the boy nicknamed "Bobo." Forty-five years later, there were few signs that Americans were unwilling to forget the longer but still too short life of a man nicknamed "Toe." (And ten years later, it is clear that he is largely forgotten.) The American media would do better, in the face of a readership demanding and consuming stories that give us a false familiarity with other people's lives, to complement those stories with portraits of brutality, pictures of violent deaths.

———

That, of course, did not happen, and it was highly unlikely that it had any chance of happening. There were no pictures of this lynching in the public domain, and for some good reasons. Publishing those photographs would have hurt a family already hurt by the crimes it was trying to understand and the loss it was trying to comprehend. And because those photographs would also have made his body, not his self, a visual representation of the injustice he suffered, we would with equal certainty have reduced James Byrd to a symbol. Moreover, there is considerable concern that publishing such pictures would harm rather than help the cultivation of a healthier public discourse about race and racial violence. That complaining New York Times reader represents what I suspect is a fairly large constituency of well-meaning individuals who would be moved to disgust rather than activism by representations of violence inflicted on human bodies. There is also a larger question about whether we ought to desire to move people to concern or action through methods that threaten to inure us to further acts of less grotesque violence. Representations of violence might not produce the desired results of a more agitated and therefore activated citizenry. As likely a result would be apathy in the face of an already jaded spectatorship or repulsion for a sensitive one.

Finally, such pictures would also undoubtedly feed a white supremacist movement that is well-organized and draws on an estimable amount of free-floating racist sentiment. Websites devoted to white supremacist causes and groups have made Byrd's murderer John William King a hero and set up tributes to him on the Internet. One featured a cartoon of a truck dragging a black man; in one chat room, an individual talked about how "fascinating" a death by dragging must be and wished that the event had been videotaped. Consider also that three months after Byrd's lynching New York City police officers and firefighters parodied the murder by imitating it in a Labor Day parade float. In the midst of the first Jasper trial in February, a Washington radio disc jockey made a joke about dragging black people behind trucks. In a climate where racist hatred exists so easily, where people respond with humor rather than horror, pictures of James Byrd's body would probably have done nothing more than feed the appetite and satisfy the perverted fascination of people like the chat room visitor.[62]

Given all these very possible outcomes, what potential good might have come from showing a picture of James Byrd lynched? For one thing, such powerful visual images of Byrd's decapitated and virtually decimated body would likely have affected even the most apathetic or inured viewer, provoking, one hopes, a politicized response in making us work toward disabling such crimes.[63] There is evidence that we have not been left entirely without sensitivity to ghastly human suffering, that pictures of graphic violence do have an effect on us yet. Members of the juries found the pictures of Byrd's body almost unbearable, having to prod themselves to turn the page to look at the next photograph as the prosecution presented its case. Indeed, one Jasper resident suggested that the lynchers should be sentenced to a life in a cell "with pictures of James Byrd's body parts pasted all over the walls," indicating, I think, that there would be a sobering effect on murderers forced to confront the facts of their crime, to be reminded continually of what they had done.[64]

That might not have been a bad idea for the public at large. It would have been more difficult for the New York policemen and firemen and the Washington disc jockey to joke about the murder of James Byrd when their jokes would remind their audiences of the pictures of just what horrific things they were taking so lightly. While pictures on the jail cell walls probably would not have had a penitential effect on the murderers, they would have a salutary effect on a public that would arguably become less tolerant of indecent attempts at humor and irreverence.[65]

A second benefit, a very real and absolutely essential one if our public discourse about race and racial violence is to have any meaning, would be that such pictures would counter so many of the media representations of people of African descent. This is not the place for a history of the full gamut of visual stereotypes of black people. It is worth noting, however, that at least in part because of that long history of portraying African Americans as either comic buffoons or dangerous criminals, a large segment of this nation remains incapable of imagining black suffering.

Consider this potent example of the effect of that failure of imagination for many white Americans. The most exhaustive study of racial discrepancy in death penalty sentencing concluded that while there is "neither strong nor consistent" evidence of discrimination against black defendants because of their race, there is compelling statistical evidence showing that the race of the *victim* matters greatly in juries' decisions to sentence a murderer to death. Without controlling for explanatory variables other than race, those murderers who kill a white victim are 11 times more likely to be condemned to death than those who kill a black victim; after controlling for all possible nonracial variables, the study concluded that the chances of being sentenced to death are 4.3 times greater for killing a white instead of a black person. Explaining how it is that by 1999 only 8 whites had been executed for murdering black Americans since the resumption of the death penalty in 1977, while 123 blacks have been put to death for murdering whites, the litigator Richard Burr noted that it is easier for whites to sympathize with white people than with black people. "We imagine the pain of white victims more easily, the suffering of their families more easily," Burr comments, because "we can more easily imagine it happening to us."[66]

The death penalty for white criminals with black victims is a rarity because predominantly white juries are not able to make the imaginative leap necessary to comprehending and having sympathy for a black person's suffering. Photographic evidence of that suffering is not likely to change so sad and widespread a phenomenon, but it would have some impact in at least countering the far more common representations of what black people's pain and death looks like, which for Americans is usually pictures of masses of African dead. A historian of photography at Cooper Union noted that pictures of "dead bodies in Africa are more tolerated" among American viewers because they are not close to home; but surely the color of those bodies plays at least as large a role as distance in explaining that tolerance.[67] Pictures of individual black bodies brutalized by violence could conceivably remind us of the very intensely personal way each body, each black body, suffers.

The dangers and costs I have outlined above are grave ones that cannot be taken lightly. To have wounded the Byrd family any more would have been intolerable; and pictures of their relative's body would have wounded them. To have created conditions that served to satisfy the blood lust of white supremacists and ideologues of hatred would have been criminal; and photographs of the remains of James Byrd would have given them glee rather than chastened them. To have lowered the already intolerably low level of public discourse would be shameful; and publishing more photographs of violence is not likely to elevate it. But we cannot determine what strategies might best work toward ending hatred by accounting for how much they would serve those who purvey it. That individual who was fascinated rather than sickened by the crime, who wished a video of it had been available, is not the one by whom we can gauge what to do or not do about promoting a form of social discourse whose ultimate aim is to diminish racial inequities.

If there is evidence that responsible use of photographic representations would work to foster a climate where people became more responsive to the racism of the society, where they became less tolerant of grossly inappropriate humor about racial violence, where people of African descent are not too readily perceived as criminals or masses but are seen as individuals, each of whose lives is a precious thing, then perhaps we might better follow the example of Mrs. Mamie Till Bradley than of the newspaper editors who have been wary of offending their readerships. A citizenry at least aware of the fullness of the horror of hate crimes, if not galvanized against hatred and actively working toward its demise as those who viewed pictures of Emmett Till's body were, would be compensation enough.

CONCLUSION

What might the absence of a photographic record tell us about our contemporary understanding of lynching, our contemporary denial about both the pervasiveness of the beliefs that motivated and continue to motivate lynchings, and about our abiding commitment to the end-of-lynching discourse? It is telling, I believe, that two years after the lynching of James Byrd, the first museum exhibit of lynching photographs and postcards was mounted first at the Roth Horowitz Gallery, then the New-York Historical Society, and then at museum sites in different cities across the nation, including the Andy Warhol Museum in Pittsburgh and the Martin Luther King Jr. National Historic Site in Atlanta. The mounting of a museum exhibit, I think it fair to say, marks a particular stage in the trajectory of a thing. Being placed into a museum makes a thing an archival property, not a living concern. Museums house things that are ancient, alien, and arcane. Museums or museum exhibits of past human horrors, those documenting the Holocaust or, soon, American slavery, for instance, are museums whose purpose is to commemorate that horror so that we do not forget. Even these museums mark the events as unalterably past, things we remember but do not expect.

The exhibiting of postcards and photographs of lynchings in museum spaces demonstrates just how completely the end-of-lynching discourse has succeeded. It has made it self-evident that lynchings are inexorably events that are archived and documented in the sepia tones of history. One CNN commentator who attended the first exhibit noted that the "most recent photo" in the collection was dated 1960.[68] It was a comment meant to show us that these are events that are not that far in the past, but that they are nonetheless distinctly in the past. Like the granite slabs marking where a "last" lynching occurred, these are artifacts of our wish to show the discontinuity of the practice. These are events we will find in a museum or at a tourist site, not images we will expect or countenance in our daily newspapers.

That discourse, as I have shown, has shaped how we deny, how we misinterpret, how we employ all sorts of euphemisms and faulty logic in order to maintain our illusion that we have already witnessed the last American lynching. That illusion of discontinuity—that lynching is so much in the past that it has to be denied in the present—is costly. We remain horrified by examples of the kind of racism that led to the murder of James Byrd. So, for instance,

we were likely shocked that within a week of Byrd's murder, there were two
reports of copycat crimes, one of three white men who taunted a Louisiana
black man with racial epithets while trying to drag him alongside their car,
and the other of three Illinois white youths who yelled racial slurs at a black
teenager they were attempting to drag beside their truck.[69] We were likely
dismayed that on the same day the New York Times informed us of the jury
verdict in the first Jasper trial, February 24, 1999, it also ran two other related
stories, one of a jury conviction of a white Virginia teenager who had burned
a cross on the lawn of an interracial couple, and the other of a white man in
Louisiana sentenced to twenty years for trying to set fire to two cars with
black motorists in them.[70]

Horrified, dismayed, or shocked most of us may have been, but we were
also not directed or habituated to think of what continuity there may be
between these events and what happened to James Byrd. Too long committed
to thinking of the discontinuity between a history of lynching and our present, we were not able to identify what happened to James Byrd as a lynching,
nor to see how the same kind of white supremacy that underwrote lynching
continues in our own day to inspire would-be lynchers. What we have inherited from the end-of-lynching discourse—a circumscribed definition, a
scripted debate, and a patriotic sensibility—has made our belief that lynchings are over as durable as the granite markers that show where they ended.

We saw how the celebrants of the end of lynching noted that the decline
and extinction of lynching signified what they called the nation's "growing
maturity and fading barbarism." The end of lynching, like the rise of civil
rights, became a symbol of how our era was distinguished from earlier,
benighted ones. There is, however, another way for us to think about these
issues, for us neither to deny the obvious truth that we live in an era that is
considerably different and in many significant ways better for African
Americans and other groups previously marginalized and subject to more
regular and persistent racist violence, nor to deny the transformed existence
of particular historical forms of violence residually in our midst. There is
another way, in other words, to see and celebrate historical change and
yet to recognize the continued presence of historical patterns in our culture.
That way, I suggest, might be found in those intellectuals who instead of
attempting to mark the "last" were instead dismally forced to record the "first
lynchings."

There was an annual ritual in which black publications would record the
inaugural lynching of the year. So, for instance, the African American historian L. D. Reddick wrote in the Crisis about "the first lynching of 1949."
The famous African American educator Horace Mann Bond, likewise, had

earlier recorded "the first lynching of 1935."[71] We, happily, no longer live in the time when each new year was inaugurated at some point with a violent act of collective violence, something sadly to mark that this was yet another year that would not be "lynch-free." But the intent of writers like Reddick and Bond, and other writers of African descent who shared their historical and political vision, was to show that the things that happened in the past mattered for what they told us about the present.

Consider how Bond began what would turn out to be an unfinished manuscript ethnography of Washington Parish, Louisiana, by writing: "More than fourteen hundred Negroes have been lynched since 1904, the date of my birth." Lynching, Bond hints, was something that so preoccupied the mind of every African American that it became a way of reckoning the passage of life, in every sense, a way of marking time as surely as birthdays. But the time marked is not just personal; it is collective time, time in the sense of a whole community's passage of life. So when Bond concludes the book by telling "the story of the first lynching of 1935, begun in 1865," he is making the point that while lynching may be an immediate event, a culminating act of racial violence affecting a specific life and county, it is also and most emphatically a product of a long past in a continuum that began in slavery.[72]

There is a deeply valuable lesson for us in this understanding of historical continuities, just as there is a deeply important lesson for us in the complicity models' insistence on the continuities of responsibility. We would do well to reject what the end-of-lynching discourse entails for us, and instead appreciate the continuities and better understand the transformations in particular social practices like lynching. We would do well to eschew believing that there are clean breaks from one epoch to another or holding one event up as a transcendent symbol of racial progress. We are not one "last" lynching away from redemption, nor are we one "first" lynching away from damnation. Lynchings are no longer the operas of white civilization, but neither are they gone forever.

CONCLUSION

THE SUBJECT OF LYNCHING

In the 1970s, George Sharp was hired at the Fisher Body plant in Marion, Indiana. Shortly after he got the job, the foreman at the plant, a Klan member, required Sharp to purchase a photograph of the 1930 lynching of Tom Shipp and Abe Smith, the famous Beitler photograph we discussed in chapter 2. According to Sharp, the whole exchange—the requirement to buy a copy of the photograph from a known Klan member—was "to prove that he was 'okay.'"[1] He would be "okay," that is, because he had expressed support for the ideology that the lynching and the photograph of the lynching represented. By buying the photograph, he bought into the beliefs of his foreman.

Consider what this exchange tells us about the ideas I have been discussing in this book—about complicity, about lynching photographs, and about the continuity of lynching after the 1940s. Here is a case where an individual is essentially made complicit by approvingly viewing a photograph of a local event forty years after its occurrence. He is asked to accept the sentiments that guided those who performed the lynching, to sanction the white supremacy of the Klan leader who sells him the photograph, and to become thereby a part of a workforce in a community that ritually used that historical moment, forty years later, to cement friendships through an indissoluble commitment to a set of shared ideals and shared sensibilities. The lynching in Marion in 1930 was not an irretrievably historical event that held no contemporary meaning for these men. It was a moment captured in a picture that helped them to identify who they were, to connect them to a past they continued to value, and to ensure that any outsider bought into the values and historical traditions of the community. It was Marion's last recorded lynching, but it did not mean the end of lynching, nor did it mean the demise of those beliefs that motivated lynchers. Those are precisely the kinds of connections and continuities that the advocates of the complicity models and the critics of the end-of-lynching discourse had been staunchly arguing define lynching as a practice.

That argument focusing on connections and continuities goes against the grain of much that is written today about lynching, despite the fact that such connections were and remain important for those who celebrated and those who agitated against lynchings. As I demonstrated in chapter 4, historians and other students of lynching emphasize the discontinuities. Almost all the books that look at the history of lynching conclude by tracing its decline, and many frequently end by proposing which lynching was the "last." Philip Dray's admirable book on lynching, for instance, ends with an attempt to answer the question "When did it stop?"[2] If my argument here is that lynching did not stop, it is appropriate that I explain in more detail just what that means, what it does not mean, and what benefit there is in acknowledging that continuity. In other words, what value is there in uncovering the two discourses that have been hidden—in one case by a more dominant discourse that commanded significantly greater attention, and in the other by being an unspoken part of a complex of beliefs built around selective facts and overwhelming hopes for the deeper meaning of the decline in American lynchings?

We can see those benefits in several ways. First, we can see in what ways the complicity discourse helps us achieve a more comprehensive and complete understanding of the anti-lynching movement. Second, we can appreciate how a new understanding of the dynamics of lynching photographs can help us better comprehend the range of what we think of as responsibility and agency in current events captured on film. Third, we can see how the end-of-lynching discourse has thwarted our efforts to produce a more robust and capacious history of lynching in America. Finally, we can see how the underlying principles of continuity and connection that gird the complicity models and sustain the critics of the end-of-lynching discourse provide us with more suitable equipment for appreciating what lynchings in our day mean in light of that history of lynching in America. In short, what we gain by recognizing historical continuity is the capacity to recognize historical change.

———

Let me begin with the complicity models. By recognizing this discourse, we are better able to appreciate a different and more affirmative stance that more accurately represents the anti-lynching movement at its best. The lynching-for-rape discourse handcuffed the anti-lynching movement for half a century. As we saw, the lynching-for-rape discourse was so powerful that it persuaded the most insightful critics of white supremacy to believe that the rumors of rape might be true. Once they began to discern the specific and general falseness of that charge, these critics had nonetheless to tailor their arguments to challenge the premises and insinuations of the lynching-for-rape discourse. Over and over again, they had to declare that the statistics showed the infrequency of rape as the charge that instigated the lynching; over and over again, they had to address the myth of the black beast rapist. And, as we saw, those critics had to undertake that task by first extricating themselves from the role in which the lynching-for-rape discourse cast them—for the white women of the ASWPL, the role of the woman for whom lynchings were performed; for the black women of the National Association of Colored Women (NACW) and other organizations, the role of the woman whose sexual deviance inspired the rapes that inspired the lynchings. In such a situation, then, the anti-lynching movement could not but be reactive. The terms of the debate were set for them, and in both tone and strategy the movement was defensive.

The complicity discourse represents a moment when the anti-lynching movement broke free of those restraints and was able to express itself in positive and powerful terms. Instead of having to deal with the alleged crime of the victim, it was able to turn the full glare of its focus on the lynchers. The importance of this shift in attention cannot be overstated. There emerged from this discourse the most sustained and penetrating analysis of what dynamic informed the crime of lynching—of what, in a word, a lynching actually was. It was an event that required a mob because it required ritual and viewers. By focusing on the mob, and insisting on seeing the mob as a genuine agent of the crime, the advocates of the complicity discourse were able to apportion responsibility so that it radiated outward from the scene of the killing to the accessories and supporters, to the onlookers, to the members of the community and citizens of the society. There was nothing defensive or tepid or reactive in what the complicity discourse advocates affirmed. Here was the anti-lynching movement unfettered.

By recovering the complicity discourse, then, we can better understand other dimensions of the anti-lynching movement, and appreciate a set of anti-lynching advocates who were not forced to fight a rearguard action, who did not have to disentangle their identities from the meshes and allegations of a more dominant discourse. Instead, we find a resonant set of moral ideas that profoundly explore what it means to be a member of a larger collective, what moral responsibility comes with being part of a mob, a city, a nation, a family. We find new legal terms in which the anti-lynching advocates were not just arguing for a simple "law and order" against the anarchy of lynching but were insisting on a more comprehensive understanding of what

CONCLUSION: THE SUBJECT OF LYNCHING   163

constituted legal responsibility. Finally, they also reoriented our understanding of just *when* a lynching is, by maintaining that a lynching was not a single
focal event, circumscribed in time and space, but a pervasive cultural fact punc-
tuated by serial rituals theatrically celebrating the doctrines of white supremacy
that underlie them and make them possible. These, then, are the accomplishments of the complicity models, and the value of recovering them is that we
have a richer and more robust sense of the variety of ways that anti-lynching
advocates and their heirs have thought about what lynchings are and mean.

———

Another thing the complicity models teach us to recognize is that lynching
photographs capture scenes of crimes—not in the usual sense of the "scene
of the crime" as someplace where something has happened in the past, but
scenes of ongoing, extended crimes, scenes, that is, of things that are happening as we watch them. The photographs themselves record actions—looking,
appreciating, not resisting—that are acts of participation. This knowledge of
what we see when we look at a lynching photograph not only helps us understand better what those historical photographs actually do, what work they
perform, but also helps us appreciate better the contemporary manifestations
of such photographic spectacles. What seemed to many most fully to capture
the dynamic of the lynching photographs in our own time are the Abu Ghraib
photographs.

In late April 2004, Americans who watched *Sixty Minutes II* or read the
New Yorker were able to see the photographs of American military personnel
posing with Iraqi prisoners of war who were forced to assume humiliating,
sexually explicit, and demeaning postures. It quickly became apparent to
commentators that the historical analogue of these photographs of clothed
white American soldiers ogling the bodies of naked men of color whom they
were ritually debasing was the lynching photograph that had come to the
wider nation's attention four years earlier at an exhibit first mounted at the
New-York Historical Society before beginning a national tour.

Susan Sontag was among the first to see the family resemblance. In a
New York Times Magazine article published a few weeks after the first
Abu Ghraib photographs came out, she wrote:

> If there is something comparable to what these pictures show it would
> be some of the photographs of black victims of lynching taken between
> the 1880's and 1930's, which show Americans grinning beneath the naked
> mutilated body of a black man or woman hanging behind them from a
> tree. The lynching photographs were souvenirs of a collective action whose

participants felt perfectly justified in what they had done. So are the pictures from Abu Ghraib.[3]

Sontag found something distinctively novel about the Abu Ghraib photographs, however, some development in them that told us something about our own time and mores. That something new was the sense of immediacy that comes with digital photography and the new social media, and the rise of an attendant voyeuristic sensibility that the new social media seems to inspire. American soldiers, she noted, have digital cameras that they use to record "their war, their fun, their observations of what they find picturesque, their atrocities," which they then swap and "email around the globe." For Sontag, that marks a difference between lynching photographs, which she argues were "trophies—taken by a photographer in order to be collected, stored in albums, displayed"—and the Abu Ghraib pictures, which were "less objects to be saved than messages to be disseminated, circulated."[4]

Hazel Carby was one of the first to correct Sontag's mistake about lynching photographs, which of course also circulated, as postcards, in a technologically less advanced way and age. Carby insisted that it is only by seeing what was *not* distinctively modern about the Abu Ghraib pictures that we can understand their function. The Abu Ghraib pictures, she argues, "are the direct descendants of the postcards of lynched black bodies: both are images and messages to be shared with those you want to warn and those with whom you want to celebrate." Both, in other words, provide "material evidence of the wielding of power, of the performance of conquest over an enemy."[5] By emphasizing the continuity from earlier practices captured on film, Carby is able to show how a colonizing racism both persists and is adapted to newer territories and goals.

Shawn Michelle Smith likewise appreciated the continuity between the two types of photographs, arguing that the Abu Ghraib pictures operate as what she calls "afterimages of American lynching photographs." What both sets of photographs reveal, she demonstrates, is a shared sensibility in those who take and circulate pictures of torture that they occupy a terrain where these pictures make sense and would appeal to a like-minded constituency. In both cases, military torture and lynching, the "perpetrators felt justified in their actions, and . . . they assumed an audience of others who would share their views."[6] These pictures, in other words, reveal something about the society the photographers think they inhabit, a society in which white women are cast as particular kinds of subjects, in need of protection from any potential transgressive sexual desire, and men of color are cast as the objects of that potential desire who must therefore be ritually punished for it.

Susan Willis agrees in noting that the Abu Ghraib pictures, which, she says, "should be read as documents of lynching," reveal the profound depths of racism in the American military. The photographs, especially the ones that stage an Iraqi man dressed in a black robe in a position of crucifixion, reveal to what extent the values and the imagery (cross, robe) of "the KKK saturate our military." Willis also agrees with Sontag in seeing in the Abu Ghraib pictures (and lynching photographs) a kind of compulsive voyeuristic disorder in which people need to share and tell of their deeds. Like the lynching photograph in which a son identifies himself in a postcard mailed to his parents, or one an aunt sends to her teenage nephew, the Abu Ghraib pictures that soldiers sent to family and friends show us the profound need people have to make known what they do, where they are, and, to those who share or discredit their creed, what they are. As Willis astutely notes, these two types of photographs reveal the "history we repress (lynching) with the history we disavow (torture)."[7]

It is heartening that commentators who understand the dynamics that informed the production, circulation, and consumption of lynching photographs provide us with enlightening interpretations of what contemporary events like Abu Ghraib reveal about the persistence of past practices, and what place such pictures of that peculiar form of sexualized torture occupy in what Smith calls "the racialized national archive bequeathed by lynching."[8] Two things seem to me to be worth adding to this discussion. First, as Sontag and Willis note, the development of new digital and social media is not unimportant. As I suggested in chapter 4, we must learn to seek out the "spectacles" that mobs used to constitute in older modes of lynching in other places—including, especially, the Internet where these photographs circulated, first covertly as celebration, and then publicly as condemnation.

A second point worth making is the insight that the complicity models provide about what such photographs capture—a staged moment in a crime whose theatricality requires both an audience (those to whom these photographs were e-mailed) and a visual record of the event (the photographs themselves). What we see when we look at the white men and women in the uniform of the United States military and the naked brown men subject to inhuman indignities and sexual humiliation inflicted on them by those uniformed soldiers is part of the process of torture. What we see in these photographs is not soldiers who are taking a break from "enhanced interrogation" techniques, who are whiling away the boredom of torturing these prisoners of war by entertaining themselves with their digital cameras. What we see is part of the torture itself, part of the military strategy of systematically eviscerating the humanity of their victims. In other words, as in the case of the lynching photographs, we see complicity. We see torture and torturers.

Such an insight should not seem startling, but, in the wake of the military's and the Bush administration's extended attempt to suggest that Abu Ghraib was the work of "a few bad apples" rather than an extension of the military's strategy, it became necessary to affirm just what these photographs captured. When the secretary of defense, Donald Rumsfeld, testified before Congress a week after the Abu Ghraib pictures became public, he addressed what he called the "mistreatment" of the Iraqi prisoners by distancing it from everything "American." "It was inconsistent with the values of our nation, it was inconsistent with the teachings of the military to the men and women of the armed forces, and it was certainly fundamentally un-American." It was, in other words, an anomaly, and, most emphatically, an anomaly (a "mistreatment") that was not "torture." Indeed, when pressed on this issue during his testimony, he challenged the representative who called the actions "torture." "I don't know if the—it is correct to say what you just said, that torture has taken place," he temporized before concluding lamely: "I'm not going to address the torture word."[9] Whatever these photographs captured, it was not systematic torture in line with American history or American military policy.

As with lynching photographs, it became too easy to discredit our own eyes and to deny the complicity of those who are there, surrounding the bodies, looking shamelessly at the work of torture and inhumanity. It became possible, with the insistence of the ultimately responsible military and government, to see pranks where our eyes behold horror, to see a few rogue soldiers where our intuition recognizes the symptomatic failure of a regime that had resorted to torture. What the complicity models teach us about photographs, then, is that they are often the sites where we can detect where responsibility should be placed—both in the people in the photographs themselves, and in those officials who attempt to explain away what those photographs so clearly reveal.

––––––

When we turn to the end-of-lynching discourse, we find ourselves in a somewhat different position. Here, the act of recovering this hidden discourse allows us to recognize that the end-of-lynching discourse is just that—a discourse and not simply common sense or a fact. It is a discourse that arose at a particular historical moment and has since flourished because it served particular cultural needs. By acknowledging that it is indeed a discourse and then dismantling it to examine the makeup of its tenets, we are able to see three important things: how it compels assent by obfuscating the history of lynching, how it misserves us in understanding the dynamics of what are contested and denied lynchings, and how it in fact misleads us in assessing what people like to call the "state of race relations" today.

Once we challenge the belief that the decline in the frequency of lynchings is in fact an inevitable prelude to the "last" lynching, and that the "last" lynching bears great cultural meaning about the national temper and mores, we are better able to appreciate how lynchings have undergone significant transformations in their formal properties and ideological imperatives throughout the long history of extralegal, collective violence in America. We will then have a fuller, more accurate history of lynching that values the important and informative continuities in the practice, without denying the significant ways that the apparent discontinuities also reveal important truths about what lynchers thought and did.

In addition, we will be significantly better positioned to understand what a contemporary lynching means once we acknowledge how the end-of-lynching discourse has generated a scripted dialogue with a rote debate between those who affirm and those who deny that a particular event is a lynching. Consider this case: in 2008, Brandon McClelland, a twenty-four-year-old African American man, was killed when two white men ran over him and dragged his mutilated corpse about forty feet with their pickup truck. Some newspapers called the event a "lynching" almost immediately, especially since it evoked the Jasper, Texas, lynching of James Byrd Jr. and happened on the tenth anniversary of that event. Those charges were buttressed when the earliest reports alleged that the two men had connections to white supremacist groups and had been concerned about the victim's relationship with a white girl. There were also the predictable efforts by civic officials and police spokespersons to downplay the event. Indeed, the police even went so far as to deny that it was "racial" at all, claiming that the victim and his killers were "friends."[10]

In a paradigmatic way, then, following precisely the script I described at length in chapters 3 and 4, the town engaged in a divisive debate about whether or not this event was a lynching, and whether or not it was racial. At a rally in January 2009, younger African Americans accused the local authorities of racism, while "older black residents" chided the youth for "comparing the problems of today with those of the Jim Crow era." The white mayor of the town—with a total population of 26,000, about 5,700 African American—dismissed the charges of racism and noted that the town had previously elected a black mayor and currently had a black mayor pro tem.[11] This episode, I think, reveals that complex state of being haunted by and yet freed from the past, bound to and yet not bound by the history of a place. The town where Brandon McClelland was killed and maybe lynched was Paris, Texas—the same town where the lynching of Henry Smith in 1893 prompted Ida B. Wells to comment on what she called "an entirely new form" of lynching, the spectacle lynching.[12]

Here we can take up the third point I mentioned above, how the end-of-lynching discourse misleads us in our assessment of contemporary race relations. Paris, Texas, in 2008 is not the same town it was in 1893; and the crime committed there in 2008 is not the same crime committed there in 1893. Those elder African Americans who maintain that racial dynamics now are not the same as they were in the era of Jim Crow are right; and so too is the mayor who notes the significance of the town's having elected a black mayor. But those who define this as a lynching because of its apparent racist dynamics may also prove to be right, as those who presciently identified what happened to Garnett Johnson Jr. in Elk Creek, Virginia, in July 1997, James Byrd in Jasper, Texas, in July 1998, and H. W. Walker in Emory, Texas, in June 1999 turned out to be right.[13] And the answer to what happened to Brandon McClelland, whatever it may be, is not going to prove either side on this debate wrong—because they really are talking about different things. And that, too, is part of the legacy of the history of lynching in America.

When one side insists that an event is a lynching, they are insisting on the continuation of certain kinds of social violence intended to terrorize black Americans. And when the other side insists that the event is not a lynching, they are claiming that American society has changed in its racial mores and values, that it is no longer the same kind of place where raw violence was regularly used to enforce social and physical immobility. Their argument is not ultimately about whether or not a lynching happened; their argument is about how to assess change and stasis in race relations. Their argument is about whether American history is repeating itself (because things have not changed) or repealing itself (because there has been social change and progress).

They are talking about different things—and yet using the same event to do it—because that event, a lynching, has been invested with an excessive surplus of cultural meaning that it simply cannot now bear. There was a time when lynchings were a prime barometer of the waning health of white supremacy, when the statistics about lynchings could tell us something about how black people's lives were subject to terroristic forces in a way that informed us about the society that sanctioned those forces. That time is past, and it is past for the reasons that the Tuskegee Institute noted in 1954; there are more meaningful measures now for assessing those things. Lynchings no longer possess that kind of meaning, nor do they express the sensibility of the larger society. But because the end-of-lynching discourse has confused the question of lynching and the state of the nation's race relations, it has burdened those debates (in their rote form) with a weight they cannot carry. By recognizing the end-of-lynching discourse that generated and continues to reproduce this rote script, we can better renounce it and promote better, more informative dialogues about our contemporary state in relation to our past one. In addition, we can also better understand what contemporary lynchings *do* mean, what they reveal about those who commit them, those who deny them, and the social and technological changes that render them what they are.

―――――

Let me conclude, then, with one final, extended example that demonstrates the value of uncovering and dismantling the end-of-lynching discourse. The benefit that will come from our seeing it as a discourse, as a complex of ideas and sentiments and rote scripts that determines and limits our options for thinking and talking about the subject, is that we can then actually make more meaningful distinctions between those manifestations of the end-of-lynching discourse (that do not promote our understanding of our current social condition) and the other accounts of the nation's progress in racial matters (that do promote our understanding).

It is clear that the candidacy and election of President Barack Obama have altered the terrain on which we can think about the dynamics of race and racism in this country. In the face of such a remarkable new beginning, scholars and thinkers have begun reconsidering the question of endings, asking what has changed, what been eschewed, what ended, and how this historic election can be thought of in light of an American history of race-based thinking and race-based violence. Two different accounts that consider this question reveal the two ways of talking about contemporary race relations that I have highlighted above.

The first raises a substantial question about how we ought to narrate the story of African American life in light of this august development, the first black president. In the summer of 2008, in a profound, meditative essay entitled "The End of the Black American Narrative," Charles Johnson reconsidered the fate of what he called the "old black American narrative of pervasive victimization." Johnson saw the value this narrative had formerly assumed in African American life, "reminding each generation of black Americans of the historic obligations and duties and dangers they inherited and faced." Now, however, Johnson concluded, the narrative had "outlived its usefulness as a tool of interpretation" and had become detrimental. It was a narrative that denied historical changes over the course of generations, persistently seeing repeated assaults against people of African descent instead of an evolving social order that made possible the emergence of such new things as a black president—and the legal and social changes, a Voting Rights Act and a conscientious white electorate, that such new things required and presupposed.

Johnson proposed replacing the "old black American narrative" with a more flexible set of "new and better stories, new concepts, and new vocabularies and grammar based not on the past but on the dangerous, exciting, and unexplored present, with the understanding that each is, at best, a provisional reading of reality, a single phenomenological profile that one day is likely to be revised, if not completely overturned." Johnson's proposal, then, is for us to dispense with grand narratives (in this case, what used to be called "the Black Experience") and to generate smaller and more diverse "narratives that do not claim to be absolute truth, but instead more humbly present themselves as a very tentative thesis that must be tested every day in the depths of our own experience and by all the reliable evidence we have available, as limited as that might be."[14]

Those sentiments were echoed about a month before the general election in another engaging essay on the meaning of this change in the social order. Gerald Early noted that his mother, a seventy-nine-year-old African American, stated what many of us felt: "I never thought I would live to see the day when I could vote for a black man for president and he actually has a chance to win." Her son summed up his mother's tone, arguing that she "says this as if that fact signifies the end of America's racial history, or at least the end of race as we knew it." That "racial history," as Early clarifies, is the "black American meta-narrative of heroic or noble victimization"—the account of African American history from middle passage to slavery to freedom, from segregation to civil rights. In a thoughtful meditation on what would be lost and gained from the retirement of that narrative, Early concludes that while the "black narrative of victimization may have outlived its historical need and its psychological urgency," it "still may have a kind of cultural work to do as a tale of redemption and an example of salvation history."[15]

Early and Johnson, with differing emphases but a common imperative, argue for the retirement of that narrative of black American victimization. Early would place it in the category of biblical narratives (a tale of redemption, a history of salvation), where it would be employed less to inform present political or social thinking, and evoked more to reveal important ethical truths like the victory of justice and the amelioration of a national character. Johnson would replace it with more revealing and experiential essays that would be premised on and reveal an entirely different sense of one's place in a historical trajectory.

The argument proposed by Professors Johnson and Early—I will call it the *end-of-victimization argument*—might seem entirely at odds with the argument I have made regarding the dangers of premature celebration of alleged "progress" in American racial dynamics, which, in the particular case I took up, were embodied in those enthusiastic claims of the "last American lynching." Moreover, the subject of this study, the history of lynching of African Americans, occupies, along with slavery, the most central place in the old narrative of black American victimization. I would like to clarify in just what ways the two arguments are not really opposed, and can indeed happily share and support each other on the same grounds.

I will start with the question of whether the subject of lynching belongs irretrievably to the victimization narrative. The answer to that question, I believe, is presupposed in the way we formulate our guiding questions, how, in other words, we choose to analyze the phenomenon of lynching in historical context. The complicity models proposed altering the grounds for understanding anti-black violence and changed the question of the meaning of lynching. While apologists for lynching maintained that lynching was an act of chivalry in protection of white women, and many white anti-lynching advocates argued that it was an act of extralegal vengeance that weakened the legal apparatus of the nation-state, it was the remarkable achievement of those anti-lynching advocates like Ida B. Wells and John Jay Chapman and James Weldon Johnson to assert that lynching was centrally about those who were lynchers and their widespread accomplices—those who watched in idle curiosity, those who read their newspapers without unease, those who viewed photographs of lynching with complacency.

By revising what lynching exposed, Wells and Johnson and the others who made complicity an essential question in their anti-lynching writings challenged the nature of the lynching narrative, and its relationship to the national narrative. The narrative of America was no account of triumph, of establishing a shining city on a hill, of manifest destiny in the conquest of the frontier; it was the story of exploitation, of rampant racism, and of barbarity. With that change, Wells and Johnson also make lynching not just another episode in the black American narrative of victimization. They assert that lynching is less about its victims and more about its purveyors and its accomplices and its seemingly innocent bystanders. The story of lynching, as they proposed it in their tracts and pamphlets, is ultimately about what Johnson called "the saving of black America's body and white America's soul."[16]

By shifting the focus from the physical victims of lynching, from how these events affect black communities, to the moral standing of a lynching culture, to the potential damning of white America's soul, the potential guilt of white America's civilization, these intellectuals make it clear that the subject of lynching, as Wells had earlier put it, placed "the white man's civilization and the white man's government . . . on trial."[17] By reorienting how we look at lynching, how we think about the deeper significance of the practice and the culture that condones it, these intellectuals render the subject of lynching less about black victims and more about national cultural mores. With that shift in focus, I believe we can think about the subject of lynching in ways that do not make it exclusively about black victimization; and instead we can pose historical and ethical questions about the dynamic of a society in which certain kinds of responsibility and sympathy were difficult to imagine or accept.

We can take up now the other question, which involves the differences between the end-of-victimization argument and the *premature celebration argument*. The premature celebration argument reveals the hope that some event is transcendently transformative, and thereby the advent of an altered and immediately ameliorated society. The end-of-victimization argument, on the other hand, exposes the limitations of meta-narratives that derive their illusive strength from playing on a singular theme and do not adequately account for the flux and flow of historical change. It was precisely on those very grounds that Barack Obama himself criticized the Reverend Jeremiah Wright in his speech on race in Philadelphia. Reverend Wright was not wrong to talk about the persistence of racism in our society, Obama noted; he was wrong to talk "as if no progress has been made," as if this country remained "irrevocably bound to a tragic past."[18]

We can better appreciate the differences between the two arguments by taking up now the second example of an Obama-inspired meditation on endings. The final example comes in the form of a documentary by Ted Koppel for the Discovery Channel, in which he interviews three individuals who were witnesses to the history of racial violence: Representative Robert Filner, who had suffered imprisonment in Mississippi's infamous Parchman prison after participating in the Freedom Rides in 1961; Lizzie Jenkins, a schoolteacher, who recalled that her grandfather had witnessed a lynching of five African Americans in the Rosewood, Florida, massacre in 1923; and Representative Artur Davis, who had worked in the 1980s to prosecute the Klan in his native Alabama. All three were also delegates to the 2008 Democratic National Convention, allowing Koppel to place into counterpoint the history of anti-black violence in America and the epochal convention that would nominate the first African American Democratic Party candidate for president. The event the documentary makes central to its story is the Klan hanging of

Michael Donald in Mobile, Alabama, in 1981. The title of the documentary is *The Last Lynching.*[19]

Koppel's intent was not to downplay the history or future possibilities of racial violence. Indeed, it was partly to offset the fantasies of people who talked about what he called a "post-racial" period in American history that he created the documentary. "Simply because we have a black candidate running for president doesn't mean that the racial era is over," he told an interviewer from the *Alabama Press-Register.* It was important to see both the "racial harmony" Americans were working hard to achieve and the festering wounds and dangers still lurking in our midst.[20] To a large extent, Koppel succeeded in capturing that tension. The documentary, as the *New York Times* reviewer noted, celebrates an event many of us did not expect in our lifetimes, but at the same time "conveys how close to the surface racial resentments can lie, and how easily they can be channeled into blind rage." As the reviewer rightly concluded, the documentary was "as much cautionary tale as celebration."[21] By focusing on an event that was still alive, and by interviewing people who participated in it, as lynchers and prosecutors of lynchers, Koppel wanted to show the continuing salience of racial violence. As he put it in his interview, "I think people look upon all of this as being a chapter that's so far in the past that we don't really need to pay it a whole lot of never mind." By showing that there was a "lynching just twenty-seven years ago," he made it clear that we cannot be complacent.[22]

Although the Koppel documentary is nuanced and careful to challenge the popular idea of our living in a "post-racial" world, its very framing (last lynching, first African American Democratic presidential nominee) threatens to raise the specter of that same continued hope that the "last lynching" (whenever it may be) reveals the exaltation of those better angels in our nation's character. For the advocate of premature celebration, then, the election of President Obama *is* the positive evidence of a wholly altered national character, the ultimate meaning of that "last lynching."

We can see, then, the material distinction between the premature celebration argument and the end-of-victimization narrative argument. The one is based on a desire to find elusive historical events to which are ascribed a burden of significance they cannot bear. The other, though, is based on a desire to develop new conceptual languages to describe those historical events in front of us. For the advocate of the end-of-victimization narratives, the election of President Obama demonstrates the need for accounts more open to the positive social, cultural, and political changes that made it possible. But that is not to say that the end-of-victimization argument refuses to recognize either the historical force of those past actions, their residual legacy in producing a discourse of anti-black sentiment, or the flare-ups that feed on and attempt to give renewed strength to that discourse, insofar as these incidents too represent a diminishing but persistent presence in our society. To ignore those would be to skew the picture in the other way, to show the new world we inhabit as if it had no relation to the older world we inherited.

———

The end-of-lynching discourse is marked by that profound desire to claim some event as the "last lynching" in America and the corollary hope for a transformative moment in which the nation's most glaring and festering wound—the violence done to racial and ethnic minorities in the name of white supremacy—is healed through the recognition that that was the last of something, the end of that regime, and that this is the first of something else, the inauguration of another, better nation. But that wound, always festering, seems just one symbolic action or one material, tragic event away from recrudescence.

The ethical lesson to be taken here is that the hope for a "last lynching" is delusive, as delusive as the hope for a "post-racial" world, or, in Dinesh D'Souza's facile words, "the end of racism." Likewise, the lesson to be taken here is that the hope the three Jasper, Texas, white supremacists had for fomenting a racial war and returning us to an older social order is equally delusive. What they share is a desire for a decidedly transformative moment, a single event that changes everything. It is a misguided desire because social transformations just do not work that way, and we are not and never again can be just one lynching away from becoming a redeemed anti-racist nation or becoming an irredeemably racist nation. That kind of social transformation is not possible because we as a society, on the one hand, have moved well beyond the kind of nation that regularly performed and justified lynchings, or other acts of extralegal vigilante violence, and also because, on the other, we have indeed inherited a particular set of discourses about race and racial violence, which do not control or limit our thinking about the subjects of race and racial violence, but do indeed inform and haunt it. It is not easy to understand or make understood what it means to be both haunted and yet not limited by a set of discourses about race and violence, just as it is not clear what it means to be both inheritors of and yet relatively alienated from an earlier world that to some extent created this one.

What is clear, and discernibly important, is that for us to be fair to our past and to our present, we must simultaneously remember what did in fact happen on this soil, create new forms and ways of talking about the world we did and now occupy, and recognize the important and meaningful shifts in the historical trends we trace. Two additional imperatives that have guided this study are that we must also temper our national tendency to celebrate prematurely any sign of our evolving better national self, and to recognize, as we have been reminded by those powerful anti-lynching advocates who wrote about complicity, that there is a deep human value in our striving for a heightened sense of responsibility for things we did not do.

NOTES

PREFACE

1. Anita Miller, ed., *The Complete Transcripts of the Clarence Thomas–Anita Hill Hearings: October 11, 12, 13, 1991* (Chicago: Academy Publishers, 1994), 118.

2. W. Fitzhugh Brundage, *Lynching in the New South: Georgia and Virginia, 1880–1930* (Urbana and Chicago: University of Illinois Press, 1993), 1.

3. Ibid, 258.

4. That book is Joel Williamson, *The Crucible of Race: Black-White Relations in the American South Since Emancipation* (New York: Oxford University Press, 1984).

5. Joel Williamson, "Wounds Not Scars: Lynching, the National Conscience, and the American Historian," *Journal of American History* 83 (March 1997): 1229, 1235, 1232, 1251, 1252. The editors of the *Journal of American History* created a unique roundtable discussion on Williamson's essay, in which they published the six readers' reports, unrevised, and then had one last historian produce a summary afterword on the entire debate (same issue, 1254–1270).

6. See, for example, Ken Gonzales-Day, *Lynching in the West, 1850–1935* (Durham, NC: Duke University Press, 2006); Jean Pfaelzer, *Driven Out: The Forgotten War Against Chinese Americans* (Berkeley: University of California Press, 2008); and William D. Carrigan, *The Making of a Lynching Culture: Violence and Vigilantism in Central Texas, 1836–1916* (Urbana and Chicago: University of Illinois Press, 2004).

INTRODUCTION

1. Daniel Jonah Goldhagen, *Hitler's Willing Executioners: Ordinary Germans and the Holocaust* (New York: Alfred A. Knopf, 1996), 80.

2. Col. William Campbell to Col. Arthur Campbell, July 25, 1780, in Louise Phelps Kellogg, *Frontier Retreat on the Upper Ohio, 1779–1781* (Madison: State Historical Society of Wisconsin, 1917), 236–240; reprinted in *Lynching in America: A History in Documents*, ed. Christopher Waldrep (New York: New York University Press, 2006), 33–34.

3. Thomas Jefferson to Charles Lynch, August 1, 1780, in *The Papers of Thomas Jefferson*, ed. Julian P. Boyd (Princeton, NJ: Princeton University Press, 1951), 3:523, reprinted in Waldrep, *Lynching in America*, 34. For a more nuanced account of Jefferson's struggles as a war governor trying to control the militia, see Merrill D. Peterson, *Thomas Jefferson and the New Nation: A Biography* (New York: Oxford

University Press, 1970), 166–240, esp. 194, on Jefferson's limited role in Charles Lynch's handling of the lead miners and the legislative act of immunity that the militia received for that handling.

4. Col. Charles Lynch to Col. William Preston, August 17, 1780, in Kellogg, *Frontier Retreat*, 250–251, reprinted in Waldrep, *Lynching in America*, 36. Col. Charles Lynch to William Hay, May 11, 1782, in Governors' Letters Received, Library of Virginia, Richmond, reprinted in ibid., 36–37.

5. James Elbert Cutler, *Lynch-Law: An Investigation into the History of Lynching in the United States* (New York: Longmans, Green, 1905), 36, 39. Christopher Waldrep, *The Many Faces of Judge Lynch: Extralegal Violence and Punishment in America* (New York: Palgrave Macmillan, 2002), 25. Some have attempted to recuperate Charles Lynch's reputation; see Thomas Walker Page, "The Real Judge Lynch," *Atlantic Monthly* 88 (December 1901): 731–743. Page represents Lynch as sentencing the Tories to jail and fining them, not hanging them.

6. John Winthrop, "A Declaration in Defense of an Order of Court Made in May, 1637," in *Puritan Political Ideas*, ed. Edmund S. Morgan (Indianapolis: Bobbs-Merrill, 1965), 144.

7. It is perhaps for this reason that Governor Jefferson was not as emphatic as he would have been under conditions of peace in alerting Colonel Lynch to this breach of protocol and justice. It is also perhaps for this reason that the Virginia legislature would indemnify Lynch and his fellow militia members in a 1782 act that tactfully praised them for suppressing the "conspiracy" by "timely and effectual measures" that while "not . . . strictly warranted by law" were nonetheless "justifiable from the imminence of the danger." This Act of Indemnity left the Bedford militia members "exonerated of and from all pains, penalties, prosecutions, actions, suits, and damages." Should they ever be indicted or prosecuted for their extralegal violence, they could "plead in bar, or the general issue, and give this act in evidence." Ironically, then, the lawmakers of the state placed beyond the reach of the law the first American lynchers, the first under that name to usurp the role of courts and executioners. See William Waller Hening, *The Statutes at Large: Being a Collection of all the Laws of Virginia* (Richmond, 1809–1823), 11:134–35. The Virginia legislature offered similar Acts of Indemnity to other Virginians in 1777, 1779, and 1784. Albert Matthews, "The Term Lynch Law," *Modern Philology* 2.2 (October 1904): 173–195, esp. 193–194.

8. Edmund Morgan, *Inventing the People: The Rise of Popular Sovereignty in England and America* (New York: W. W. Norton, 1988), 122–148, 153–173.

9. While we are making a mild distinction between these two claims, they do belong to the same system of values, and in discussions of lynching were more often conflated than distinguished. The reason for us to make the distinction at all is that it reveals the different strands of pro-lynching rhetoric and reveals the differing emphases placed by some on situation (frontier) and by others on democratic values (popular sovereignty). The notable difference, perhaps, is that the frontier argument rests on the supposition that the situation will inevitably change—lynchers perform justice that one day will be performed by more civilized and established systems—while the popular sovereignty argument rests on an attitude of perpetual confrontation to those established systems. Representative politics for the popular sovereignty argument is not simply a formal system with annual or biennial elections; it is a system in which "consent" can be

given by a fraction of the population to self-proclaimed executors of the public will in ad hoc acts of directed collective violence.

10. "The Vicksburg Tragedy," *Vicksburg Register*, July 9, 1835. The Vicksburg lynching was widely covered across the nation. See, for example, "Frightful Affair," *Portsmouth Journal of Literature and Politics*, August 1, 1835; "Lynch Law—Five Gamblers Hung Without Trial," *Connecticut Courant*, August 3, 1835; "Lynch Law, as It Is Called at the West," *New-Hampshire Sentinel*, July 30, 1835; "Southern Atrocities," *New Bedford Mercury*, August 7, 1835. For a fuller historical account of the Vicksburg lynchings, see Waldrep, *The Many Faces of Judge Lynch*, 27–32; and for a shorter one with different numbers of victims, see David Grimsted, *American Mobbing, 1828–1861* (New York: Oxford University Press, 1998), 12. Dickson D. Bruce Jr., *Violence and Culture in the Antebellum South* (Austin: University of Texas Press, 1979), 111, discusses the apologists who saw the lynching as a response to the failures of the law.

11. "Lynch Law," *New Hampshire Patriot and State Gazette*, August 24, 1835. "Lynch Law," *New Bedford Mercury*, September 4, 1835.

12. "The Vicksburg Tragedy," *Vicksburg Register*, July 9, 1835.

13. Ibid.

14. Ibid.

15. Waldrep, *The Many Faces of Judge Lynch*, 52–53. Richard Maxwell Brown, *Strain of Violence: Historical Studies of American Violence and Vigilantism* (New York: Oxford University Press, 1975), 136–139. Hubert Howe Bancroft, *Popular Tribunals*, vol. 2, in *The Works of Hubert Howe Bancroft* (San Francisco: History Company, 1887), 37:166. The 1851 Committee Constitution, quoted in Frank Soule, John H. Gihon, and James Nisbet, *The Annals of San Francisco, Together with the Continuation, Through 1855*, comp. Dorothy H. Huggins (Palo Alto, CA: Lewis Osborne, 1966), 569. The 1856 Committee Constitution, quoted in Bancroft, *Popular Tribunals* 2:111–112. Bancroft, *Popular Tribunals* 2:541, 643–649. Brown, *Strain of Violence*, 139.

16. Bancroft, *Popular Tribunals*, vol. 1, in *The Works of Hubert Howe Bancroft* (San Francisco: History Company, 1887), 36:261. Bancroft, *Popular Tribunals* 2:91. Brown, *Stain of Violence*, 134–135. Waldrep, *The Many Faces of Judge Lynch*, 66. For the influence of the San Francisco Committees on other vigilante movements, see Soule, Gihon, and Nisbet, *Annals*, 586; and Bancroft, *Popular Tribunals* 1:429–729.

17. Richard Slotkin, *The Fatal Environment: The Myth of the Frontier in the Age of Industrialization, 1800–1890* (1985; Norman: University of Oklahoma Press, 1994), 37–38, 211, writes that America's mythical "Frontier experience" is in reality constituted of six or seven major frontier expansions, starting with the seventeenth-century transoceanic crossing and the establishment of settlements on the eastern seaboard of North America, then from the seaboard to the Alleghenies, succeeded by the trans-Allegheny frontier and then the Mississippi Valley frontier, the Mexican frontier (Texas), then the Oregon and California acquisitions, and then finally the development of the Great Plains as an "internal" frontier by the 1880s. Many forces were at work in stimulating these successive expansions, including "geometrically multiplied populations, coupled with advances in the technology of transportation and the development of newer, more efficient modes of economic and political organization." Each of these large-scale frontiers, and each of the more local frontiers within them, contained its own dynamic and was marked by particular sets of conflicts (of social classes, economic

interests, and slave- and free-soil partisans). Yet, despite the particulars of each frontier, we might discern a general pattern that helps us define the frontier experience of collective violence.

18. Richard Maxwell Brown, "Western Violence: Structure, Values, Myth," *Western Historical Quarterly* 24.1 (February 1993): 5–20, esp. 5–8.

19. For studies of the patterns and stages of lynchings on American frontiers, see Brown, "Western Violence: Structure, Values, Myth"; Stephen J. Leonard, *Lynching in Colorado, 1859–1919* (Boulder: University Press of Colorado, 2002); William D. Carrigan, *The Making of a Lynching Culture: Violence and Vigilantism in Central Texas, 1836–1916* (Urbana and Chicago: University of Illinois Press, 2004); Frederick Allen, *A Decent, Orderly Lynching: The Montana Vigilantes* (Norman: University of Oklahoma Press, 2004); Paul Walton Black, "Lynchings in Iowa," *Iowa Journal of History and Politics* 10.2 (1912): 151–254; Genevieve Yost, "History of Lynchings in Kansas," *Kansas Historical Quarterly* 2.2 (1933): 182–219; and Michael J. Pfeifer, *Rough Justice: Lynching and American Society, 1874–1947* (Urbana and Chicago: University of Illinois Press, 2004). Pfeifer gives a more detailed list of the phases of Wyoming lynching history, which has five phases (not four) and exposes the debate between advocates of rough justice and of due process (29–30).

20. See Bancroft, *Popular Tribunals* 2:84–85; Brown, *Stain of Violence*, 137–141; and Grimsted, *American Mobbing*, 240.

21. John Temple Graves, "An Appeal to Negro Leaders, to Stop the 'Reign of Terror' for Southern White Women," *Atlanta Georgian*, August 21, 1906. This editorial was widely reprinted.

22. Ida B. Wells, *Crusade for Justice: The Autobiography of Ida B. Wells*, ed. Alfreda M. Duster (Chicago: University of Chicago Press, 1970), 64, 72. Wells also noted the British belief in her newspaper articles. See Wells, "Ida B. Wells Abroad. Lectures in Bristol, England, on American Lynch Law," *Daily Inter-Ocean* (Chicago), May 19, 1894: "It is true that they had read of lynchings, and while they thought them dreadful had accepted the general belief that it was for terrible crimes perpetrated by negro men upon white women."

23. Ida B. Wells, *A Red Record: Tabulated Statistics and Alleged Causes of Lynchings in the United States, 1892–1893–1894* (Chicago: Donohue & Henneberry, 1895), 8–10. Cf. Frederick Douglass, *Why Is the Negro Lynched?* (1894), in *The Life and Writings of Frederick Douglass*, ed. Philip S. Foner (New York: International Publishers, 1955), 4:501–503.

24. Wells, *A Red Record*, 98.

25. Jacquelyn Dowd Hall has superbly delineated the ways in which the threat of rape and lynching worked intimately together to dramatize "hierarchical power relationships based both on gender and on race." See Jacquelyn Dowd Hall, *Revolt Against Chivalry: Jessie Daniel Ames and the Women's Campaign Against Lynching*, rev. ed. (New York: Columbia University Press, 1993), 129–157, esp. 149–156; and Hall, "'The Mind That Burns in Each Body': Women, Rape, and Racial Violence," in *Powers of Desire: The Politics of Sexuality*, ed. Ann Snitow, Christine Stansell, and Sharon Thompson (New York: Monthly Review Press, 1983), 328–349.

26. Philip A. Bruce, *The Plantation Negro as a Freeman: Observations on His Character, Condition, and Prospects in Virginia* (New York: G. P. Putnam's Sons, 1889), 53, 26, 84, 19. Myrta Lockett Avary, *Dixie After the War: An Exposition of Social Conditions Existing in*

the South, During the Twelve Years Succeeding the Fall of Richmond (New York: Doubleday, Page, [1906]), 395. Cf. Hall, *Revolt Against Chivalry*, xxvi–xxvii. Angela Davis, *Women, Race, and Class* (New York: Random House, 1981), 172–201, was one of the first modern scholars to analyze the myth of the black rapist, which she does with exquisite insights, and among the first to demonstrate how the "fictional image of the Black man as rapist" has as its "inseparable companion" the "image of the Black woman as chronically promiscuous" (182).

27. *Lynchings and What They Mean: General Findings of the Southern Commission on the Study of Lynching* (Atlanta: the Commission, [1931]), 5.

28. Graves, "An Appeal to Negro Leaders." Cf. Thomas Nelson Page, *The Negro: The Southerner's Problem* (New York: Charles Scribner's Sons, 1904), xi, 87, 111, 113, 98, 115, who suggests that "all Negroes" are certainly responsible for rapists by noting "the absence of a strong restraining public opinion among the Negroes of any class" and the complicity of the black intelligentsia. Not only have intellectual "leaders of the Negro race . . . rarely, by act or word, shown a true appreciation of the enormity of the crime of ravishing and murdering women," but the spiritual leaders in black churches condone and give sanction to rapists, both by failing to provide for them a practical moral code and by harboring black criminals and refusing to surrender them to white police. Indeed, concludes Page, "the real sympathy of the race" resides "mainly with the criminal rather than his victim," and the crime of rape will simply not be "done away with while the sympathy of the Negroes is with the ravisher."

29. Wells, *A Red Record*, 26.

30. According to historian Grace Elizabeth Hale, the lynching of Henry Smith in 1893, which she describes as the "first blatantly public, actively promoted lynching of a southern black by a crowd of southern whites," was indeed the "founding event in the history of spectacle lynchings." For the next forty years, until the lynching of Claude Neal in 1934 "signaled the end of the gruesome southern practice," spectacle lynchings became the most resonant of the rituals of violence against African Americans. Lynchings, it is important to note, actually decreased in frequency after 1892, and spectacle lynchings were not as common as the more private lynchings with smaller mobs that occurred on average approximately once a week, every week, for the forty years between the lynching of Henry Smith and the lynching of Claude Neal. Yet these spectacle lynchings, as Hale notes, assumed greater cultural power even as the actual numbers of lynchings decreased, because they became not only spectacles for more participants in the significantly larger lynch mobs but also mediated spectacles for the consumers of the newspaper reports and photographs that circulated after the lynchings. See Grace Elizabeth Hale, *Making Whiteness: The Culture of Segregation in the South, 1890–1940* (New York: Random House, 1998), 207, 222, 201. The statistics of lynchings from 1893 to 1934 are taken from Stewart E. Tolnay and E. M. Beck, *A Festival of Violence: An Analysis of Southern Lynchings, 1882–1930* (Urbana: University of Illinois Press, 1995), 271–272, ix. Cf. Joel Williamson, *The Crucible of Race: Black-White Relations in the American South Since Emancipation* (New York: Oxford University Press, 1984), 117–118.

31. Wells, *A Red Record*, 24. Wells, "Ida B. Wells Abroad. Speaking in Liverpool Against Lynchers of Negroes," *The Daily Inter Ocean* (April 9, 1894). Wells, *Southern Horrors. Lynch Law in All Its Phases* (New York: New York Age, 1892), 14, 21.

32. David Bromwich, "Moral Imagination," *Raritan* 27.4 (Spring 2008): 4–33, esp. 14, 31, 32. I would like to thank my friend Rochelle Gurstein for directing me to this article,

and for her innumerable kindnesses in reading the manuscript and helping me think through the questions the topic raises.

CHAPTER 1 — THE ACCOUNTANT AND THE OPERA HOUSE

1. Michael Fedo, *The Lynchings in Duluth* (1979; St. Paul: Minnesota Historical Society Press, 2000), 101–102. I am using Fedo's characterization of Johnson's emotions and bodily responses. It is not clear whether this is poetic license or based on an interview.

2. Philip Dray, *At the Hands of Persons Unknown: The Lynching of Black America* (New York: Random House, 2002), ix–x. Although absent from the physical space itself, this fifth element, according to Dray, is fully responsible and its "complicity" essential to the lynching.

3. Dennis B. Downey and Raymond M. Hyser, *No Crooked Death: Coatesville, Pennsylvania, and the Lynching of Zachariah Walker* (Urbana and Chicago: University of Illinois Press, 1991), 16, 19–20, 23, 31–32.

4. "Desperado Burned to Crisp," *Montgomery Advertiser*, August 15, 1911, reprinted in *100 Years of Lynchings*, ed. Ralph Ginzburg (1962; Baltimore: Black Classic Press, 1988), 73–74. Downey and Hyser, *No Crooked Death*, 34–36; the picture of the charred remains of Zachariah Walker in the box is found on 37. I would like to acknowledge here my deep indebtedness to *No Crooked Death*, the definitive history of the Coatesville lynching.

5. Downey and Hyser, *No Crooked Death*, 1, 2. In 1919 the NAACP listed 71 lynchings in 1911, 63 of African Americans; in 1929 White amended these numbers to 80 and 72, respectively, while in 1995 Tolnay and Beck, focusing exclusively on the ten Southern states, put the numbers at 52 and 50. See National Association for the Advancement of Colored People, *Thirty Years of Lynching in the United States, 1889–1918* (New York: NAACP, 1919), 29; Walter White, *Rope and Faggot: A Biography of Judge Lynch* (New York: Alfred A. Knopf, 1929), 231; Stewart E. Tolnay and E. M. Beck, *A Festival of Violence: An Analysis of Southern Lynchings, 1882–1930* (Urbana and Chicago: University of Illinois Press, 1995), 271. These statistics are deceptive and do not include victims of race riots or racial pogroms that were often seen as mass lynchings.

6. *New York Times*, quoted in Downey and Hyser, *No Crooked Death*, 45. There was a lynching in Oklahoma that same day, which the *New York Times* covered in its back pages. See Robert F. Worth, "The Legacy of a Lynching," *American Scholar* 67.2 (Spring 1998): 71. According to one contemporary, there were apparently telephone messages "bearing invitations to the lynching" before Walker was caught, and telegrams "were sent to certain papers in New York and Philadelphia, asking how many words they would run in a lynching-story." See Albert Nock, "What We All Stand For?" *American Magazine* 75.4 (1913): 53–57, esp. 54.

7. Downey and Hyser, *No Crooked Death*, 52–55, 49–50, 55, 61, 51, 81, 86, 88, 113.

8. Ibid., 55, 68 n. 29, 103, 84.

9. Ibid., 88, 110–111, 112, 113.

10. Ibid., 55, 68 n. 30, 72, 85, 86, 115.

11. *Pittsburgh Dispatch*, quoted in "The Reign of Terror," *Crisis* 2.6 (October 1911): 235.

12. Downey and Hyser, *No Crooked Death*, 84.

13. *New York Times*, quoted in *Crisis* 3.1 (November 1911): 13. *Philadelphia Inquirer*, quoted in *Crisis* 4.2 (June 1912): 71.

14. Michael Tonry, *Malign Neglect: Race, Crime, and Punishment in America* (New York: Oxford University Press, 1995), 33.

15. Arthur F. Raper, *The Tragedy of Lynching* (Chapel Hill: University of North Carolina Press, 1933), 12, 47; cf. 5, 47, 332. Downey and Hyser, *No Crooked Death*, 80, 81. Theodore Roosevelt, "Lynching and the Miscarriage of Justice," *Outlook* 99 (November 25, 1911): 706–707.

16. For Berry, see Downey and Hyser, *No Crooked Death*, 19, 30, 86–88; for Markward, see ibid., 29, 76.

17. Ida B. Wells, *A Red Record: Tabulated Statistics and Alleged Causes of Lynchings in the United States, 1892–1893–1894* (Chicago: Donohue & Henneberry, 1895), 30–32. Downey and Hyser, *No Crooked Death*, 158–159.

18. Both the *Brooklyn Eagle* and the *Pittsburgh Dispatch* are quoted in "Opinion," *Crisis* 4.2 (June 1912): 71.

19. The articles from the *Continent* and the *Cressett Magazine* are quoted in Downey and Hyser, *No Crooked Death*, 56, 153.

20. For Chapman's anniversary visit to Coatesville, see M. A. DeWolfe Howe, *John Jay Chapman and His Letters* (Boston: Houghton Mifflin, 1937), 214–220; Richard B. Hovey, *John Jay Chapman: An American Mind* (New York: Columbia University Press, 1959), 209–212; Jacques Barzun, "Introduction," *The Selected Writings of John Jay Chapman*, ed. Barzun (New York: Farrar, Straus and Cudahy, 1957), v–x; and Downey and Hyser, *No Crooked Death*, 118–119.

21. "John Jay Chapman on Lynching," *Southern Workman* 42.1 (January 1913): 55–58. "A Penitent at Coatesville," *Literary Digest* 45.14 (October 5, 1912): 566–567. "Sackcloth and Ashes," *Crisis* 5.2 (December 1912): 87–88. "A Nation's Responsibility," *Educational Review* 44.5 (December 1912): 460–465.

22. John Jay Chapman, "Coatesville," in *Unbought Spirit: A John Jay Chapman Reader*, ed. Richard Stone (Urbana and Chicago: University of Illinois Press, 1998), 1, 3.

23. Ibid., 2–3.

24. Ibid., 4.

25. Chapman himself had an extremely heightened sense of responsibility. Indeed, in one famous incident he atoned for his beating of a rival in love by burning his hand until it had to be amputated. See Hovey, *John Jay Chapman*, 38–57. Edmund Wilson understated the point when he noted that there "can have been few codes of morality ever formulated so individualistic as John Jay Chapman's." Quoted in Worth, "The Legacy of a Lynching," 73.

26. Chapman, "Coatesville," 4.

27. Ibid. "Address of John Jay Chapman," *Harper's Weekly*, September 29, 1912: 6. The prefatory matter is not included in *Unbought Spirit* but is in most of the contemporary reprintings of the address.

28. Chapman, "Coatesville," 3.

29. *John Jay Chapman and His Letters*, 220.

30. Jessie Daniel Ames, *The Changing Character of Lynching: Review of Lynching, 1931–1941* (Atlanta: Commission on Interracial Cooperation, 1942), 19. Jacquelyn Dowd Hall, *Revolt Against Chivalry: Jessie Daniel Ames and the Women's Campaign Against Lynching*, rev. ed. (New York: Columbia University Press, 1993), 208.

31. Lily Hammond, quoted in J. William Harris, *Deep Souths: Delta, Piedmont, and Sea Island Society in the Age of Segregation* (Baltimore: Johns Hopkins University Press, 2001), 208–209.

32. Worth, "The Legacy of a Lynching," 66, 71, 72–73.

33. Ibid., 66, 75, 65, 65–66.

34. Ashraf H. A. Rushdy, "Seeking Family, Seeking Forgiveness: The Memoirs of Slaveholders' Great-Grandsons," *Southern Review* 35.4 (1999): 789–805; Rushdy, "Apologies and Amnesia in the Guilted Age," *Newsday*, October 31, 1999, B6, B15; and Rushdy, "Ghosts of Sorrow: The Haunted Dialectic of Historical Apologies," in *Postcolonial Ghosts/Fantômes Postcoloniaux*, ed. Mélanie Joseph-Vilain and Judith Misrahi-Barak, with poems by Gerry Turcotte (Montpellier, France: Presses universitaires de la Méditerranée, 2008), 31–45.

35. For more on apologies for past events, see Elazar Barkan, *The Guilt of Nations: Restitution and Negotiating Historical Injustices* (New York: W. W. Norton, 2000); and Roy L. Brooks, ed., *When Sorry Isn't Enough: The Controversy over Apologies and Reparations for Human Injustice* (New York: New York University Press, 1999).

36. Worth, "The Legacy of a Lynching," 74–75.

37. Ibid., 75–76.

38. Ibid.

39. Ibid., 76–77.

40. Ibid.

41. Nock, "What We All Stand For," 57.

42. French Criminal Code, Article 223. See, for example, the Virginia good Samaritan law, Code of Virginia, Section 8.01-225 (as amended 1999). For a list of European countries with good Samaritan laws, see Aleksander W. Rudzinski, "The Duty to Rescue: A Comparative Analysis," in *The Good Samaritan and the Law*, ed. James M. Ratcliffe (Garden City, NY: Doubleday Anchor Books, 1966), 92. The French law was passed during the Vichy regime, in response to a horrifying incident in which fifty hostages were killed as a reprisal for the murder of a German officer. It was declared void after the Liberation by an ordinance of June 25, 1945, but the ordinance strengthened rather than eliminated the good Samaritan provisions. See André Tunc, "The Volunteer and the Good Samaritan," ibid., 46–47; and John F. Dawson, "Rewards for the Rescue of Human Life?" ibid., 71.

43. Lord Thomas Macauley, "Notes on the Indian Penal Code," in *Works*, 8 vols. (New York: Longmans, Green, 1897), 7:497, quoted in Joel Feinberg, *Harm to Others* (New York and Oxford: Oxford University Press, 1984), 135.

44. The Continental tradition, as opposed to the tradition of English common law, can be represented by the sixteenth-century statement of Phillippe du Plessis-Mornay, who held that "there are two species of injustice. The first is to commit injustice. The second is to fail to defend another from attack and injury if one is able to do so." See Phillippe du Plessis-Mornay, *Vindiciae contra tyrannos*, trans. and ed. Julian H. Franklin, in *Constitutionalism and Resistance in the Sixteenth Century: Three Treatises by Holman, Beza, and Mornay* (New York: Pegasus, 1969), 198. I would like to thank Felicity Enayat for bringing this passage to my attention. The tract was originally published pseudonymously in Basel in 1579.

45. Feinberg, *Harm to Others*, 129–130.

46. Ibid., 126–186. Cf. Michael Moore, *Placing Blame: A General Theory of the Criminal Law* (Oxford: Clarendon Press, 1997), 262–286.

47. Bertram Wyatt-Brown, *Southern Honor: Ethics and Behavior in the Old South* (New York: Oxford University Press, 1982), 439.

NOTES TO PAGES 46–54

48. Frank Soule, John H. Gihon, and James Nisbet, *The Annals of San Francisco* (New York: D. Appleton & Co., 1855), 315.

49. Tom Watson, "The Voice of the People Is the Voice of God," *Jeffersonian*, August 26, 1915, in *Lynching in America: A History in Documents*, ed. Christopher Waldrep (New York: New York University Press, 2006), 195. The title is of course an English translation of the Latin proverb *Vox populi, vox dei.*

50. *Philadelphia Inquirer*, quoted in *Crisis* 4.2 (June 1912): 71.

51. *Scimitar* (Abbeville, LA), February 1, 1917, quoted in Dray, *At the Hands of Persons Unknown*, 227.

52. Judge Luke Lawless, quoted in *Missouri Republican*, May 26, 1836, in Waldrep, *Lynching in America*, 55–57. Judge Lawless concluded this sanction for lynching by noting that McIntosh was evidently influenced by abolitionists and proceeded to read from the anti-slavery *St. Louis Observer*, edited by Elijah Lovejoy. Inspired by his words, and in response to Lovejoy's critique of Lawless, a mob destroyed the printing press of the newspaper. Lovejoy left St. Louis and established his newspaper in the town of Alton, across the river in Illinois. A year later, a mob killed Lovejoy as he was protecting his printing press from being destroyed for the fourth time in a year. The Lovejoy episode is widely discussed in many histories; see Leonard L. Richards, *"Gentlemen of Property and Standing": Anti-Abolition Mobs in Jacksonian America* (New York: Oxford University Press, 1970), 101–111.

53. Abraham Lincoln, "Address Before the Young Men's Lyceum of Springfield, Illinois," January 27, 1838, in *The Collected Works of Abraham Lincoln*, ed. Roy P. Basler (New Brunswick, NJ: Rutgers University Press, 1953–1955), 1:108–115.

54. Reverdy Ranson, quoted in William Ziglar, "'Community on Trial': The Coatesville Lynching of 1911," *Pennsylvania Magazine of History and Biography* 106.2 (April 1982): 245–270, esp. 258.

55. Kelly Miller, *As to the Leopard's Spots: An Open Letter to Thomas Dixon, Jr.* (Washington, DC: Kelly Miller, [1905]), 20.

56. "The Shame of America," *New York Times*, November 23, 1922. The advertisement was reprinted in "The Shame of America," *Crisis* 25.4 (February 1923): 167. James Weldon Johnson, "An Open Letter to Every Senator of the United States," December 13, 1922, James Weldon Johnson Papers, Yale University Library, quoted in Dray, *At the Hands of Persons Unknown*, 272.

57. Christopher Waldrep, *The Many Faces of Judge Lynch: Extralegal Violence and Punishment in America* (New York: Palgrave Macmillan, 2002), 135. Dora Apel, *Imagery of Lynching: Black Men, White Women, and the Mob* (New Brunswick, NJ: Rutgers University Press, 2004), 51. James Elbert Cutler, *Lynch-Law: An Investigation into the History of Lynching in the United States* (New York: Longmans, Green, 1905), 276. For a full account of the NAACP's work with Representative Leonidas Dyer and the congressional fate of the Dyer Bill, see Robert L. Zangrando, *The NAACP Crusade Against Lynching, 1909–1950* (Philadelphia: Temple University Press, 1980), 42–71.

58. Frederick Douglass, *Christian Recorder*, August 11, 1892, cited in *A Documentary History of the Negro People in the United States*, vol. 2, ed. Herbert Aptheker (New York: Citadel Press, 1951), 794–795.

59. Wells, *A Red Record*, 24. Wells, *Southern Horrors. Lynch Law in All Its Phases* (New York: New York Age, 1892), 14, 21.

60. Wells, *A Red Record*, 98.

61. W.E.B. Du Bois, "The Shape of Fear," *North American Review* 223 (June 1926): 291–304, reprinted in *Writings by W.E.B. Du Bois in Periodicals Edited by Others*, ed. Herbert Aptheker (Millwood, NY: Kraus-Thomson Org., 1982), 3:282–290, esp. 284.

62. A. A. Brill, quoted in White, *Rope and Faggot*, 61.

63. George Schuyler, *Black No More* (1931; Boston: Northeastern University Press, 1989), dedication, 203–204, 216–217, 217–218.

64. White, *Rope and Faggot*, 43.

65. Oliver Cromwell Cox, *Caste, Class and Race: A Study in Social Dynamics* (1948; New York: Monthly Review Press, 1970), 549, 555, 554.

66. Schuyler, *Black No More*, 217. Contemporary and later commentators would elaborate on these points. In 1931, the Southern Commission on the Study of Lynchings noted that lynchings provided "an opportunity for all so inclined to share in the orgy, some by directly taking part in the affair and others through the vicarious participation of justifying or condoning the lynching." A decade later, the Princeton University psychologist Hadley Cantril noted that the spectators in a lynching derive their "chief satisfaction" from "their prolonged feeling of participation." See *Lynchings and What They Mean: General Findings of the Southern Commission on the Study of Lynching* (Atlanta: the Commission, 1931), 24. Hadley Cantril, *The Psychology of Social Movements* (New York: John Wiley & Sons, 1941), 116.

67. The *New York Times* reported the story in articles on April 21 and 22, 1911; the NAACP recorded it in its minutes of the executive committee for May 2, 1911. See the accounts in George C. Wright, *Racial Violence in Kentucky, 1865–1940: Lynchings, Mob Rule, and "Legal Lynchings"* (Baton Rouge and London: Louisiana State University Press, 1990), 118–119; and Herbert Shapiro, *White Violence and Black Response: From Reconstruction to Montgomery* (Amherst: University of Massachusetts Press, 1988), 142.

68. "Real Murder on the Stage," *Philadelphia Inquirer*, April 24, 1911.

CHAPTER 2 — DATE NIGHT IN THE COURTHOUSE SQUARE

1. James H. Madison, *A Lynching in the Heartland: Race and Memory in America* (New York: St. Martin's Press, 2001), 116, 119. Cynthia Carr, "The Atrocity Exhibition," *Village Voice*, March 28, 2000, 63. "The Man Who Was Almost Lynched," *Ebony*, April 1980, 148–153. "Lynching," in *Encyclopedia of Black America*, ed. W. Augustus Low and Virgil A. Clift (New York: McGraw-Hill, 1981), 542. Philip Dray, *At the Hands of Persons Unknown: The Lynching of Black America* (New York: Random House, 2002). Dora Apel and Shawn Michelle Smith, *Lynching Photographs* (Berkeley: University of California Press, 2007). James Cameron, *A Time of Terror: A Survivor's Story* (1982; Baltimore: Black Classic Press, 1994). Cynthia Carr, *Our Town: A Heartland Lynching, a Haunted Town, and the Hidden History of White America* (New York: Crown Publishers, 2006). David Margolick, *Strange Fruit: The Biography of a Song* (2000; New York: HarperCollins, 2001), 21. Shawn Michelle Smith has also recently found the photograph in a 1997 French textbook used for teaching English to high school students and in an anti-abortion campaign poster by the pro-life group Justice for All. See Apel and Smith, *Lynching Photographs*, 28, 35.

2. Madison, *A Lynching in the Heartland*, 11, 64, 111–112.

3. ABC, *Compass*, http://abc.net.au/compass/series/1996/legacy.htm. Madison, *A Lynching in the Heartland*, 116. Part of the reason that the Beitler photograph has

assumed such prominence as "*the* generic lynching photograph" is that it captures what we think of as the essential tableau of a lynching: hanging bodies, Southern setting. Of course, this lynching did not occur in the South, where 82 percent of all lynchings happened during the 1880s and 95 percent during the 1920s. Yet so persistent is the belief that lynching is a Southern phenomenon that in at least one famous instance the photograph has been incorrectly labeled to indicate that the lynching occurred in Missouri rather than Indiana; it is also worth noting that the first words of the song inspired by this picture are "Southern trees."

4. Michael Ayers Trotti, "Murder Made Real: The Visual Revolution of the Halftone," *Virginia Magazine of History and Biography* 111.4 (2003): 379–410, esp. 407. Cf. Trotti, *The Body in the Reservoir: Murder and Sensationalism in the South* (Chapel Hill: University of North Carolina Press, 2008), 176–177, 280 n. 60, where Trotti warns of the dangers of historians' making too much of the cultural role played by these photographs, given the paucity of extant images.

5. Amy Louise Wood, *Lynching and Spectacle: Witnessing Racial Violence in America, 1890–1940* (Chapel Hill: University of North Carolina Press, 2009), 88. Shawn Michelle Smith, *Photography on the Color Line: W.E.B. Du Bois, Race, and Visual Culture* (Durham, NC: Duke University Press, 2004), 118; cf. 139.

6. Wood, *Lynching and Spectacle*, 94. John H. Holmes, "Holmes on Lynching," *Crisis* 3.3 (January 1912): 109.

7. Wood, *Lynching and Spectacle*, 85, 99.

8. Ibid., 93, 75.

9. Jacquelyn Dowd Hall, *Revolt Against Chivalry: Jessie Daniel Ames and the Women's Campaign Against Lynching*, rev. ed. (New York: Columbia University Press, 1993), xx, 150. Ida. B. Wells, *A Red Record: Tabulated Statistics and Alleged Causes of Lynchings in the United States, 1892–1893–1894* (Chicago: Donohue & Henneberry, 1895), 55–56. Leon F. Litwack, *Trouble in Mind: Black Southerners in the Age of Jim Crow* (1998; New York: Random House, 1999), 287. Smith, *Photography on the Color Line*, 122; cf. 127. Leigh Renee Raiford, "'Imprisoned in a Luminous Glare': History, Memory, and the Photography of Twentieth-Century African American Social Movements" (PhD diss., Yale University, 2003), 21. Raiford, *Imprisoned in a Luminous Glare: Photography and the African American Freedom Struggle* (Chapel Hill: University of North Carolina Press, 2010), 43.

10. Wood, *Lynching and Spectacle*, 88. Smith, *Photography on the Color Line*, 114–145. Dora Apel, *Imagery of Lynching: Black Men, White Women, and the Mob* (New Brunswick, NJ: Rutgers University Press, 2004), 42.

11. Both quoted in Wood, *Lynching and Spectacle*, 108.

12. *American Magazine* (December 1906), quoted in Mark Bauerlein, *Negrophobia: A Race Riot in Atlanta, 1906* (San Francisco: Encounter Books, 2001), 65.

13. Raiford, *Imprisoned in a Luminous Glare*, 42, 43. Smith, *Photography on the Color Line*, 138.

14. Raiford, *Imprisoned in a Luminous Glare*, 45, 63, 89, 90.

15. Wood, *Spectacle and Lynching*, 89.

16. Leigh Renee Raiford, "Ida B. Wells and the Shadow Archive," unpublished manuscript, 24, 27. I thank Leigh Raiford for generously allowing me to quote from this paper.

17. Joel Williamson, *The Crucible of Race: Black-White Relations in the American South Since Emancipation* (New York: Oxford University Press, 1984), 188. The Holmes postcard was published in *Crisis* 3.3 (January 1912): 110. Cf. Litwack, *Trouble in Mind*, 283–284.

18. Ida B. Wells, *Southern Horrors. Lynch Law in All Its Phases* (New York: New York Age, 1892). Wells, *A Red Record*, 39, 55–56, 98. For more on civilization in Wells's anti-lynching campaign, see Gail Bederman, *Manliness and Civilization: A Cultural History of Gender and Race in the United States, 1880–1917* (Chicago and London: University of Chicago Press, 1995), 45–76. Raiford, *Imprisoned in a Luminous Glare*, 41–42, 56, reminds us that Wells used lynching images in her 1893 essay "Lynch Law," which served as the foundation of *A Red Record*.

19. For Catherine Impey and Sir Edward Russell, see Vron Ware, *Beyond the Pale: White Women, Racism and History* (London: Verso, 1992), 174–175; and Paula J. Giddings, *Ida: A Sword Among Lions: Ida B. Wells and the Campaign Against Lynching* (New York: HarperCollins, 2008), 259, 289. For Reverend Aked, see Dray, *At the Hands of Persons Unknown*, 103. Ida B. Wells, *Crusade for Justice: The Autobiography of Ida B. Wells*, ed. Alfreda M. Duster (Chicago: University of Chicago Press, 1970), 178. Wells's description of this breakfast meeting originally appeared in Wells, "Ida B. Wells Abroad: A Breakfast with Members of Parliament," *Daily Inter-Ocean* (Chicago), June 25, 1894, 10.

20. Litwack, *Trouble in Mind*, 287. James Allen, "Notes on the Plates," in *Without Sanctuary: Lynching Photography in America* (Santa Fe, NM: Twin Palms Publishers, 2000), 195; the postcard is reproduced in plates 74 and 75. "Second Annual Report, NAACP," 1911, in *A Documentary History of the Negro People in the United States*, vol. 3, ed. Herbert Aptheker (1973; New York: Citadel Press, 1990), 38–39.

21. Raiford, *Imprisoned in a Luminous Glare*, 53.

22. Litwack, *Trouble in Mind*, 287. Wood, *Lynching and Spectacle*, 186.

23. Photograph of Will Stanley in *Crisis* 11.3 (January 1916): 145. Drawing of Lee County, Georgia lynching in *Crisis* 11.6 (April 1916): 303. "The Waco Horror," Supplement to *Crisis* 12.2 (July 1916): 1–8, esp. 7–8. "Our Lynching Culture," *Crisis* 12.6 (October 1916): 283–289.

24. Raiford, *Imprisoned in a Luminous Glare*, 36–41.

25. Hall, *Revolt Against Chivalry*, 210. David Levering Lewis, *W.E.B. Du Bois: The Fight for Equality and the American Century, 1919–1963* (New York: Henry Holt & Co., 2000), 1. Jacqueline Goldsby, *A Spectacular Secret: Lynching in American Life and Literature* (Chicago: University of Chicago Press, 2006), 250–251. Cf. Raiford, *Imprisoned in a Luminous Glare*, 41–43.

26. Tillman in *Congressional Record*, 59th Cong., 2d sess. (January 21, 1907), 1441. Senator Clark, quoted in Wood, *Lynching and Spectacle*, 197.

27. Representative Fish, quoted in Wood, *Lynching and Spectacle*, 216.

28. "Do Lynching Pictures Create Race Hatred?" *Crisis* 44.2 (February 1937): 61 and 44.3 (March 1937): 93. Wood, *Lynching and Spectacle*, 202.

29. The description of the second postcard sent to Reverend John H. Holmes is taken from Aptheker, *A Documentary History of the Negro People in the United States* 3:142. The postcard was sent in 1916.

30. Raiford, *Imprisoned in a Luminous Glare*, 81.

31. For the *Chicago Defender* cartoon, see Wood, *Lynching and Spectacle*, 205.

32. Ibid., 184.

33. Arthur F. Raper, *The Tragedy of Lynching* (Chapel Hill: University of North Carolina Press, 1933), 114–115, 420. Howard Smead, *Blood Justice: The Lynching of Mack Charles Parker* (New York: Oxford University Press, 1986), 114–115.

34. Madison, *A Lynching in the Heartland*, 113.

35. Ibid., 11, 64, 111–114. Arthur Bruner, "Marion Report of Bruner," n.d., Box 20, James Ogden Papers, Indiana State Archives, Indianapolis, is quoted on 112.

36. *Chicago Defender*, August 16, 1930. *Crisis* 37.10 (October 1930): 348. Cf. Madison, *A Lynching in the Heartland*, 73, 113–114; and Apel and Smith, *Lynching Photographs*, 20–23.

37. Madison, *A Lynching in the Heartland*, 113. Contemporary artist Ken Gonzales-Day has produced a series of chromogenic prints in which he erases the body of the lynch victim from lynching photographs, showing what a mob looks like surrounding empty air. For examples, see "Erased Lynching (c. 1910–15)" and "Erased Lynching (1935)," in Gonzales-Day, *Lynching in the West: 1850–1935* (Durham, NC: Duke University Press, 2006), [21], [61].

38. *Chicago Defender*, August 23, 1930; see Madison, *A Lynching in the Heartland*, between 114 and 115.

39. *Chicago Defender*, June 4, 1927, and May 9, 1936, both quoted in Wood, *Lynching and Spectacle*, 192–193.

40. *Chicago Defender*, August 16, 1930, *New York World*, August 24, 1930, both quoted in Madison, *A Lynching in the Heartland*, 115. *Crisis* 37.10 (October 1930): 348.

41. Cameron, *A Time of Terror*, 74–75. Deeter forgave his assailants on his deathbed. There is great confusion about whether or not Mary Ball was raped. Cameron says that Ball testified that she "was not raped. No attempt was made to rape her," and she did not remember seeing Cameron at the crime scene at all. Madison claims that Ball "testified that she was assaulted," but that the night "was too dark to identify Cameron as one of the rapists." Carr, noting that the trial transcripts from Cameron's case had disappeared long ago, drew on the two newspapers that covered the case, noting their discrepancies, but also noting that both had Ball testify that she was "assaulted." See Cameron, *A Time of Terror*, 135–151, 146 quoted; Madison, *A Lynching in the Heartland*, 103–108, 107 quoted; and Carr, *Our Town*, 325.

42. Cameron, *A Time of Terror*, 74–75. Madison, *A Lynching in the Heartland*, 10.

43. Cameron, *A Time of Terror*, 84. The first edition was published by T/D Publications, Milwaukee.

44. Ibid., 74. Bessie Jones, *For the Ancestors: Autobiographical Memories*, coll. and ed. John Stewart (Athens and London: University of Georgia Press, 1989), 41–43.

45. Cameron, *A Time of Terror*, 54–55, 132.

46. Jacquie Jones, "How Come Nobody Told Me about the Lynching?" in *Picturing Us: African American Identity in Photography*, ed. Deborah Willis (New York: New Press, 1994), 152–157, esp. 155. Cf. Apel and Smith, *Lynching Photographs*, 26.

47. Madison, *A Lynching in the Heartland*, 84–85.

48. "Patricia J. Williams, "Without Sanctuary," *Nation* 270.6 (February 14, 2000): 9. Hilton Als, "GWTW," in Allen, *Without Sanctuary*, 38–44, esp. 40.

49. "Death by Lynching," *New York Times*, March 16, 2000.

50. "My Grandfather's Deathbed Secret," *New York Post*, January 16, 2000. Carr, "The Atrocity Exhibition." Carr, *Our Town*, 29.

51. Carr, *Our Town*, 32, 31–32, 202, 234–235, 462.

52. Ibid., 455–461, 320–322.

53. Ibid., 27.

54. Ibid., 462.

55. Ibid.

56. Ibid., 26–27.

57. Ibid., 462.

58. Ibid., 6, 64.

59. Ibid., 462, 204, 461–462.

60. James Harmon Chadbourn, *Lynching and the Law* (Chapel Hill: University of North Carolina Press, 1933), 162. The Indiana law is cited from a 1926 code. Alabama, from a code dated 1928, has the same provision (149). The Indiana law on lynching dates to 1899 and was revised in 1901 (to make the sheriff more accountable for all persons in his custody). See James Elbert Cutler, *Lynch-Law: An Investigation into the History of Lynching in the United States* (Longmans, Green, 1905), 241–243. There is one other section of the Indiana code that is relevant here to our consideration of the mob's possible complicity in lynching. It states that "if any such bystander or other person so requested by the sheriff to aid him shall fail or refuse to assist in defending such prisoner, the person so failing or refusing shall be deemed guilty of a misdemeanor" (Chadbourn, *Lynching and the Law*, 163).

61. Carr, *Our Town*, 31, 67, 38. Also see Madison, *A Lynching in the Heartland*, 89–92.

62. Cameron, *A Time of Terror*, 150.

63. *Black's Law Dictionary*, 8th ed. (St. Paul, MN: Thompson-West, 2004), 15.

64. Allen, "Notes on the Plates," 177.

65. Madison, *A Lynching in the Heartland*, 115, 114, 153. Allen, "Notes on the Plates," 176. Apel and Smith, *Lynching Photographs*, 60. Also see Apel, *Imagery of Lynching*, 20–23.

66. Carr, *Our Town*, 37–38, 116.

67. Wood, *Lynching and Spectacle*, 94, 193, 199.

68. Madison, *A Lynching in the Heartland*, 8, 13, 115.

69. Wood, *Lynching and Spectacle*, 199.

70. Ray Stannard Baker, *Following the Color Line: American Negro Citizenship in the Progressive Era* (1908; New York: Harper & Row, 1964), 186–187.

71. Wood, *Lynching and Spectacle*, 85.

72. John Hammond Moore, *Carnival of Blood: Dueling, Lynching, and Murder in South Carolina, 1880–1920* (Columbia: University of South Carolina Press, 2006), 76–77.

73. Madison, *A Lynching in the Heartland*, 8–10. Cameron, *A Time of Terror*, 62. Carr, *Our Town*, 384–385, records that many observers she interviewed in Marion think that Smith was alive when he was hanged from the tree.

74. *Houston Chronicle and Herald*, quoted in Apel, *Imagery of Lynching*, 32.

75. John Jay Chapman, "Coatesville," in *Unbought Spirit: A John Jay Chapman Reader*, ed. Richard Stone (Urbana and Chicago: University of Illinois Press, 1998), 4.

76. Raper, *The Tragedy of Lynching*, 2, 12, 47, 41; cf. 5, 47, 332.

77. Ibid., 45, 47.

78. "Maryland Witnesses Wildest Lynching Orgy in History," *New York Times*, October 19, 1933, reprinted in *100 Years of Lynchings*, ed. Ralph Ginzburg (1962; Baltimore: Black Classic Press, 1988), 200–202. "Heart and Genitals Carved from Lynched Negro's Corpse," *New York World-Telegram*, December 8, 1933, reprinted in

ibid., 211–212. "Girls in Teens Take Part in Raid on Funeral Home," *New York Post*, May 25, 1937, reprinted in ibid., 231–232. Dray, *At the Hands of Persons Unknown*, 359–360.

79. Jessie Daniel Ames, *The Changing Character of Lynching: Review of Lynching, 1931–1941* (Atlanta: Commission on Interracial Cooperation, 1942), 2, 5, 8–9.

CHAPTER 3 — THE END OF AMERICAN LYNCHING

1. Maybelle Trout, "The Last Mob Lynching: Central Texas Town Recalls 'Santa Claus' Case 65 Years Ago," *Houston Chronicle*, October 16, 1994. According to one Texas tourist website, the pole inside the picket fence surrounding the Eastland granite memorial is the one used to hang Ratliff. See John Troesser, "The Day Eastland, Texas Hanged Santa Claus," http://www.texasescapes.com/FEATURES/Eastland_Texas_Hanged_Santa_Claus/Eastland_hanged_santa.htm (accessed July 13, 2010).

2. "Foresees End of Lynching," *New York Times*, January 12, 1930, reprinted in *100 Years of Lynchings*, ed. Ralph Ginzburg (1962; Baltimore: Black Classic Press, 1988), 181.

3. Jessie Daniel Ames, *The Changing Character of Lynching: Review of Lynching, 1931–1941* (Atlanta: Commission on Interracial Cooperation, 1942), 29. Cf. Linda O. McMurry, *Recorder of the Black Experience: A Biography of Monroe Nathan Work* (Baton Rouge and London: Louisiana State University Press, 1985), 127; and Christopher Waldrep, *The Many Faces of Judge Lynch: Extralegal Violence and Punishment in America* (New York: Palgrave Macmillan, 2002), 147–149.

4. Ames, *The Changing Character of Lynching*, 30. On the NAACP, see Waldrep, *The Many Faces of Judge Lynch*, 2.

5. Ames, *The Changing Character of Lynching*, 2, 5, 8–9.

6. The Commission on Interracial Cooperation had published a tract that used the term "underground lynching" to describe the shift from spectacle to secretive events in the 1930s. See Philip Dray, *At the Hands of Persons Unknown: The Lynching of Black America* (New York: Random House, 2002), 383–383.

7. Horace B. Davis, "A Substitute for Lynching," *Nation* 130.3365 (January 1, 1930): 12–14.

8. "When Is a Lynching?" *Christian Century* 55.32 (August 10, 1938): 957.

9. Jonathan Daniels, "A Native at Large," *Nation* 151.11 (September 4, 1940): 219. Cf. "Terror Against the Negro People," *Equal Justice* 15.3 (1941): 52–54.

10. Henry Wallace, "Violence and Hope in the South," *New Republic* 117.23 (December 8, 1947): 14–16, esp. 15.

11. *Rome [Georgia] News-Tribune*, quoted in "Racialism and Violence," *Race Relations: A Monthly Summary of Events and Trends* 5.6 (1948): 137–143, esp. 137.

12. Senator Borah, quoted in Alfred Stone, "A Mississippian's View of Civil Rights, States Rights, and the Reconstruction Background," *Journal of Mississippi History* 10.3 (1948): 181–239, esp. 209.

13. Rebecca West, "A Reporter at Large: Opera in Greenville," *New Yorker* 23.17 (June 14, 1947): 31–65, esp. 33. The last passage is taken from West's revised essay published two years later. West, "Lynching Trials in America," *Medico-Legal Journal* 17.3 (1949): 90–99, esp. 92.

14. Stephen J. Whitfield, *A Death in the Delta: The Story of Emmett Till* (Baltimore: Johns Hopkins University Press, 1988), 24–25. "Designed to Inflame," *Jackson Daily News*, September 2, 1955, reprinted in *The Lynching of Emmett Till: A Documentary Narrative*, ed. Christopher Metress (Charlottesville: University of Virginia Press, 2002),

19–22, esp. 22. Howard Smead, *Blood Justice: The Lynching of Mack Charles Parker* (New York: Oxford University Press 1986), 120.

15. Whitfield, *A Death in the Delta*, 28. Smead, *Blood Justice*, 95, 165.

16. "The 'Decline' of Lynching," *Crisis* 8.1 (May 1914): 19–21, esp. 19. Ames, *The Changing Character of Lynching*, 12. John Ross, "At the Bar of Judge Lynch: Lynching and Lynch Mobs in America" (Ph.D. diss., Texas Tech University, 1983), 141, also notes the difficulty of defining "prevented lynching."

17. For Ames's attempt to designate a lynch-free year, see Waldrep, *The Many Faces of Judge Lynch*, 127, 134; and Jacquelyn Dowd Hall, *Revolt Against Chivalry: Jessie Daniel Ames and the Women's Campaign Against Lynching*, rev. ed. (New York: Columbia University Press, 1993), 256. For more on Ames's and the ASWPL's tensions, see the CIC-published, Ames-edited magazine *The Southern Frontier* for January 1942, which was both hopeful and cautious in its celebration. It noted that there had been almost three years since the last lynching in Mississippi (May 11, 1939) and prophesied that "another year and no lynchings will become a habit in that State." The more cautious tone appeared in its story on Texas, where the headline "No Lynching in Texas" was meant to prevent any "cause for rejoicing" in the sixth year without a recorded lynching in that state, since the story was primarily an account of the variety of "new methods" for killing African Americans.

18. "Tuskegee Omits 'Lynching Letter,'" *New York Times*, December 31, 1953. The *Crisis* responded to the announcement by Tuskegee that 1952 was a lynch-free year by noting that the Tuskegee definition of "lynching" was "too technical and doctrinaire," and that the claim of the "end of lynching" would actually weaken the cause of those who hoped to end "lynching, less technically defined." Marguerite Cartwright, "The Mob Still Rides—Tuskegee Notwithstanding," *Crisis* 60.4 (April 1953): 222.

19. "End of Lynching," *Washington Post*, January 2, 1954, reprinted in Ginzburg, *100 Years of Lynchings*, 240.

20. William S. McFeely, "Afterword," *Under Sentence of Death: Lynching in the South*, ed. W. Fitzhugh Brundage (Chapel Hill: University of North Carolina Press, 1997), 318. Cynthia Carr, *Our Town: A Heartland Lynching, a Haunted Town, and the Hidden History of White America* (New York: Crown Publishers, 2006), 198. Ross, "At the Bar of Judge Lynch," 140. Burran cited in ibid., 151. Dominic J. Capeci Jr., *The Lynching of Cleo Wright* (Lexington: University Press of Kentucky, 1998), 193.

21. William S. McFeely, "Afterword," *Under Sentence of Death*, 318. Whitfield, *A Death in the Delta*, 127. Smead, *Blood Justice*, 205. Dray, *At the Hands of Persons Unknown*, 457. John Ross, "At the Bar of Judge Lynch," 159, 164–169.

22. Capeci, *The Lynching of Cleo Wright*, 193. Laura Wexler refers to the 1946 mob murder of two African American couples as the "last mass lynching in America" (but here "mass" likely refers more to the number of victims than the size of the mob). See Laura Wexler, *Fire in a Canebrake: The Last Mass Lynching in America* (New York: Scribner, 2003). Dray, *At the Hands of Persons Unknown*, 457. Whitfield, *A Death in the Delta*, 127. Smead, *Blood Justice*, xi, 205.

23. Lewis Blair, "Lynching as Fine Art," *Our Day* 13.76 (1894): 307–314, esp. 307, 313. James Elbert Cutler, *Lynch-Law: An Investigation into the History of Lynching in the United States* (Longmans, Green, 1905), 1. Ida B. Wells, *A Red Record: Tabulated Statistics and Alleged Causes of Lynchings in the United States, 1892–1893–1894* (Chicago: Donohue & Henneberry, 1895), 14.

24. B. O. Flowers, "The Rise of Anarchy in the United States," *Arena* 30.3 (September 1903): 305.

25. National Association for the Advancement of Colored People, *Thirty Years of Lynching in the United States, 1889–1918* (New York: NAACP, 1919), 5. "The Great American Specialty," *Crisis* 27.4 (February 1924): 168. "My Country, 'Tis of Thee," *Crisis* 41.11 (November 1934): 342.

26. Dray, *At the Hands of Persons Unknown*, 191. Mark Twain, "The United States of Lyncherdom," in *Mark Twain: Collected Tales, Sketches, Speeches, and Essays, 1901–1910* (New York: Library of America, 1992), 479–486, esp. 486. Twain's essay was written in 1901, published posthumously in 1923; he sent it to an editor as a proposal for the multi-volume work but changed his mind about the project. See L. Terry Oggel, "Speaking Out About Race: 'The United States of Lyncherdom' Clemens Really Wrote," *Prospects: An Annual of American Cultural Studies* 25 (New York: Cambridge University Press, 2000), 129.

27. John P. Fort, "The Mind of the Lynching Mob," *Forum* 76.6 (December 1926): 818–822, esp. 822, 819, 821.

28. "Interracial Activities," *Southern Workman* 59.10 (1930): 434–444.

29. Charles S. Mangum Jr., *The Legal Status of the Negro* (Chapel Hill: University of North Carolina Press, 1940), 307.

30. Hodding Carter, *Where Main Street Meets the River* (New York: Rinehart, 1952), 228, 244.

31. Ken Hammond, "Lynchings in Texas: The Awful Violence of Frontier 'Justice,'" *Texas Magazine*, December 1, 1985. The magazine is an insert in the *Houston Chronicle*.

32. David Bradley, "Commentary: Perspective on the Texas Murder," *Los Angeles Times*, June 11, 1998. In 1996, numerous Southern music retailers refused to stock a rap group's CD that had on its cover a picture of the charred remains of a black man lynched in Pennsylvania in 1911. See Richard Harrington, "Cover Stories: Photos Used on Two Albums Stir Controversy," *Washington Post* (March 27, 1996).

33. Richard Stewart, "Dragged into Infamy: Murder Case Forces Jasper to Revisit Horror of Slaying in June," *Houston Chronicle*, January 24, 1999.

34. Ibid.

35. Patty Reinert, "Byrd's Slaying Called the Basis for Hate Group: Prosecutor Says King Wanted 'Respect' for New Racist Gang," *Houston Chronicle*, February 17, 1999. Jeff Franks, "Texas Race Murder Was Publicity Ploy—Prosecutor," Reuters, February 16, 1999.

36. Lee Hancock, "Defense Expects Inmates to Testify Dragging Plan Started in Prison," *Dallas Morning News*, January 28, 1999. Bob Hohler, "Texas Prison Is School for Hatred: Behind Bars, Jasper Suspects Were Free to Embrace Racism," *Boston Globe*, June 27, 1998.

37. David Firestone, "A Life Marked by Troubles, but Not by Hatred," *New York Times*, June 13, 1998.

38. James Gunter, affiant, "Affidavit of Probable Cause," June 9, 1998.

39. Ibid.

40. Stewart, "Racist Guilty of Jasper Murder: Defendant Pens Verdict with Letters," *Houston Chronicle*, February 24, 1999.

41. Martin McLaughlin, "Racial Violence and the Social Forces in America That Fuel It," World Socialist website, June 13, 1998.

42. Hohler, "Texas Prison Is School for Hatred."

43. The federal judge's order had been issued in 1980.

44. Allan Turner, "Racial Hate Crimes Sordid Past of State History," *Houston Chronicle*, June 10, 1998.

45. T. J. Milling, "Hymn Offers Counterpoint to Klan Rally," *Houston Chronicle*, June 28, 1998.

46. Rick Sarlat, "Area Groups Raising Funds for Relatives of Dragging Victim," *Philadelphia Tribune*, June 26, 1998.

47. Firestone, "A Life Marked by Troubles, but Not by Hatred."

48. "Black Teen Dragged by Truck," *Washington Post*, June 14, 1998. "A Third Car-Dragging Incident Is Reported," *New York Times*, June 15, 1998.

49. "Anti-Defamation League to Honor Family," *Houston Chronicle*, September 3, 1998.

50. Richard Stewart, "Symbol of Racial Division Tumbles: Jasper Dismantles Iron Fence That Split Cemetery into Black, White," *Houston Chronicle*, January 21, 1999. Rick Lyman, "As Trial in Dragging Opens, Town Talks of Reconciliation," *New York Times*, January 26, 1999. Paul Duggan, "Tearing Down a Fence and More: Racist Killing Forces Jasper, Tex., to Look Hatred in the Eye," *Washington Post*, January 26, 1999.

51. John William King, "Logical Reasoning," *Dallas Morning News*, November 12, 1998.

52. "King's Second Letter to the News' Reporter," *Dallas Morning News*, December 5, 1998. "King's Letter to *Jasper NewsBoy* Editor," *Dallas Morning News*, January 27, 1998.

53. Patty Reinert and Richard Stewart, "Pathologist Tells How Byrd Suffered, Died: Prosecutors Rest Case Against White Supremacist," *Houston Chronicle*, February 23, 1999.

54. Ibid.

55. Lee Hancock and Bruce Tomaso, "Jasper Man Guilty of Murder," *Dallas Morning News*, February 24, 1999.

56. Bruce Tomaso, "Suspect in Jasper Case Bragged About Slaying, Prosecutors Say," *Dallas Morning News*, September 14, 1999. Patty Reinert, "Jasper Suspect Said He Was 'Hero,'" *Houston Chronicle*, September 13, 1999.

57. Bruce Tomaso, "Prosecution Rests in 2nd Jasper Trial," *Dallas Morning News*, September 17, 1999.

58. Patty Reinert, "Suspect Tells Jury He Blames Co-Defendant for Byrd's Death," *Houston Chronicle*, September 17, 1999.

59. Patty Reinert, "3rd Suspect Blames Other Two," *Houston Chronicle*, September 28, 1999.

60. Richard Stewart, "Attorney: Defendant Not Racist," *Houston Chronicle*, October 25, 1999.

61. Patty Reinert, "Prosecutors in Dragging Trial Seek to Subpoena TV's Rather," *Houston Chronicle*, October 27, 1999. C. Bryson Hull, "Court Allows Hearing over CBS Videotapes," *Houston Chronicle*, November 1, 1999. Richard Stewart, "Give Up Tapes or Go to Jail, Judge Tells CBS Producer," *Houston Chronicle*, November 2, 1999. Stewart, "Jail Considered for CBS Producer," *Houston Chronicle*, November 4, 1999. Stewart, "Jury Picked to Hear Last Jasper Case/CBS Producer Avoids Jail in Tapes Dispute," *Houston Chronicle*, November 5, 1999. Patty Reinert, "CBS Posts Interview on Internet," *Houston Chronicle*, November 10, 1999.

62. Stewart, "Attorney: Defendant Not Racist."

63. Patty Reinert, "Berry Was at Wheel in Jasper, Jury Told," *Houston Chronicle*, November 10, 1999. Reinert and Richard Stewart, "Footprints Add to the Evidence Against Berry," *Houston Chronicle*, November 11, 1999.

64. Patty Reinert and Richard Stewart, "Defense Expert Offers New Theory in Jasper," *Houston Chronicle*, November 15, 1999. Terri Langford, "Friends Say Berry Showed No Racist Tendencies," *Dallas Morning News*, November 16, 1999.

65. Patty Reinert and Richard Stewart, "Jasper Defendant Blames Others for Dragging Death in Testimony," *Houston Chronicle*, November 16, 1999.

66. Patty Reinert and Richard Stewart, "3rd Defendant Gets Life Sentence in Jasper Man's Dragging Death," *Houston Chronicle*, November 18, 1999.

67. Richard Stewart, "Family Remembers Byrd, Looked for 'Closure,'" *Houston Chronicle*, November 19, 1999. *Both Sides with Jesse Jackson*, CNN, June 14, 1998, transcript 98061400V49. Patty Reinert, "Fate of 3rd Jasper Defendant Now in Jury's Hands," *Houston Chronicle*, November 17, 1999.

CHAPTER 4 — THE LAST AMERICAN LYNCHING

1. For Tuskegee definition, see "The Lynching Records at Tuskegee Institute," in *Eight Negro Bibliographies*, comp. Daniel T. Williams (New York: Kraus Reprint, 1970), 4. For the 1940 definition, see Jessie Daniel Ames, *The Changing Character of Lynching: Review of Lynching, 1931–1941* (Atlanta: Commission on Interracial Cooperation, 1942), 29; Linda O. McMurry, *Recorder of the Black Experience: A Biography of Monroe Nathan Work* (Baton Rouge and London: Louisiana State University Press, 1985), 127; and Christopher Waldrep, *The Many Faces of Judge Lynch: Extralegal Violence and Punishment in America* (New York: Palgrave Macmillan, 2002), 147–149. For the 1968 Civil Rights Bill as an anti-lynching bill, see Barbara Holden-Smith, "Lynching, Federalism, and the Intersection of Race and Gender in the Progressive Era," *Yale Journal of Law and Feminism* 8.1 (1996): 31–78, esp. 44 n. 75.

2. Richard Stewart and T. J. Milling, "FBI Joins in Probe of Murder: 3 White Men Held in Black Man's Death," *Houston Chronicle*, June 9, 1998.

3. Ricardo C. Ainslie, *Long Dark Road: Bill King and Murder in Jasper, Texas* (Austin: University of Texas Press, 2004), 118.

4. Sylvia Moreno, "Man Plea-Bargains for Life Prison Term in Beheading Case," *Houston Chronicle*, May 30, 1998. Tony White, "Chances for Death Penalty Bleak," *Baltimore Afro-American*, June 19, 1998.

5. "National News Briefs: Life Term for White Man in Killing of Black Man," *New York Times*, November 8, 1998.

6. There are exceptions to these scripted dialogues between public officials and civil rights advocates. Consider the case of Mike Christofeno, the chief deputy prosecutor in Elkhart County, Indiana, who responded to the murder of Sasezley Richardson by two white supremacists by immediately calling it "racially motivated." The Elkhart County branch of the NAACP praised the prosecutor for identifying the murder as a "true hate crime" and called for calm in the community. Jo Thomas, "White Teenagers Charged in Killing That Is Called Racial," *New York Times*, November 24, 1999.

7. Dina Temple-Raston, *A Death in Texas: A Story of Race, Murder, and a Small Town's Struggle for Redemption* (New York: Henry Holt, 2002), 110–111. Joyce King, *Hate Crime: The Story of a Dragging in Jasper, Texas* (New York: Pantheon, 2002), 59, 116, 196,

201. King makes a couple of allusions to lynching in a reference to earlier "night riders with a preference for ropes and horses" and mentions that the DA received a photograph of a lynching in an anonymous letter (28, 208). Ainslie, *Long Dark Road*, 1, 48, 201, 6. In the final paragraph, Ainslie does note in a reflection on the prosecutor's story of a 1920s lynching that just as "upstanding citizens" proved "capable of lynching people," so too "anyone might become capable of monstrous cruelty" (235–236). Likewise, the Showtime film of the event, *Jasper, Texas*, directed by Jeff Byrd, written by Jonathan Estrin (2003), does not use or evoke the term.

8. Philip Dray, *At the Hands of Persons Unknown: The Lynching of Black America* (New York: Random House, 2002), 458. Orlando Patterson, *Rituals of Blood: Consequences of Slavery in Two American Centuries* (Washington, DC: Civitas/ Counterpoint, 1998), xvii, 172. Patterson does elsewhere refer to Byrd as "America's most recent lynch victim" (171). Cf. Laura Wexler, *Fire in a Canebrake: The Last Mass Lynching in America* (New York: Scribner, 2003), 265: "how similar Jasper, Texas, in 1998 was to Monroe, Georgia, in 1946—and how different." (Monroe is where four African Americans were lynched in 1946.)

9. Waldrep, *The Many Faces of Judge Lynch*, 12, 182, 9, 186, 9, 191. Cf. Christopher Waldrep, *African Americans Confront Lynching: Strategies of Resistance from the Civil War to the Civil Rights Era* (Lanham, MD: Rowman & Littlefield, 2009), 125–126: "Journalists who first traveled to Jasper, for example, thought the dragging of James Byrd by three men qualified as a lynching. But ultimately they decided Byrd's murder was not a lynching."

10. *Both Sides with Jesse Jackson*, CNN, June 14, 1998, transcript 98061400V49. "Shocking to the Soul," *Miami Times*, June 18, 1998. "A Wake-Up Call," *Bay State Banner*, June 18, 1998. "The Gruesome Texas Killing," *Baltimore Afro-American*, June 19, 1998. Thomas Novel, "Still Lynching After All These Years," *Community Contact*, June 24, 1998. "The Issue of Race in America," *Washington Informer*, June 24, 1998. "Hatred and the James Byrd Murder," *Caribbean Today*, June 30, 1998. David Bradley, "Commentary: Perspective on the Texas Murder," *Los Angeles Times*, June 11, 1998. Dorothy Bruce, "A Time to Kill: When a Black Man Was Brutally Lynched in Texas This Week, African Americans Were Enraged at the Prospect of the White Suspects Escaping the Death Penalty," *Journal*, June 12, 1998. Clarence Page, "Sadly, There's Still Plenty of Hate to Go Around," *Chicago Tribune*, June 14, 1998. Sheryl McCarthy, "Racism Bubbles Up in Large and Small Ways," *Newsday*, June 15, 1998. Carl Rowan, "What Jasper Murder Tells Us About America," *Houston Chronicle*, June 13, 1998. William Raspberry, "Redemption in East Texas," *Washington Post*, June 19, 1998. Tony White, "Chance for Death Penalty Bleak," *Baltimore Afro-American*, June 19, 1998. Lovell Beaulieu, "No Longer Surprised by Racial Hate Crimes," *Des Moines Register*, June 20, 1998. Novel, "Still Lynching After All These Years." Bernhardt Dodson Jr., "Miami Vigil Pays Its Respect to James Byrd," *Miami Times*, June 25, 1998. Karen A. Holness, "Byrd Slaying Symbolic of Ongoing Racism," *Miami Times*, June 25, 1998. Joseph H. Brown, "All Murders Merit Similar Outrage," *Tampa Tribune*, June 28, 1998. "Race Hate in Texas," *Irish Times*, June 12, 1998.

11. Lee Hancock, "Arguments to Begin in Jasper Trial," *Dallas Morning News*, February 16, 1999.

12. Stanley Crouch, "Power of Racists Is Waning," *New York Daily News*, February 28, 1999.

13. Patterson, *Rituals of Blood*, 172–173.

14. *Cincinnati Enquirer*, July 14, 1903, quoted in Rayford W. Logan, *The Betrayal of the Negro: From Rutherford B. Hayes to Woodrow Wilson*, rev. ed. (New York: Da Capo Press, 1997), 393.

15. J. M. Early, *"An Eye for an Eye"; or, The Fiend and the Fagot. An Unvarnished Account of the Burning of Henry Smith at Paris, Texas, February 1, 1893, and the Reason he Was Tortured* (Paris, TX: Junius Early, n.d.), 71.

16. *Marshall Democrat*, August 26, 1859, quoted in Thomas G. Dyer, "'A Most Unexampled Exhibition of Madness and Brutality': Judge Lynch in Saline County, Missouri, 1859: Part 2," *Missouri Historical Review* 89.4 (1995): 367–383, esp. 374.

17. Margaret Vandiver, *Lethal Punishment: Lynchings and Legal Executions in the South* (New Brunswick, NJ: Rutgers University Press, 2006), 37. Stephen J. Leonard, *Lynching in Colorado, 1859–1919* (Boulder: University Press of Colorado, 2002), 51. George C. Wright, *Racial Violence in Kentucky, 1865–1940: Lynchings, Mob Rule, and "Legal Lynchings"* (Baton Rouge and London: Louisiana State University Press, 1990), 65. Juanita C. Crudele, "A Lynching Bee: Butler County Style," *Alabama Historical Quarterly* 42.1–2 (Spring/Summer 1980): 59–71. William D. Carrigan, *The Making of a Lynching Culture: Violence and Vigilantism in Central Texas, 1836–1916* (Urbana and Chicago: University of Illinois Press, 2004), 164.

18. Mary Louise Ellis, "'Rain Down Fire': The Lynching of Sam Hose" (PhD diss., Florida State University, 1992), 110–111; cf. Dray, *At the Hands of Persons Unknown*, 11. Yohuru R. Williams, "Permission to Hate: Delaware, Lynching, and the Culture of Violence in America," *Journal of Black Studies* 32.1 (September 2001): 3–29, esp. 14.

19. W. Fitzhugh Brundage, *Lynching in the New South: Georgia and Virginia, 1880–1930* (Urbana and Chicago: University of Illinois Press, 1993), 223–224.

20. James M. SoRelle, "The 'Waco Horror': The Lynching of Jesse Washington," *Southwestern Historical Quarterly* 86.4 (April 1983): 517–536, esp. 529, 531. Carrigan, *The Making of a Lynching Culture*, 190–191.

21. William Ziglar, "'Community on Trial': The Coatesville Lynching of 1911," *Pennsylvania Magazine of History and Biography* 106.2 (April 1982): 245–70, esp. 253.

22. Monte Akers, *Flames After Midnight: Murder, Vengeance, and the Desolation of a Texas Community* (Austin: University of Texas Press, 1999), 129–130.

23. *Tampa Daily Times*, June 1, 1927, quoted in Robert P. Ingalls, *Urban Vigilantes in the New South: Tampa, 1882–1936* (1988; Gainesville: University Press of Florida, 1993), 165.

24. Brundage, *Lynching in the New South*, 238, 236, 242.

25. *Montgomery Advertiser*, April 15, 1895, quoted in Crudele, "A Lynching Bee," 69.

26. Dray, *At the Hands of Persons Unknown*, 228–229.

27. Wexler, *Fire in a Canebrake*, 125. Howard Smead, *Blood Justice: The Lynching of Mack Charles Parker* (New York: Oxford University Press, 1986), 118, 184, 77.

28. Smead, *Blood Justice*, 79, 97.

29. Stephen J. Whitfield, *A Death in the Delta: The Story of Emmett Till* (Baltimore: Johns Hopkins University Press, 1988), 142–144, 47.

30. James Elbert Cutler, *Lynch-Law: An Investigation into the History of Lynching in the United States* (Longmans, Green, 1905), 276.

31. Edmund S. Morgan, *Inventing the People: The Rise of Popular Sovereignty in England and America* (1988; New York: W. W. Norton, 1989), 59.

32. Ronald W. Powell, "Perceptions in Black and White; Hate Crime Reactions Bare a Cultural Rift," *San Diego Union-Tribune*, March 1, 1999.

33. Another important issue involves the number of people required to constitute a mob. We should perhaps modify the anti-lynching provisions of the 1968 Civil Rights Act and add to the definition of lynching those acts of terror that replicate the formal features of earlier lynchings. It is assuredly not for lack of a third person in the party that Garnett Johnson wasn't lynched and James Byrd was. They were both lynched, one by two people and the other by three.

34. Jacqueline Goldsby, *A Spectacular Secret: Lynching in American Life and Literature* (Chicago: University of Chicago Press, 2006), 106. Ida B. Wells, *Mob Rule in New Orleans: Robert Charles and His Fight to the Death* (1900), reprinted in *Selected Works of Ida B. Wells-Barnett*, ed. Trudier Harris (New York: Oxford University Press, 1991), 316. Elliot Jaspin, *Buried in the Bitter Waters: The Hidden History of Racial Cleansing in America* (New York: Basic Books, 2007), 128. "Lynch Victim's Father Called to Clear Away Son's Ashes," *St. Louis Argus*, November 25, 1921, reprinted in *100 Years of Lynchings*, ed. Ralph Ginzburg (1962; Baltimore: Black Classic Press, 1988), 156. Grif Stockley, *Blood in Their Eyes: The Elaine Race Massacres of 1919* (Fayetteville: University of Arkansas Press, 2001), 230. *Lynchings and What They Mean: General Findings of the Southern Commission on the Study of Lynching* (Atlanta: the Commission, 1931), 45. "Lynching Carried Off Almost as Advertised," *Birmingham Post*, October 27, 1934, reprinted in Ginzburg, *100 Years of Lynchings*, 222–224. Dominic Capeci Jr., *The Lynching of Cleo Wright* (Lexington: University of Kentucky Press, 1998), 20–24. Crystal Nicole Feimster, "'Ladies and Lynching': The Gendered Discourse of Mob Violence in the New South, 1880–1930" (PhD diss., Princeton University, 2000), 136–137, details the participation of women in dragging lynchings.

35. Gloria Rubac, "Outrage over Texas Lynching," *Workers World*, June 25, 1998.

36. Waldrep, *The Many Faces of Judge Lynch*, 155.

37. *Lynchings and What They Mean*, 41.

38. "Heart and Genitals Carved from Lynched Negro's Corpse," *New York World-Telegram*, December 8, 1933, reprinted in Ginzburg, *100 Years of Lynching*, 211–212.

39. Lee Hancock, "Arguments to Begin in Jasper Trial," *Dallas Morning News* (February 16, 1999).

40. Andrew Sullivan, "What's So Bad About Hate," *New York Times Magazine*, September 26, 1999.

41. Bruce Tomaso, "Suspect in Jasper Case Bragged About Slaying, Prosecutors Say," *Dallas Morning News*, September 14, 1999. Patty Reinert, "Jasper Still Waiting to Learn Killer's Fate," *Houston Chronicle*, September 22, 1999.

42. Michael Berryhill, "Prisoner's Dilemma: Did the Texas Penal System Kill James Byrd?" *New Republic*, December 23, 1999.

43. "Interview with Shawn Berry," *CBS News: 60 Minutes II*.

44. James Gunter, affiant, "Affidavit of Probable Cause," June 9, 1998.

45. Andrew Macdonald, *The Turner Diaries*, 2nd ed. (New York: Barricade Books, 1996). Macdonald, *Hunter*, 2nd ed. (Hillsboro, WV: National Vanguard Books, 1998). "Andrew Macdonald" is Pierce's nom de plume.

46. Jo Thomas, "New Face of Terror Crimes: 'Lone Wolf' Weaned on Hate," *New York Times*, August 16, 1999.

47. Lee Hancock, "Jasper Killer Becoming Extremists' Hero," *Dallas Morning News*, March 7, 1999.

48. Ibid.

49. Jim Henderson, "Teen Pleads Guilty in Burning Death of Black Man; Defendant Says Hate Crime Was Not Motive," *New York Times*, August 17, 1999. Jim Lane, "Texas Lynching Stirs Outrage," *People's Weekly World*, August 28, 1999.

50. Felicity Barringer, "Giving Outrage a Face; Breaking a Taboo, Editors Turn to Images of Death," *New York Times*, October 25, 1998.

51. Carol Marie Cropper, "Black Man Fatally Dragged in a Possible Racial Killing," *New York Times*, June 10, 1998. Bob Hohler, "Brutal Slaying Tears at a Texas Town," *Boston Globe*, June 12, 1998.

52. Barringer, "Giving Outrage a Face."

53. Hancock, "Jasper Killer Becoming Extremists' Hero."

54. There are varying accounts of what precisely Mamie Till Bradley said at the train station, although there is a great deal of consistency in the tenor of what she said. Cf. her accounts in *Voices of Freedom: An Oral History of the Civil Rights Movement from the 1950s through the 1980s*, ed. Henry Hampton and Steve Fayer (New York: Bantam Books, 1990), 5–6; and Mamie Till-Mobley and Christopher Benson, *Death of Innocence: The Story of the Hate Crime That Changed America* (New York: Random House, 2003), 128–137. Also see the insightful essay on the whole scene by Ruth Feldstein, "'I Wanted the Whole World to See': Race, Gender, and Constructions of Motherhood in the Death of Emmett Till," in *Not June Cleaver: Women and Gender in Postwar America, 1945–1960*, ed. Joanne Meyerowitz (Philadelphia: Temple University Press, 1994), 263–303.

55. Feldstein, "'I Wanted the Whole World to See,'" 275–276.

56. Ibid., 289. Whitfield, *A Death in the Delta*, 145. Also see Dora Apel and Shawn Michelle Smith, *Lynching Photographs* (Berkeley: University of California Press, 2007), 61–64.

57. Joyce Ladner, quoted in Feldstein, "'I Wanted the Whole World to See,'" 289. Cleveland Sellers and Robert Terrell, *The River of No Return: The Autobiography of a Black Militant and the Life and Death of SNCC* (1973; Jackson and London: University Press of Mississippi, 1990), 14–15.

58. Kareem Abdul-Jabbar, *Black Profiles in Courage* (1996), quoted in *The Lynching of Emmett Till: A Documentary Narrative*, ed. Christopher Metress (Charlottesville: University of Virginia Press, 2002), 277. Muhammad Ali with Richard Durham, *The Greatest: My Own Story* (New York: Random House, 1975), 34–35, 341–346. Not all responses contained such positive resolve, of course. For other accounts, see *The Lynching of Emmett Till: A Documentary Narrative*, 226–288.

59. John Edgar Wideman, "The Killing of Black Boys," in Metress, *The Lynching of Emmett Till: A Documentary Narrative*, 278–288, esp. 279.

60. Lee Hancock, "Hard-Fighting DA Didn't Hesitate to Take Byrd Case," *Dallas Morning News*, January 24, 1999.

61. "Jasper Killer's Father Remembers Own Brother's 1939 Murder Trial," *Houston Chronicle*, March 2, 1999. Lee Hancock, "Roots of Hatred Elude King's Father," *Dallas Morning News* (February 27, 1999).

62. "A Sick Tradition," *New York Times*, September 14, 1998. Kit R. Roane, "Suspended Police Officer Apologizes, Calling Float 'a Big Mistake,'" *New York Times*, September 13,

1998. Roane, "New York Officer Fired over Racist Float," *Houston Chronicle*, October 11, 1998. Frank Ahrens, "D.C. Radio Shock Jock Fired for Racist Remark," *Houston Chronicle*, February 26, 1999. John W. Gonzalez, "Net's Chat Weighs in on Slaying: Some Say 3 Suspects in Jasper Are 'Heroes,'" *Houston Chronicle*, June 12, 1998.

63. One way to judge the effect of these photographs is to know the response of those who have seen them. For two eyewitness accounts of how the jury responded to the photographs, see Temple-Raston, *A Death in Texas*, 200–201, and King, *Hate Crime*, 120–121. King also viewed the photographs and recorded her response (124–127).

64. James T. Campbell, "Hope for a Better World in Troubled Jasper," *Houston Chronicle*, July 6, 1998.

65. It is worth noting that they might have a penitential effect. During his trial for the murder of James Byrd, Lawrence Russell Brewer recoiled from the prosecutor approaching him with the album of photographs of Byrd's corpse, crying and crying out, "I don't want to look at those pictures." Reinert, "Suspect Tells Jury He Blames Co-Defendant for Byrd's Death."

66. Bruce Tomaso, "Death Penalty for White Killer of Black Man an Exception," *Dallas Morning News*, February 28, 1999.

67. Barringer, "Giving Outrage a Face."

68. Maria Hinojosa, "Exhibit of Lynching Photos Is a Harsh Display of Hatred," *CNN.com*, January 18, 2000, http://archives.cnn.com/2000/US/01/18/lynching.photography/ (accessed July 26, 2010).

69. "Black Teen Dragged by Truck." "A Third Car-Dragging Incident Is Reported."

70. "Man Sentenced to 20 Years in Louisiana Hate Crime," *New York Times*, February 24, 1999. "Jury Convicts Man of Cross-Burning at Home of Interracial Couple," *New York Times*, February 24, 1999.

71. L. D. Reddick, "The Lynching of Pickie Pie," *Crisis* 57 (March 1950), reprinted in *A Documentary History of the Negro People in the United States, 1945–1951*, vol. 5, *From the End of World War II to the Korean War*, ed. Herbert Aptheker (New York: Carol Publishing, 1993), 431–436, esp. 431. Horace Mann Bond and Julia W. Bond, *The Star Creek Papers*, ed. Adam Fairclough (Athens and London: University of Georgia Press, 1997), 130.

72. Bond and Bond, *The Star Creek Papers*, 3, 130.

CONCLUSION

1. Cynthia Carr, *Our Town: A Heartland Lynching, a Haunted Town, and the Hidden History of White America* (New York: Crown Publishers, 2006), 32–33.

2. Philip Dray, *At the Hands of Persons Unknown: The Lynching of Black America* (New York: Random House, 2002), 457.

3. Susan Sontag, "Regarding the Torture of Others," *New York Times Magazine*, May 23, 2004.

4. Ibid.

5. Hazel Carby, "US/UK's Special Relationship: The Culture of Torture in Abu Ghraib and Lynching Photographs," *NKA: Journal of Contemporary African Art* 20 (Fall 2006): 60–71, esp. 67–68.

6. Shawn Michelle Smith, "Afterimages: White Womanhood, Lynching, and the War in Iraq," *NKA: Journal of Contemporary African Art* 20 (Fall 2006): 72–85, esp. 73, 78.

7. Susan Willis, *Portents of the Real: A Primer for Post 9/11 America* (New York and London: Verso, 2005), 124, 129, 135–136, 120.

8. Smith, "Afterimages," 81.

9. Donald Rumsfeld testimony before Congress, quoted in Mark Gibney and Niklaus Steiner, "Apology and the American 'War on Terror,'" in *The Age of Apology: Facing Up to the Past*, ed. Mark Gibney, Rhoda E. Howard-Hassman, Jean-Marc Coicaud, and Niklaus Steiner (Philadelphia: University of Pennsylvania Press, 2008), 287–297, esp. 292–293.

10. Howard Witt, "Was His Death a Hate Crime?" *Chicago Tribune*, October 5,2008.

11. James C. McKinley Jr., "Killing Stirs Racial Unease in Texas," *New York Times*, February 15, 2009.

12. Ida. B. Wells, *A Red Record: Tabulated Statistics and Alleged Causes of Lynchings in the United States, 1892–1893–1894* (Chicago: Donohue & Henneberry, 1895), 26.

13. Jim Henderson, "Teen Pleads Guilty in Burning Death of Black Man; Defendant Says Hate Crime Was Not Motive," *Houston Chronicle*, August 17, 1999. Jim Lane, "Texas Lynching Stirs Outrage," *People's Weekly World*, August 28, 1999. Another related but different case occurred as I was writing the conclusion. In Newberry, South Carolina, Anthony Hill, a black man, was shot dead and then dragged behind a pickup truck for eleven miles by a white man, Gregory Collins. The case devolved into the same debates over whether it was or was not a hate crime, whether or not it was "racially motivated." Collins apparently acted alone. See Shaila Dewan, "Call for Justice Sets Off a Debate," *New York Times*, July 18, 2010.

14. Charles Johnson, "The End of the Black American Narrative," *American Scholar* 77.3 (Summer 2008): 32–42. It must be said in fairness to Professor Johnson that he has been proposing these ideas for far longer than the candidacy of President Obama; these are arguments he has been eloquently and persistently making since the 1980s.

15. Gerald L. Early, "The End of Race as We Know It," *Chronicle of Higher Education*, October 10, 2008, http://chronicle.com/article/The-End-of-Race-as-We-Know-It/3343 (accessed September 12, 2011).

16. James Weldon Johnson, *Along This Way: The Autobiography of James Weldon Johnson*, ed. Sondra Kathryn Wilson (1933; New York: Penguin, 1990), 318.

17. Wells, *A Red Record*, 98.

18. "Barack Obama's Speech on Race," transcript, *New York Times*, March 18, 2008.

19. Ted Koppel, *The Last Lynching*, Discovery Communications, 2008.

20. Mike Brantley, "Ted Koppel Looks Back on 1980s Lynching in Mobile," *Alabama Press-Register*, October 12, 2008.

21. Daniel M. Gold, "In the Bad Old Days, Not So Very Long Ago," *New York Times*, October 12, 2008.

22. Brantley, "Ted Koppel Looks Back on 1980s Lynching in Mobile."

INDEX

ABOUT THE AUTHOR

Ashraf H. A. Rushdy is the author of *The Empty Garden: The Subject of Late Milton* (1992), *Neo-Slave Narratives: Studies in the Social Logic of a Literary Form* (1999), and *Remembering Generations: Race and Family in Contemporary African American Fiction* (2001). He teaches in the African American Studies Program and the English Department at Wesleyan University.